An encounter with Rumi is akin to chasing an elusive melody; one is perpetually left yearning for more. Yet, within the pages of *rumi roaming*, we are graced with a masterful intervention that confronts the crises of our modern age—a crisis rooted in language and its intricate dance of translation. Seamlessly weaving modern renditions of Rumi's ghazals with a tapestry of contemporary creative nonfiction, melodious poetry, scholarly musings, immersive photo essays, and haunting videos, this collection addresses a void I've perennially sensed in my engagements with Rumi's diverse oeuvre, from the poetic to the visual. The Algorithmic encounter that concludes this journey offers a wry nod, a poignant irony, underscoring the pressing relevance and urgency of such a groundbreaking endeavor.

Zainub Verjee, artist, critic and scholar, Governor General's Award recipient and Member of the Order of Canada

rumi roaming is the long-awaited work that finally addresses some of the most questionable aspects of the popular Rumi. That the popularity of Rumi's bestselling translations in English remains unaffected by a rise in racism towards people who share his region and culture is a clear indication that the best-selling translations are failing profoundly, a failure felt most acutely by people of Persian and Central Asian origin. Sensitive to post-colonial problematics of translation and without avoiding the most challenging and potentially offensive aspects of Rumi's oeuvre, in *rumi roaming* a diversity of creative thinkers bare their souls in the spirit of the poet himself to connect directly and transparently with their audience about how his poetry resonates with them in the present moment. This multi-media volume is far more sophisticated and nuanced in its vision of Rumi than criticisms that have focused simply on the stripping of Islamic references in popular translations. *rumi roaming* provides a much richer and more creative re-reading of Rumi than has been previously available.

Jawid Mojaddedi, professor of religion at Rutgers University and translator of *The Masnavi* for Oxford World's Classics

rumi roaming masterfully shines a light on the complex and contradictory legacies of Rumi both past and present, and inevitably, the future. Artists, scholars, and activists bring themselves to the figure of Rumi and grapple with the various dimensions of Rumi's life, social context, and literary outputs, especially as it has interjected their lives, such as his poetry that evoked love and longing, sexist, and patriarchal stories, and calls for revolution. The essays, poems, and art in these pages are multi-dimensional, multi-linguistic, and global. They challenge easy ideas of translation and transmission. Though Rumi remains a popular spiritual icon today, this volume and its contributors showcase that this popularity should not be taken at face value but needs to be interrogated and disentangled. The contributors to the volume and Hashemi have done a great service in taking this important and difficult first step for us the readers, but as with any mystical path, including that of Rumi's, the rest depends on what we the readers do with this knowledge.

M. Shobhana Xavier, professor of religion and diaspora at Queen's University and author of *The Dervishes of the North: Rumi, Whirling, and the Making of Sufism in Canada*

rumi رومی

در پرسه roaming

indigenous folks, migrants, settler descendents, refugees, transnationals, and guests from india, iran, afghanistan, turkey, syria, egypt, italy, cuba, mexico, and turtle Island,

the contributors variously live and work on

the colonized region of yucatan, ancestral land of the maya

unceded lands of tiohtià:ke, home of the kanien'kehá:ka nation

the mississaugas of the credit treaty 13 land claim region of t'karonto, also traditional territory of the huron-wendat and the haudenosaunee covered by 'dish with one spoon' and 'the two row' wampum belt agreements

the territories of the xʷməθkʷəy̓əm, sḵwx̱wú7mesh and səlilwətaɬ

the traditional territories of the nuu-chah-nulth peoples, the ha-houlthee of the ƛaʔuukʷiʔatḥ tla-o-qui-aht and the yuułuʔiłʔatḥ first nations

nogojiwanong (place at the foot of the rapids) and the otonabee (river that beats like a heart) region originally stewarded by michi saagig nishnabeg

anacostia and potomac, the ancestral land of the piscataway, pamunkey, nentego (nanichoke), mattaponi, chickahominy, monacan, and powhatan

nanzuhzaugewazog, treaty 14 and treaty 22 lands and territory of the mississaugas of the credit and the traditional territory of the huron-wendat and the haudenosaunee

occupied serachtague (place of the swift water), ancestral land of the mohawk, mohican, oneida, and abenaki peoples

treaty 6 territory, traditional lands of the anishinaabek, haudenosaunee, lūnaapéewak, and chonnonton peoples

we are grateful to the indigenous caretakers and stewards of these lands and waters

we learn from the steadfast land reclamation and water protection by indigenous peoples and their allies

we honour the continued connections with past, present, and future
and the aromas of earth and water that give life

زبان خانه است language is home اللغة بيت el idioma es el hogar भाषा घर है la lingua è casa

rumi roaming

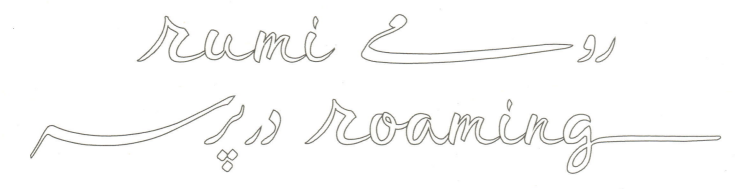

contemporary engagements and interventions

curated and edited by gita hashemi

poetry and translation editor and editorial consultant: elena basile

GUERNICA World EDITIONS

subversivepress

GUERNICA AND SUBVERSIVEPRESS
TORONTO—CHICAGO—BUFFALO—LANCASTER (U.K.)
2025

contents

titles with ↖ include link to media content

online media

go to online index

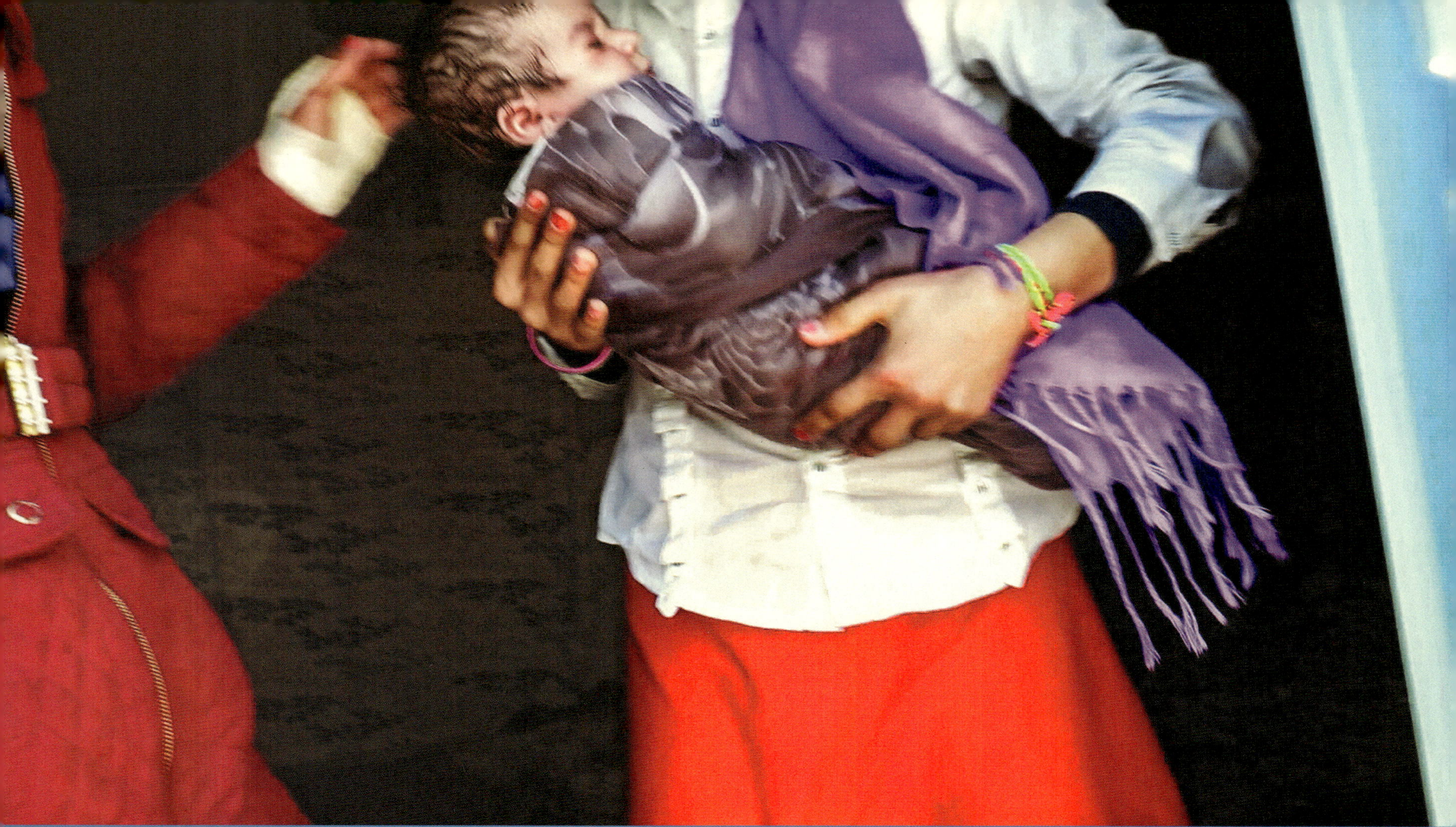

nasrin and her sisters | tabanovce refugee camp, april 8, 2016 | from the series *nth movement*, part of the *declarations diptych* | gita hashemi | 2016

http://hdl.handle.net/10315/41083

dawn of existence

oneness of being, 3 | gita hashemi | 2022

recorded at bellamy ravine and scarborough bluffs, unceded territory of the mississauga of the credit first nation

The dawn of existence has only one sun
its oneness of being sustains every particle
Yet because it reveals new facets
at each dawn and dusk it looks as an other

Rumi, ghazal 458

Sobh-e vojud rā be joz in āftāb nist
bar zarre zarre vahdat-e hosnash moghararist
Ammā bedān sabab ke be har shām-o har sabuh
ashkāle now namāyad guyi ke digarist

صبح وجود را به جز این آفتاب نیست
بر ذره ذره وحدت حسنش مقرریست
اما بدان سبب که به هر شام و هر صبوح
اشکال نو نماید گویی که دیگریست

مولوی، غزل ۴۵۸

to begin

Dear reader, thank you for coming to these pages. This book is a large spread with offerings by old and new friends, collaborators and allies. *rumi roaming* is not solely about Rumi—it is an intervention in processes of cultural appropriation and depoliticization of spirituality. Drawing attention to diverse geographies of Rumi's circulation, *rumi roaming* invites you to think about Rumi in lower case and as a dynamic and questionable cross-cultural force, and to sense your way through the cultural and spiritual challenges of this moment of collective and individual dis/placements and longings. The project started in early 2020 amidst the "curves and twists of the sea"—soon after the downing of the Flight 752 and the formal declaration of the COVID as a pandemic. Initially, it was imagined as a series of place-based (rather than stage-based) embodied performances in collaboration with poets, spoken word, and movement artists. In the immediate period after the pandemic lockdowns dis-placed creative making and forced collaborations into virtual spaces, pulling off performances involving real bodies in real spaces became far too demanding. This became glaringly obvious after we managed the one live performance that is included in this volume in video. *rumi roaming* then morphed into a "book"—still aiming to maintain the original multi-modality and transdisciplinarity—as we whirled through the injustices of inadequate healthcare and social welfare systems (ongoing), surges in the refugee population in the world (ongoing), and racist backlash against poor dark-skinned displaced people (ongoing). The formative gestures and textures of the book took shape during the Russian war in Ukraine (ongoing), and the Black Lives Matter and Every Child Matters uprisings on Turtle Island (ongoing). The tonalities were shaped by rising environmental disasters (ongoing)—now in the global north as well as the south—and by settling in and taking hold of the realization that our human impact has been irreversibly calamitous not only for us but for all our animal and plant kin. The last major strokes were put down after the second coming of the Taliban (ongoing) and the WomanLifeFreedom Revolution (ongoing). The book's publication date was postponed twice since (with different publishers). With each delay, this opening expanded to include a larger list of global trials that touched this volume's contributors in direct and indirect ways. The first time I thought I was done with this paragraph, the earthquake in Kahramanmaraş, Turkey was top of the news. The second time was a few months through the new war in Sudan; some months after Masoud Eskandari, one of the contributors, passed away suddenly; and 83 days through Israel's livestreamed war on Gaza and the escalating threat of another attack on Lebanon. Now, 222 days through Israel's (ongoing) genocide of Palestinians (or is it seventy-six years?) and 7 days since the fires in Northern British Columbia (ongoing), I know that these words are dated as soon as typed. And there are yet several months to go before this book is out in the world. For the contributors to this volume (and perhaps for you), these were/are not just news headlines. These were/are experiences that we *live with/through* and grieve (grief ongoing) as racialized people carrying ongoingly the weight of belonging to multiple histories and places marked with multiple colonialisms and injustices. With all these goings on why then engage with Rumi? From the distance of eight centuries, what could Rumi's mystical thought and poetics bring to this mayhem world? Haven't we had enough Rumi? From entertainment to what masquerades as "inner attainment," given all the hallmark-ish Rumi memes circulating in the (cyber)world, all the musical productions with Rumi in their title, all the neo-mystic prophets and spiritual profiteers claiming Rumi, and all the translations of Rumi by "translators" who do not know his language, not to mention all the scholarly productions hashing out everything Rumi, isn't the sheer number of cultural products dedicated to Rumi—part exalted, part exotic; part hyper-specialized, part hyper-banalized—reason enough against another production engaging with Rumi?

In the hearts and minds of most Persian-speaking people there is a sacred place for poetry and in that place Jalal al-Din Mohammad Balkhi—aka Molavi, Molana, Mevlevi and Rumi—occupies the altar alongside Hafez, Sa'adi, and Ferdowsi. These four poets pin down the four corners of the Persianate identity, if not of its very soul. But, I must admit, reading Rumi's ghazals, which held profound truths for me when I was younger and in Iran, now that I am in my sixties and nearly forty years in exile is often infuriating, more so because the deep aesthetic/affective impact of his movingly musical words opens my senses to desire a more exalted realm than this senseless tattered world of greed, violence, and hate that binds me. Neither *Love* nor *Longing*, neither *Truth* nor *Virtue*, neither *God* nor *Sufi*—capitalized as abstract and absolute concepts as they often appear in translations of Rumi—can solace the pain of injustices lived and ever-increasingly witnessed. In fact, I no longer believe that Rumi himself had ever been able to transcend his own materially-bound and historically-conditioned limitations and attain anything near the kind of exaltation that we attribute to him, as is abundantly clear from his doctrinal masterpiece, the *Masnavi*, that promotes and propagates the patriarchal and multi-prejudicial world-view of his time (ongoing). Why this project then? Simple, really. Because Rumi's name immediately conjures an intercultural space rarely afforded any other cultural figure from the East or the West. Rumi is arguably the best-selling poet in the English language, and the one poet from the East whose words have been translated in all populous languages in the world—even if often emptied of much of their historical burdens, cultural bearings, and nuanced intimations. Reading Rumi, we enter a *noplace*, a place with no temporal and no spatial specificity, a space so full that it is empty, allowing us to enter it with our own *situatedness*, our own *projections* and *imaginations*, our own *longings* and *belongings*, and find ourselves reflected, somehow, somewhere there. When the pandemic hit and we became more isolated in our survival struggles, I wanted to hold a space for communing across the distances and distancings. Rumi's name worked the magic. In essence, he became the reed flute whose voice we hear at the opening of the *Masnavi*:

> Since I was cut off from the reed bed
>   in my cry men and women have wailed
> I want hearts torn to shreds by separation
>   so I can reveal the pain of longing
> Whoever was parted from their origin
>   seeks the season of their reunion[1]

A re/union this volume became as the contributors brought a decolonial lowercase rumi-ness to our diverse contexts and communities and created much-needed spaces for thinking about cultural/spiritual heritage and its connection to our contemporary concerns and conditions. Here, artists, poets, scholars, and thinkers from different disciplines and cultural backgrounds—activists one and all—take off from Rumi's

1 Rumi, *Masnavi* 1.1. See the original and translation in this volume, page 14. All translations are mine unless otherwise noted.

poetry toward nurturing critically alert and spiritually aware relations in our world. The contributions cover a wide range of interconnected and urgent themes, including global displacements and relations to land and water, translingual poetics and translation politics, indigenous language revitalization and diasporic language reclamation, and interrogations of spirituality, healing, and social justice. Inspired by Rumi's itinerant life trajectory across (present-day) Afghanistan, Iran, Turkey, and Syria, the contributors reflect on human connections, places, histories, presents, and our own path(s) to the sacred—not the holy and the sanctified—through engaging overtly and covertly with Rumi—including with what is challenging and offensive in his work for our present societies and sensibilities—exploring his relevance to our concerns and resistant practices, and sometimes walking away from Rumi altogether and declaring him irrelevant. Rather than laying claim to "spirituality," the contributors claim the spirit of the world they encounter, with and without Rumi.

The "book" is in print, virtual, and real spaces. It includes auto-ethnographic and performative prose, poetry, scholarly and critical essays, photo essays, performances, videos, audio readings, as well as new English translations of some of Rumi's ghazals. For most of the contributors in this volume English is a second (for some, third or fourth) language, and those who are native to English come from different communities and usage traditions. I chose not to homogenize and standardize their Englishes—a violent and colonial editorial practice that aims to erase histories and contexts from language—but to maintain the specific accent of each piece. The structure of the book too does not adhere to organizing conventions based on thematic and/or formal classifications. Instead, it is built on tenuous and evocative associations, the stuff of poetry, memory, and identification. Some threads will be more tangible and visible than others, and some readers may find their own unique connections. Overall, the order of offerings is not linear and prescriptive but is meant to invite multiple ways of roaming through. So, dear reader, this content is yours to sample and remix.

I am deeply honoured by the community of artists and intellectuals who contributed to this volume. They came here variously through solid friendships and relations of solidarity—the intricate weave that holds us together in times that fray our individual and collective resilience. I am deeply grateful to Elena Basile for her manifold editorial labour, particularly for gifting her remarkably sensitive ears and rigorously decolonial handling of the poetry and translations, as well as for keeping all this up from almost the beginning to the end, starting as the editor of the series of which this book was to be the first, and remaining with the project and fully committing to seeing it through in the demanding process of moving to a new publisher and out into your hands.

The story of every project precedes and exceeds its product. This one started as an experiment in intercultural and interdisciplinary collaboration. Some collaborations did not sprout or were short-lived. There were mistimings, misunderstandings, miscommunications, missteps and other misses. But all the people who entered this place left their mark on it and absences became the well-spring for presences. This has been a process of communal learning and acquisition and a true aesthetic experiment. If we walk back to the Greek roots of aesthetic we find *aisthanesthai*, meaning to *feel* or to *perceive*. If we walk further back, we arrive at the Avestan *avish* and Sanskrit *avih*, meaning *openly*. Thus, *to feel and perceive openly*. Courageously. Such has been the gift of this project. What more could we ask of rumi?

As I close this opening, the project has exceeded the limits of this book with seasons-based appearances in Ucluelet, British Columbia, over the course of the year; rumi roaming (ongoing)

— gita hashemi
16 may 2024
t'karonto
where there are trees in the water

notes on translation, transliteration, and pronunciation

On Translation

Unless otherwise noted, I selected and translated all of Rumi's works in this volume. This is not a book of translations however, and my selections are by no means representative of the expanse of his work. Every translation is ultimately an interpretation, and no translation is fully transparent. As I am not a Rumi or Sufi scholar, I walked away from approaches that modulate word choices with the interpretive conventions rooted in the compendia of Sufi symbology. Raised in the Persian language, I read Rumi's ghazals in particular because they touch me deeply with their evocative imagery and moving music, both carried through the language of the everyday, a language that remains highly accessible even to a lay person from the distance of eight hundred years. The power of Rumi's ghazals, unlike most of his *Masnavi*, is in their affective and visceral impact rather than any doctrinal teachings. In addition to their relevance—or not, as Mahdi Tourage argues in this volume—to some of the contemporary issues we grapple with, I selected the included poems for their impactful imagery. Because my creative base is in visual arts, in translating I prioritized capturing the images in the simplest and most direct language. Perhaps at times even risking literalness, I opted to remain loyal to the image and its affect rather than to the intellect and doctrinal interpretation.

As in most classical Persian verse, ghazals are composed of a string of lines, each consisting of two interdependent hemistiches, and every line ending with the dominant rhyme. The music of Rumi's poetry in Persian—what Fatemeh Keshavarz calls its "sonic surface"—is characterized by distinct affect-based word choices carrying unparalleled rhymes *within* each line as well as at the end of the line. These characteristics are all lost in translation. Here I tried to keep a semblance of (more like a gesture toward) the beat through the visual spacing and segmenting of the lines. The convention in classical Persian verse—predominantly composed in *masnavi*, *ghazal*, or *roba'i* forms—is to write the hemistiches in equal lengths on the same baseline separated by a gap between them. This convention underpins the visual texture and character of Persian poetry manuscripts and calligraphic works. Here, in order to connect visually the Persian, the transliteration, and the English translation, I have used a contemporary typographic convention by putting the hemistiches on successive lines, with the second hemistich indented to indicate its dependence on the first. I also maintained the structure and order of the original lines rather than break them into smaller lines that are re-ordered—as many translators have done to make the reading easy. Lastly, punctuation marks were certainly not a thing in Rumi's work and his time, and I decided not to colonize his time with mine, so I kept the impulse to use them at bay. The labour of understanding then is on the reader who has to slow down to attune to the emotional, spatial, and visual registers of the poems. In order to make the "sonic surface" accessible to those who do not read Persian, in addition to the original Persian and the English translation, I have included them also in Pinglish/Finglish (Persian/Farsi transliterated in English). See it, sound it, feel it. ببین، بخوان، دریاب *bebin, bekhān, daryāb*.

All poems of Rumi and selections from *Fih ma Fih* are from digital collection of Ganjoor.Net. The poems have been compared with print copies including Mowlana Jalal al-Din Mohammad Balkhi, *Masnavi Ma'navi*, be tashih-e Reynold Nicholson (Tehran: Amir Kabir, 1366/1988); and Jalal al-Din Mohammad Molavi Rumi, *Koliyātt-e Divān-e Shams-e Tabrizi*, be tashih-e Badi' al-Zaman Foruzānfar (Tehran: Amir Kabir, 1358/1979). I have also consulted Mowlana Jalal al-Din Mohammad Balkhi, *Gozide-ye Ghazaliyat-e Shams* be kushesh-e Mohammad Reza Shafiei-Kadkani (Tehran: Amir Kabir, 1365/1987).

On Transliteration and Pronunciation

The transliterations offered here alongside Rumi's poems in Persian and English translation use a modified Romanization scheme mostly based on the ALA-LC (American Library Association – Library of Congress) standards that are commonly used in North American formal and academic transliteration. In the scheme used in this volume the modifications aim for simplification and are inspired by the common practices in text-based electronic communication by Pinglish/Finglish users who, favouring rapid typing in the most readily available keyboard layouts, do away with all diacritical marks in the ALA-LC system and use multi-letter equivalents for Persian-specific letters and/or sounds. Persian uses an abjad writing system similar to Arabic. In this system only consonants are represented in the writing and the vowel sounds are inferred by the reader. In this volume, the ALA-LC system of vowel equivalency is also simplified, and only one diacritical mark—*ā* differentiated from *a*—is used to ease the sounding of the transliteration for those unfamiliar with Persian.

Persian—called Farsi in Iran, Dari in Afghanistan, and Tajiki in Tajikistan—is the native language of over 70 million and the (imposed) language of education or required second language for nearly 40 million people living in 6 countries. Its sounds and usage are different from one locality to another. The Rumi transliterations here are based on the pronunciations that are most common in central Iran and standardized in the Dehkhoda Lexicon. Standardization was part of the project of modernization in Iran in the early- to mid-20th century. Like all such projects, it has a colonial impulse and masks the lived diversity of the language. Having grown up in central Iran myself, these pronunciations are for the most part native to me, but by no means do they represent the way all Persian readers and speakers hear and vocalize Rumi's language.

Finally, Persian and Arabic, although they are vastly different languages, share the same script as well as some vocabulary that has mostly entered into Persian from Arabic via Islam. Many shared words, however, are pronounced differently in the two languages, owing to the fact that there are sounds that they do not share. These words would therefore have different transliteration depending on whether they are brought in from Persian or Arabic. Rather than imposing an arbitrary standardization, in this volume where Arabic or Persian words are used within English text, we maintain the transliteration that the author has used, thus acknowledging the diversity of the languages and their contextual transliteration. For example, وجد is pronouned *wajd* in Arabic and *vajd* in Persian which does not have the *w* sound. Also, where a Persian or Arabic word is in common use in English—or Spanish as in the case of one of the chapters—we have kept the transliteration that is most common in the host language.

sounding guide

a as in ***a***pple and c***a***t
ā as in ***A***mish and t***a***r
e as in ***e***rgo and sh***e***d
i as in ***i***nfidel and rav***i***ne
u as in ***U***panishad and t***u***t***u***
o as in ***O***mar and m***o***re
ow as in gl***ow***
y as in ***y***ear

Consonants are pronounced as in English.

The following are used for sounds not found in English or not specifically represented in its writing system:
zh as in a***z***ure and fu***s***ion
kh is a fricative sound close to Ba***ch*** in German
gh is a hard fricative g pronounced in the throat, close to ***r***ue in French

Unless appearing in one of the above combinations, ***h*** is aspirated and voiced in all positions as in
hammer and Kanda***h***ar.

Doubling a letter indicates overpronouncing the letter:
avval read closer to *av val*

A single prime ʼ before a letter should be read as a very short pause and often points to the letter ع *eyn* in Persian:
mo'āven is pronounced close to *mo āven*

Ou used alone is pronounced as in ***u*** in t***u***t***u*** and stands for the third-person singular pronoun for humans او which in Persian is genderless.

A dash **-** at the end of a word often followed by ***e***, ***ye***, or ***o*** indicates a relation of association between the surrounding words: *sobh-**e** vojud* (dawn of existence) or *shab-**o** ruz* (night and day) or *sine-**ye*** mashruh (unraveled heart)

Affixes and prefixes are indicated with a dash **-** as in:
dane-ha (plural of *dane* seed) or *al-Majnun* (the Arabic article *al* preceding a name)

Contracted words and phrases—sometimes written without contraction but pronounced with—are transliterated as pronounced.

Generally, the transliteration aim has been to simplify reading, as is often the case for Pinglish/Finglish users, rather than to be precise.

rumi

masnavi, book one, section 1

Hear this reed as it moans
    telling tales of separation
Since I was cut off from the reed bed
    in my cry men and women have wailed
I want hearts torn to shreds by separation
    so I can reveal the pain of longing
Whoever was parted from their origin
    seeks the season of their reunion
I moaned in every crowd
    I coupled with the unhappy and the content
Each befriended me with their own assumptions
    None sought my secrets from inside me
My secrets are not far from my cry
    yet eyes and ears lack the insight
Body is not veiled from soul nor soul from body
    still no body is allowed to see the soul
The reed's call is fire not air
    Whoever has not this fire be naught

lines 1-14 read by zainab amadahy

مولوی

مثنوی، دفتر اول، بخش ۱

Beshnow in ney chon shekāyat mikonad
    Vaz jodāyi-hā hekāyat mikonad
Kaz neyestān tā marā bobride-and
    Dar nafiram mard-o zan nālide-and
Sine khāham sharhe sharhe az farāgh
    Tā beguyam sharh-e dard-e eshtiyāgh
Har kasi ku dur mānd az asl-e khish
    Bāz juyad rozegar-e vasl-e khish
Man be har jam'iyati nālān shodam
    Joft-e bad-hālān-o khosh-hālān shodam
Har kasi az zann-e khod shod yār-e man
    Az darun-e man najost asrār-e man
Serr-e man az nāle-ye man dur nist
    Lik chashm-o gush rā ān nur nist
Tan ze jān-o jān ze tan mastur nist
    Lik kas rā did-e jān dastur nist
Ātash ast in bāng-e nāy-o nist bād
    Harke in ātash nadārad nist bād

بشنو این نی چون شکایت می‌کند
    از جدایی‌ها حکایت می‌کند
کز نیستان تا مرا ببریده‌اند
    در نفیرم مرد و زن نالیده‌اند
سینه خواهم شرحه شرحه از فراق
    تا بگویم شرح درد اشتیاق
هر کسی کو دور ماند از اصل خویش
    باز جوید روزگار وصل خویش
من به هر جمعیتی نالان شدم
    جفت بدحالان و خوش‌حالان شدم
هر کسی از ظن خود شد یار من
    از درون من نجست اسرار من
سر من از نالهٔ من دور نیست
    لیک چشم و گوش را آن نور نیست
تن ز جان و جان ز تن مستور نیست
    لیک کس را دید جان دستور نیست
آتش است این بانگ نای و نیست باد
    هر که این آتش ندارد نیست باد

read in persian by hajar hussaini

Fire of love imbued the reed
    Heat of love infused the wine
The reed is a rival to whoever was ripped from a lover
    Its reverbs revealed our veil and cover
Whoever heard of a poison and antidote like the reed
    Whoever saw a confidant and a seeker like the reed
The reed tells of the path covered in blood
    It tells of Majnun's fabled love
Privy to this knowledge is but whoever lost all sense
    The tongue has no customer but the eager ear
In our heartache every day became time-less
    Every day became companion to anguish
Let them go if days are gone   don't fear
    You who are purer than all   you remain
"Whoever is not a fish"[1]   is sated in this water
    "Whoever is without daily bread"[2]   their day drags on
Whoever is raw doesn't get the experience of the ripe
    Thus my discourse should be brief and that's enough
O child   break the bonds and be free
    How long will you be chained to silver and gold
If you pour the sea into a jar
    does it hold more than a day's ration
The eye of the greedy is never filled
    The oyster doesn't make pearl until it surrenders
Whoever tore their robes for love
    is cleansed of all greed and flaw
Be happy   o love   our sweet dreamer
    love   the healer of all our maladies
You   the medicine for our vanity and our greed
    You   our Plato and our Galen
The earthly body soared to the skies from love
    The mountain bounced and broke into dance

1 Wording borrowed from Jalaluddin Rumii, *The Mathnawi*, translated by Reynold A. Nicholson (London: Cambridge University Press, 1926), 5, accessed 15 July 2021, Archive.Net

2 Ibid.

Ātash-e eshgh ast kandar ney fetād
    Jushesh-e eshgh ast kandar mey fetād
Ney harif-e har-ke az yāri borid
    Parde-hāyash parde-hāye mā darid
Hamcho ney zahri-o teryāghi ke did
    Hamcho ney damsāz-o moshtāghi ke did
Ney hadis-e rāhe por khun mikonad
    Ghesse-hā-ye eshgh-e majnun mikonad
Mahram-e in hush joz bi-hush nist
    Mar zabān rā moshtari joz gush nist
Dar gham-e mā ruz-hā bigāh shod
    Ruz-hā bā suz-hā hamrāh shod
Ruz-hā gar raft gu row bāk nist
    To bemān ey ānke chon tow pāk nist
Har ke joz māhi ze ābash sir shod
    Har ke bi-ruzist ruzash dir shod
Dar nayābad hāl-e pokhte hich khām
    Pas sokhan kutāh bāyad vas-salām
Band bogsal bāsh āzād ey pesar
    Chand bāshi band-e sim-o band-e zar
Gar berizi bahr rā dar kuze-i
    Chand gonjad ghesmat-e yek ruze-i
Kuze-ye cheshm-e harisān por nashod
    Tā sadaf ghāne' nahsod por dor nashod
Har ke rā jāme ze eshghi chāk shod
    Ou ze hers-o 'eyb kolli pāk shod
Shād bāsh ey eshgh-e khosh sodā-ye mā
    Ey tabib-e jomle 'ellat-hā-ye mā
Ey davāy-e nekhvat-o nāmus-e mā
    Ey to aflātun-o jālinus-e mā
Jesm-e khāk az eshgh bar aflāk shod
    Kuh dar raghs āmad-o chālāk shod

آتش عشق است کاندر نی فتاد
    جوشش عشق است کاندر می فتاد
نی حریف هر که از یاری برید
    پرده‌هایش پرده‌های ما درید
همچو نی زهری و تریاقی که دید
    همچو نی دمساز و مشتاقی که دید
نی حدیث راه پر خون می‌کند
    قصه‌های عشق مجنون می‌کند
محرم این هوش جز بیهوش نیست
    مر زبان را مشتری جز گوش نیست
در غم ما روزها بیگاه شد
    روزها با سوزها همراه شد
روزها گر رفت گو رو باک نیست
    تو بمان ای آن که چون تو پاک نیست
هر که جز ماهی ز آبش سیر شد
    هرکه بی روزیست روزش دیر شد
در نیابد حال پخته هیچ خام
    پس سخن کوتاه باید و السلام
بند بگسل باش آزاد ای پسر
    چند باشی بند سیم و بند زر
گر بریزی بحر را در کوزه‌ای
    چند گنجد قسمت یک روزه‌ای
کوزهٔ چشم حریصان پر نشد
    تا صدف قانع نشد پر در نشد
هر که را جامه ز عشقی چاک شد
    او ز حرص و عیب کلی پاک شد
شاد باش ای عشق خوش سودای ما
    ای طبیب جمله علت‌های ما
ای دوای نخوت و ناموس ما
    ای تو افلاطون و جالینوس ما
جسم خاک از عشق بر افلاک شد
    کوه در رقص آمد و چالاک شد

Love breathed life into the Sinai   o lover
    The Sinai is thundering drunk   and Moses fallen
Were I to join the lips of my beloved
    I would tell tales like the reed
Whoever parted from the one who speaks their tongue
    lost their tongue though filled with hundred songs
Once the bloom is gone and the garden dried
    you will not hear the nightingale's tales
The beloved is all and the lover but a veil
    The beloved is alive and the lover but a corpse
Whoever is not favoured by love
    there is a bird without wings   o woe
How could I know ahead and behind
    when the beloved doesn't shine on past and future
Love demands that these words become apparent
    If the mirror does not reflect   what good could it do
Do you know why your mirror doesn't reflect
    Because rust is not apart from its visage

rumi, masnavi, book one, section 1, translated by gita hashemi

Eshgh jān-e tor āmad āsheghā
        Tor mast-o kharr-e musā säeghā
Bā lab-e damsāz-e khod gar joftami
        Hamcho ney man goftani-hā goftami
Har ke ou az hamzabāni shod jodā
        Bi-zabān shod garche dārad sad navā
Chon ke gol raft-o golestān dargozasht
        Nashnavi z-ān pas ze bolbol sargozash
Jomle ma'shugh ast-o 'āshegh parde-i
        Zende ma'shugh ast-o 'āshegh morde-i
Chon nabāshad 'eshgh rā parvā-ye ou
        Ou cho morghi mānd bi-par vāy-e ou
Man chegune hush dāram pish-o pas
        Chon nabāshad nur-e yāram pish-o pas
'Eshgh khāhad kin sokhan birun bovad
        Āyene ghammāz nabvad chon bovad
Āyenat dāni cherā ghammāz nist
        Zān ke zengār az rokhash momtāz nist

عشق جان طور آمد عاشقا
        طور مست و خر موسی صاعقا
با لب دمساز خود گر جفتمی
        همچو نی من گفتنی‌ها گفتمی
هر که او از هم‌زبانی شد جدا
        بی‌زبان شد گرچه دارد صد نوا
چون که گل رفت و گلستان درگذشت
        نشنوی زآن پس ز بلبل سر گذشت
جمله معشوق است و عاشق پرده‌ای
        زنده معشوق است و عاشق مرده‌ای
چون نباشد عشق را پروای او
        او چو مرغی ماند بی‌پر وای او
من چگونه هوش دارم پیش و پس
        چون نباشد نور یارم پیش و پس
عشق خواهد کاین سخن بیرون بود
        آینه غماز نبود چون بود
آینه‌ت دانی چرا غماز نیست
        زآن که زنگار از رخش ممتاز نیست

raúl moarquech ferrera-balanquet

sama' zikr recuerdos remembrances

Al Zikr recuerdo de Maulana Jalal al-Din Rumi
A mi hermano y amigo Mohsen Hosseini

Bayt

He reunido ciertos pasajes de mi novela inédita Urakán con el objetivo de expresar el efecto que la obra de Maulana Jalal al-Din Rumi ha tenido sobre mi imaginario. Escribir sobre un afecto tan profundo como la intimidad entre hombres es un desafío al patriarcado monoteísta impuesto por ciertas religiones para colonizar culturas, pueblos, territorios y cuerpos.

Desde una posición crítica, reconozco cómo el destierro y la condición de refugiado me llevó en 1980 a Iowa City, ciudad situada en el Medio Oeste de los Estados Unidos. Allí logré ingresar en la prestigiosa Universidad de Iowa. Mientras trabajábamos juntos en una de las cafeterías universitarias, conocí a mi gran amigo Mohsen Hosseini. De su voz encantada por la mítica sabiduría de la lengua persa, escuché por primera vez los versos de Rumi. Aun hoy, me siento halagado por el amor de un amigo que sabe amar al otro tal y como el otro es. Mohsen Hosseini me ayudó a fortalecer mi espíritu emigrante y a solidificar esa identidad islámica heredada de Abuelo Moarkech, la cual, muchas veces, me causaba temor, en parte, por su absurdo patriarcado e inexplicable homofobia.

Cuando comencé a escribir el boceto de Urakán intentaba sanar la incertidumbre impuesta por la experiencia de vivir en la calle a mi llegada a los Estados Unidos. No tuve duda de imaginar una relación entre Ariamo Urakán y Dariush, personajes principales de la novela, basada en la desinteresada intimidad que experimenté con Mohsen y mis amigos persas[1] la cual me brindaron cuando, una vez más, estuve desamparado, sin dinero y sin techo. Mientras laboraba junto con Moshen, una tarde le confié la incertidumbre provocada por los gastos de una clase de producción de cine, pues debía escoger entre pagar la renta del apartamento y los gasto del laboratorio cinematográfico. Mi amigo entonces abrió la puerta del departamento compartido con otros sietes estudiantes persas. En aquella guarida aprendía a desoccidentalizar y desexualizar mi manera de imaginar la intimidad entre hombres. Aun hoy, cuando escucho hablar de la homofobia en las comunidades persas, me pregunto ¿cómo Mohsen y mis amigos persas, todos heterosexuales, me albergaron cuando yo más lo necesitaba?

Esta experiencia expandió mi visión del mundo e inspiró en mí la necesidad de aprender más sobre la cultura de Abuelo Moarkech. Conocer la obra y vida de Maulana Jalal al-Din Rumi abrió caminos de saberes, los cuales todavía transito mientras

1 [Nota del Editor: La designación Persa, con mayor precisión debería referirse solo a los iraníes de origen persa, una de las muchas naciones que habitan dentro del territorio de Irán, el cual también incluye kurdos, turcos (azeríes), baluchi, turcomano, árabes, gilaki, manzadarani, lur, tat, qashqai, asirios, armenios, georgianos y circasianos. El término persa se usa en este texto porque en la época que abarca la novela Urakán, muchos iraníes se identificaron como persas en público para protegerse de los ataques racistas que se intensificaron contra los iraníes que vivían en los EE. UU. después de la ocupación de la embajada estadounidense y la toma de rehenes en Teherán, 1979-1981.]

logró hacer un viaje ancestral al *zikr* y, simultáneamente, realizar una investigación histórica que alimenta el proceso creativo. Rumi, al igual que mis amigos persas y yo, experimentó la emigración y el destierro en su adolescencia. También amó a otro hombre con la intensidad afectiva manifestada por los personajes de mi novela. Contrario a la experiencia de Rumi y Shams de Tabriz, mis personajes logran crear un espacio en construcción, el cual les permite aprender de ambos y reconocer los temores, las ansias, los sueños, las luchas y los logros alcanzados para enfrentar el sistema patriarcal monoteísta que impidió la realización plena entre Jalal al-Din Rumi y Shams Tabriz.

Para la apariencia corporal del personaje de Dariush de mi novela me inspiré en un estudiante de Odontología, amigo de Mohsen, por quien me sentía atraído eróticamente, aunque nunca lo expresé. Imaginar la construcción del amor entre dos hombres conjugó el saber de mis ancestros Indígenas Kairibes,[2] Africanos y Árabes para completarme como ser. Nunca he experimentado físicamente el amor reflejado en la novela, pero al escribirla, sané las opresiones patriarcales y aprendí sobre la historia y la cultura de Abuelo Moarkech. A continuación incluyo fragmentos de *Urakán*.

Qawl I

Bailo los tiempos, creando *halqah* círculos contra reloj en espiral; percibo sonidos astrales. El éxtasis me comunica la información inscritas en mis células. *Sama'* danza vórtice tiempo, hereda de ancestros poetas, calígrafos, juristas, historiadores, hacedores de la palabra cantada. Giró contra reloj atravesando vientos transatlánticos conectando al Kairibe con Dameshq, ciudad amor. Habito un territorio junto abuelos sirios libaneses, encantados al escuchar las palabras conocimientos de ilustres maestros en la Madrasa. Junto a Maulana Jalal al-Din Rumi, idearon formas de acabar con las injusticias.

Imaginé el amor relacionado con un hombre persa, desplazado de su tierra por la guerra y el asesinato de sus padres. Imaginado en la corporalidad de un estudiante de medicina, a quien, desde la distancia, acaricié sus cejas juntas y su ingenua sonrisa. Me debatía entre el amargo temor de vivir en la calle y la protección desinteresada de un buen compañero de trabajo. Mohsen comprendió mis esfuerzos por sobrevivir las consecuencia hostiles de una emigración forzada. Mientras escribía evoqué a un hombre persa capaz de amar con la misma intensidad con la cual yo amaba, con la cual nos queríamos protegidos por el amor entre Rumi y Shams de Tabriz.

¿Será que la distancia, el exilio, el abandono y la inaptitud de amantes sin rumbos me hicieron sentir la desesperación, la partida y la ruptura? ¿Fue esa la razón por la cual necesité imaginar un amor horizontal, de tú a tú, de yo hacia el amado, de nosotros en desvelo? *Sama'* danza, en espiral contra reloj que une territorios y conocimientos. Navego rutas imaginadas hasta Dameshq, en donde mis ancestros comulgaron con Maulana Jalal al-Din Rumi. Al transcurrir versos siglos de amor, el *zikr* inscrito en mis células alivia la desesperación cuando repentinamente la epidemia del SIDA se llevó a amigos, compañeros y amantes.

¡Ahondo en la distancia inesperada!

Qawl II

Gracias a mi amigo Mohsen llegué al apartamento de dos cuartos, en el cual compartí con los estudiantes persas. Aquel grupo de jóvenes, la mayoría de clase media alta, compartían el apartamento. En una habitación dormían cinco personas porque después de la llegada al poder del Ayatollah Khomeini, sus padres no podían mandar dinero. Algunos trabajan por primera vez y otros mezclaban el trabajo y la escuela con una actividad política que justifica su exilio.

Aun recuerdo como mis compañeros persas se besaban al saludarse o descansaban la cabeza sobre el muslo del otro cuando miraban la televisión o cuando tres o cuatro de ellos se juntaban para hacer la cena y, en el piso, preparaban un mantel de periódicos viejos donde disfrutamos de *ghorme sabzi*, *kababs*, arroces con eneldo y cúrcuma, cebollas crudas, pan y té caliente. En mi mirada "occidental" caribeña, trastocada por el falocentrismo colonial, aquellos eran "maricones" y no lo querían aceptar. Me llevo mucho tiempo para darme

2 En la lengua Loko Arauhuca, *Kaire* significa isla y *be* es el nominal para el plural. En los sistemas de conocimiento indígena, la topografía juega un rol importante en la denominación de la comunidad y el colectivo. Regreso a nombre original del territorio para desligarme del nombramiento euro colonial.

cuenta como la intimidad entre los hombres persas es una condición histórica y que a los varones se le tiene prohibido acercarse a las mujeres. Su contacto corporal no era una respuesta carno sexual como yo lo había aprendido, sino un espacio fraterno e íntimo.

Algunos historiadores se refieren a las relaciones entre los hombres sufis como un "amor místico del tipo platónico; dos hombres - dos cuerpos con la misma alma". Igualdad y diferencia, relación contenida en la "unidad del amor". Nos preguntamos cual lugar ocupan las mujeres dentro del contexto histórico-social del siglo XII cuando la poesía sufi llega a yuxtaponerse con la espiritualidad masculina. Existen referencias a la poeta, santa, y mística sufi Rabi'ah al-Basri, considerada precursora del feminismo islámico, líder espíritual y destacada contribuyente al desarrollo del sufismo durante el siglo VIII.[3]

—El sultán Valad, biógrafo y segundo hijo de Rumi, poeta persa y miembro de la orden Mevlevi—me comentó Mohsen—reseña la relación que su padre tuvo con Shams de Tabriz quien, asustado por el acoso de los discípulos de Rumi, emigra a Damasco causando una pena enorme en el poeta. Valad va en busca del Shams y lo regresa junto al padre. En 1247, Shams desaparece misteriosamente y Rumi escribe "Líricas de Shams de Tabriz", una colección de poemas místicos donde se celebra la "otredad." Más tarde, Rumi vuelca su atención hacia Salah al-Din Fereydum Zarkub, su diputado asignado. Años después, Hosam al-Din Hasan Ibn Muhamed ocupa el lugar del "divino amado" en la vida y obra del poeta. Después de la muerte de Rumi, Hosam al-Din se convirtió en fundador y líder de la orden Mevlevi, la cual actualmente mantiene la tradición de Sama', danzas contra reloj acompañadas por una flauta caña y que desde su aparición son interpretadas por mujeres y hombres.

Qawl III

> *Since you have seen the dust, see the Wind; since you have seen the foam, see the Ocean of Creative Energy.*[4]

Años después apresuraba los pasos por la calle Cuarenta y Dos West, a la altura del teatro New Ámsterdam en la Ciudad de New York. *Third World Newsreel*, la distribuidora de mis películas, había convocado a una reunión urgente la noche anterior. Avancé rumbo a la esquina de la Séptima Avenida, doblé a la izquierda y continué hasta la calle Treinta y Ocho West; el olor de una mezcla de perejil, puerros, cilantro, fenogreco y cebolla sazonada en aceite de oliva me incitó a detenerme frente a la amplia ventana de cristal que precedía al Deli Isfahan.

Isfahan, la ciudad a donde regresó mi amigo Mohsen Hosseini al concluir la maestría porque sus padres le ordenaron terminar su relación con Inspiración Rangel y casarse con una mujer que ellos escogieron. Mohsen debía cumplir con su obligaciones, me explicó consternado mi amigo la noche antes de regresar a Irán.

Reparé en el muchacho al otro lado del cristal quien, utilizando un cazo de plata, vertía una porción de *ghorme sabzi* sobre un plato hondo de porcelana blanca; el joven reconoció mi curiosidad con una sonrisa; tomó una cuchara de arroz; excavó una ración de *shirin polo* de una cazuela de cobre y la colocó sobre un plato trinchero; depositó el cubierto y, con un plato en cada mano, dio media vuelta rumbo al comedor principal.

Extrañé a mi camarada persa. Mohsen estaba muy lejos, al otro lado del Mediterráneo; atravesó Estambul, Ankara, Tabriz y Teherán para llegar disfrazado a casa de sus padres; la policía de Irán no podía identificar que venía de los Estados Unidos; lo llevarían a la cárcel acusado de ser miembro del Mojahedin.[5]

Qawl IV

> *Wait for your senses to be transmuted, so that you may discern these occult presences...*[6]

Al final del segundo año, me quedé sin dinero después de pagar el revelado de un cortometraje para mi clase de producción de cine ficción y no pude costear el alquiler. Mohsen consultó con Ahmad, Saeed, Mehdi y Kurosh quienes me ofrecieron albergue en un apartamento de dos cuartos cerca de la avenida Muscatine; todos dormían en alfombras persas fabricadas, según se vanagloriaba mi amigo, en Isfahan, su tierra natal. También tuve mi alfombra y viví por un año con

3 Hijjas, Mulaika. "The trials of Rābi'a al-'Adawīyya in the Malay world: the woman Sufi in Hikayat Rabi'ah" *Bijdragen tot de taal-, land- en volkenkunde / Journal of the Humanities and Social Sciences of Southeast Asia*, 174, no. 2-3. (2018), 216-243.

4 Rumi, Jalal al-Din. "The Grief of the Dead," *Selected Poems of Rumi / Jalalu'l-Din Rumi*. Translated from the Persian with Introduction and notes by Reynold A. Nicholson. (Mienola, New York: Dover Publication, 2001), 6.

5 [Nota Editorial: Sazeman-i Mojahedin-i Khalq-i Iran (MEK, People's Mojahedin Organization of Iran), o Mojahedin, es una organización Islámica militante fundada en 1969 y oponente del régimen del Shah. Después del establecimiento de la República Islámica, el grupo fue marginado y ejecutó acciones armadas contra el gobierno durante los primeros años de la república. Más tarde establecieron base en Iraq. En 1980, un numeroso grupo de miembros Mojahedin fueron condenados en tribunales y ejecutados en las cárceles iraníes].

6 Rumi, Jalal al-Din. "Knowledge Is Power" *Selected Poems of Rumi*, 39.

estudiantes persas, hijos de buenas familias, dueños de autos Jaguares, BMW y Mercedes Benz y sin un centavo en el bolsillo. Al tomar el poder, el gobierno de la República Islámica reguló mandar larga sumas de dinero a cualquier país fuera de Irán debido al embargo impuesto por Occidente. En noviembre de 1979, un grupo perteneciente a la organización *Estudiantes Musulmanes Seguidores de la Ideología del Imam* ocuparon la embajada de Estados Unidos en Teherán y tomaron como rehenes a varios diplomáticos y ciudadanos estadounidenses. Esta crisis se alargó hasta enero de 1981 mientras mis compañeros persas estudiaban en la Universidad de Iowa. En aquel entonces, yo estudiaba Inglés en Iowa City.

Frente a la mesa de periódicos tendida sobre el piso de la sala del apartamento, cada uno sentado frente a una taza de té y una tajada de pastel de zanahoria, diseñábamos en un pedazo de papel estraza *el plan de confiscación*, cómo lo había bautizado Mehdi una tarde cuando cuestioné el robo en los supermercados y las tiendas de ropa.

—Arimao y Ahmad llegan al súper sin nada en las espaldas —Saeed iniciaba el plan con las funciones de quienes llenarían los bultos con los víveres escogidos durante la reunión del té. —Mehdi me acompañará en el Jaguar con una mochila.

—Yo conduciré mi BMW —agregaba Mohsen. —Kurosh irá conmigo y llevará otra mochila en su espalda.

—¿Qué se necesita? —Kurosh siempre organizaba la lista de productos a recabar durante la confiscación.

—Jamón serrano, caviar, salmón ahumado, carne de cordero, queso Brie, arroz, eneldo, azafrán, aceitunas de Palestina, mantequilla —enumeró Ahmad de acuerdo al menú planeado para esa semana.

—Entonces, cuando ya todos estén adentro —Mehdi contribuía con una estrategia mientras tomaba un par de cubos de azúcar de un pequeño plato blanco —Kurosh y yo le pasamos los bultos a Ahmad y a Arimao —las colocó en la pequeña taza de porcelana y se dispuso a verter una porción de té Negro. —Saeed junto con Mohsen se dedican a verificar los espejos… —Aún las cámaras de video y los circuitos de televisión cerrada no estaban instalados en los inmensos supermercados y los cristales redondos bañados de azogue que colgaban en la parte superior de cada esquina del recinto, configuraban el sistema de vigilancia—.

—Después de cargar los víveres, Arimao y Ahmad deben pasar las mochilas a los hombros de Kurosh y Mehdi —Saeed continuó el plan. —Y ustedes dos —señalaba a Kurosh y a Mehdi, —al llegar a la caja pagan por una botella de 7up y semillas de girasol mientras los chóferes vamos a comprar algún caramelo o una cajetilla de cigarros.

—Ahmad y Arimao, al abandonar el supermercado, van a caminar dos cuadras hacia el norte y esperan en la esquina a Kurosh y Mehdi—aportó Mohsen. —Allí van a intercambiar los bultos —trazó la última secuencia. —Estaré estacionado en la otra esquina dentro del BMW.

—Yo espero por Ahmad y Arimao en mi Jaguar a media cuadra —Saeed secundó la propuesta de Mohsen y así concluía el plan de confiscación.

Nadie imaginaba a esa tropa de chicos guapos, bien vestidos y dueños de autos último modelo a la cual yo pertenecía, ser estudiantes universitarios sin un centavo para comer y, al mismo tiempo, confiscadores de víveres, perfumes Cerruti, camisas y pantalones de Ermenegildo Zegna y zapatos de Mezlan Prato.

Qawl V

> *… the pipe and lute that charms our ears /*
> *Derive their melody from rolling spheres…*[7]

Una tarde, mientras estudiaba para la clase de teoría de cine sentado en el sofá de la sala, noté que Mehdi, envuelto en la depresión causada por su exilio político-religioso, acudía a Saeed en busca de consuelo, comprensión y abrazos reconfortantes. Hasta Dariush quien vivía a dos cuadras con otros tres estudiantes de medicina, cuando llegaba a cenar al apartamento, compartía esa costumbre con Mohsen. Confundí la cercanía con una homosexualidad escondida. Mi ignorancia cultural no me permitía ver el porqué la intimidad entre los hombres persas era totalmente explícita. Solo tenía de referencia la experiencia con Kamran —un estudiante persa a quien conocí en una clase de retórica y tuve un fracasado

7 Rumi, Jalal al-Din. "Remembered Music" *Selected Poems of Rumi*, 3.

affaire—y para mí, en aquel entonces, mis amigos tenían *affaires* secretos aunque se abrazaban sin reparo frente a todos.

Inspiración Rangel se enamoró de Mohsen atraída por sus ojos negros, nariz puntiaguda y sutil perspicacia; aquel fumador de tabaco francés *Gauloises* en pipa movía los hombros y las manos con una sensualidad que las putas de La Perla Tapatía, por seguro, envidiarían al ver tanto derroche de gracia y ritmo en el cuerpo de un hombre.

Cuando nos mudamos a los apartamentos de subsidio público de Mark IV, a orillas de la carretera a Coralville, Mohsen me aconsejó romper con esa historia de violencia oculta impuesta por Kamran.

—Ese tipo está loco, Urakán ––comentó Mohsen la noche cuando regresé del Lago McBride con el rostro golpeado. —Es muy difícil para los hombres persas tener una relación libre con otro hombre, pero cuando se quiere: *En el llanto, el que ama es como las nubes; en la perseverancia, como las montañas; en la postración, como el agua; en la humildad, como polvo del camino.*[8] Rumi lo tenía bien claro, ¿entiendes, *azizam*? El amor de Kamran no es amor. Para los persas, el amor por el otro hombre es encontrar esa mitad complementaria. No importa si las caricias llegan a la intimidad sexual donde has estado con Kamran. Lo carnal puede estar ahí, ¿me entiendes? Ahí, justo cuando nos besamos o dormimos sobre el pecho del otro para no sentir la soledad impuesta por estar lejos de las mujeres. A veces estás cerca del otro y te preguntas: *Se apoderó de mí el poder del amor / y me volví fiero como el león, / y después tierno como el lucero del alba.*[9] No, Kamran no te ama como aman los hombres persas y tampoco cómo se aman los occidentales, porque esa violencia viene de su inaptitud, de su baja autoestima, de su desquiciada frivolidad. *Puede que el sediento se duerma durante un rato, pero soñará con agua, con una jarra bien llena al lado de un arroyo o con el agua espiritual que se recibe de la otra persona…*[10] ¡Oh, Rumi, poeta de varones y vino, cuánta verdad guardan tus versos!

Y, al abrir sus brazos, Mohsen me cobijó para que externara el llanto y la angustia.

8 Rumi, Jalal al-Din, "Conocer el Amor," *Perfume del desierto: Tesoro de la Sabiduría Sufi*, edited by Andrew Harvey (México D.F.: Alamah, 1999), 93. [Traducido por Sebastián Patiño]

9 Rumi, Jalal al-Din. "Sublime Generosidad," *La Esencia de Rumi*, Coleman Bark, edit., (España: Ediciones Obelisco, 2002), 173. [Traducido por Alejandro Arrese. Barcelona]

10 Rumi, Jalal al-Din. "La Vigilia," *La Esencia de Rumi*, 116-117.

Wajd

Entre movimientos contra reloj, comencé a bailar en los sueños. Mis brazos conducían los ritmos vórtices alimentando el trance mientras atravesaba distancias. Logré percibir imágenes proyectada sobre las aguas del mar Caribe. Un barco mercante cruzaba olas atlánticas hasta llegar al puerto de Santiago de Cuba. El abuelo Moarkech, junto a su hermano menor, descendía de la nave que abordaron en el puerto de Santa Cruz de La Palma. Los *halqahs* aceleraban la respiración alterando mi estado anímico. De repente, sentí arcos arabescos dibujar el entorno con azules geometrías. Entrelazaban círculos reflejados en mis movimientos. Alcanzaba el *wajd* bebiendo el aire cósmico y envuelto en *Sama'* cuando, una vez más, sentí como salía de mi cuerpo para ver el *zikr*.

En el interior de la *madrasa*, la escuela donde estudiaban mis ancestros sirios libaneses junto a Jalal al-Din Rumi en Dameshq, el vórtice alimentaba los *halqahs*. Shaykh Muhammad, con palabras alentadoras, enseñaba poesía, caligrafía, leyes, historia y los *qawl* y *bayt*, himnos, los cuales, al ser cantados en *halqahs*, llevaba a alcanzar *wajd*, el embriagador éxtasis. Destellos solares penetraron el interior de la escuela. En trance, desde la distancia, reconocí los flujos cósmicos uniendo eras, migraciones y experiencias. Sentí el amor amigo instigado por Mohsen Hosseini aquellos días cuando, envueltos en la pobreza y el exilio, alimentábamos las esperanzas de crecer nuestros saberes en la Universidad de Iowa, a pesar de las vicisitudes.

El *wajd* no sólo conectaba mi memoria ancestral con la vida de Rumi, sino también traía el *zikr* afirmando la conexión con Mohsen, Dariush, Mehdi y mis compañeros persas. Entonces comprendí cómo los hombres persas aman a los hombres entre rituales lazos. Comprendí como Dariush me amaba en el reflejo de mis luchas, mis ansias, en el dolor del exilio incrustado en su alma desde la noche cuando presenció el asesinato de sus padres.

Aceleré los *halqahs* contra reloj en busca de otras respuestas y sentí los saberes de Abuelo Moarkech cargados de poesía, caligrafías, leyes y de la encantación de versos heredada de mi padre. En vórtice contra reloj percibí la huida de Abuelo Moarkech. Junto a su hermano menor abandonaba Dameshq, la tierra origen. Llevó con él lo aprendido en Sama' rituales: la poesía de Al-Mutanabbi—*Porque el corazón no tiene más remedio que disponer de su propio medio, un raciocinio que hienda la más sólida roca*[11]—junto a los versos de Jalal al-Din Rumi—*De repente, se inclinó y susurró algo al oído del otro rey y, en aquel instante, ese otro rey también se convirtió en un hombre errante. Cogidos de la mano, salieron de la ciudad, sin cintos reales ni tronos*[12]. Abuelo Moarkech y su hermano atravesaban el desierto hasta el puerto de Constantinopla. Allí, gracias a pasaportes turcos, pudieron embarcar a la Isla de Córcega. A bordo de un barco camaronero, cruzaba el Golfo de México rumbo al exilio cuando imaginé la brisa salada del Mediterráneo. Me embriagó el *zikr* mientras que en la proa de otro barco, proyecté el recuerdo del Abuelo Moarkech divisando la costa de Santa Cruz de La Palma. Al re-imaginar ese viaje, logré el éxtasis espiritual afirmando el amor de Dariush. Desapareció el temor del abandono mientras, acelerando los *halqahs* contra reloj, junto a Mohsen y Dariush comencé a cantar los versos de Maulana Jalal al-Din Rumi: *El amor está aquí; es la sangre de mis venas, mi piel. Estoy destrozado; él me ha llenado de pasión. Su fuego ha inundado los nervios de mi cuerpo. ¿Quién soy? Sólo mi nombre; el resto es Él.*[13]

11 Abul Tayib Al-Mutanabbi, "Kafur," *Poesía Árabe Clásica*, traducido por Bolado, Alfonso et. al. (Madrid, España – México D.F.: Grijalbo Mondadori S.A., 1998), 50.

12 Rumi, Jalal al-Din. "Imra'u 'L-Qays" *La Esencia de Rumi*, 121-122.

13 Rumi, Jalalu'l-Din. "El amor está aquí" *Perfume del desierto: Tesoro de la Sabiduría Sufi*, 172.

Raul Moarquech Ferrera-Balanquet, PhD (Duke University), MFA (University of Iowa), was born in Havana in 1958. He is the Co-Executive Director of Howard University Gallery of Art, and the author of *Aestesis Decolonial Transmoderna Latinx_MX* (2019). He exhibited at Haceres Decoloniales, Galeria ASAB, Bogota; and BE.a 2013, Berlin; and received grants from Critical Minded, FONCA, and Lyn Blumenthal Video Foundation.

raúl moarquech ferrera-balanquet

sama' zikr recuerdos remembrances

translated by ml papusa molina

Zikr of Malana Jalal al-Din Rumi
To my brother and friend Mohsen Hosseini

Bayt

I have gathered specific passages from my unpublished novel Urakán, aiming to express the effect that Maulana Jalal al-Din Rumi's work has had upon my imagination. Writing about an affect as deep as intimacy between men is a challenge to the monotheistic patriarchy imposed by certain religions to colonize cultures, peoples, territories, and bodies.

From a critical position, I recognize how exile, as well as my refugee status, led me to Iowa City in 1980, a city located in the Midwest of the United States. There, I managed to enter the prestigious University of Iowa. While working together at one of the university cafeterias, I met my dear friend Mohsen Husseini. It was from his voice, enchanted by the mythical wisdom of the Persian language, that I heard Rumi's verses for the first time. Even today, I am flattered by the love of a friend who knows how to love the other just as he is. Mohsen Husseini also helped me strengthen my migrant spirit and solidify that Islamic identity inherited from my Grandfather Moarkech, which often caused fear, partly due to its absurd patriarchy and inexplicable homophobia.

When I began to write the sketch for *Urakán*, I was trying to overcome the uncertainty imposed by the experience of living on the streets upon my arrival in the United States. I had no hesitation in imagining a relationship between Ariamo Urakán and Darisuh, the novel's main characters, based on the selfless intimacy I experienced with Mohsen and my Persian[1] friends—an intimacy given to me when I was once again destitute, penniless, and homeless. One afternoon, while working along Mohsen at the cafeteria, I shared my uncertainty about the costs of a film production class, as I had to choose between paying for the rent or for the film lab's costs. After this conversation my friend opened to me the door to the apartment he shared with seven other Persian students. In that hideout, I learned to de-westernize and de-sexualize how I imagined intimacy between men. Even today, when I hear others talking about homophobia in Persian communities, I wonder how Mohsen and my Persian friends, all straight, sheltered me when I most needed it.

This experience expanded my vision of the world and inspired the need to learn more about my Grandfather Moarkech's culture. Learning about the work and life of

1 [Editor's note: The designation Persian more accurately should refer only to Iranians of Persian origin, one of the many nations within Iran proper that also includes Kurdish, Turkish (Azeri), Baluchi, Turkmen, Arab, Gilaki, Mazandarani, Lur, Tat, Qashqai, Armenian, Assyrian, Georgian, and Circassian people. The term Persian is used here because in the time period of this piece many Iranians identified as Persian in public in order to protect themselves from racist attacks escalated against Iranians living in the US following the events dubbed Iran hostage crisis, November 1979 to January 1981.]

Maulana Jalal al-Din Rumi opened paths of knowledge that I still travel while managing to make an ancestral journey to *zikr* and, simultaneously, carry out historical research that feeds the creative process. Rumi, like my Persian friends and me, experienced migration and exile in his teens. He also loved another man with the same emotional intensity with which the characters in my novel love each other. However, contrary to the experience of Rumi and Shams of Tabriz, my characters manage to create a space under construction, one that allows them to learn from each other, recognizing the fears, anxieties, dreams, struggles, and achievements obtained against the monotheistic patriarchal system that prevented full realization between Jalal al-Din Rumi and Shams of Tabriz.

In my novel, for the bodily appearance of the character of Dariush, I was inspired by a friend of Mohsen who was studying dentistry, and to whom I was erotically attracted, although I never publicly expressed it. Imagining how love was constructed between two men allowed me to combine my Kairibe[2], African, and Arab indigenous ancestors' knowledge, and to become complete as a person. I have never physically experienced the love reflected in the novel, but by writing it, I healed from patriarchal oppressions and learned about Grandfather Moarkech's history and culture. What follows are fragments from *Urakán*.

Qawl I

I dance to the beats, creating counterclockwise spiral *halqahs*; I perceive astral sounds. Ecstasy communicates the information inscribed in my cells. *Sama'* time vortex dance inherited from my ancestors—poets, calligraphers, jurists, and historians, makers of the sung word. The movement turned counterclockwise, crossing transatlantic winds, connecting the Kairibe landscape with Dameshq, the city of love. I inhabit a territory with Syrian-Lebanese grandfather, enchanted to hear the words of knowledge from illustrious teachers in the *Madrasa*. Next to Maulana Jalal al-Din Rumi, my ancestors devised ways to end injustice.

I had to imagine love in relation to a Persian man, who was displaced from his land by war and the murder of his parents. I imagined him in the body of a medical student, whose close-knit eyebrows and naïve smile I caressed from a distance. I was torn between the bitter fear of living on the streets and the selfless protection of a good co-worker. Mohsen understood my efforts to survive the hostile consequences of forced migration. While writing, I evoked a Persian man capable of loving with the same intensity I loved, with the intensity with which we loved each other, as we imagined to be protected by the love between Rumi and Shams of Tabriz.

Could it be that the distance, the exile, the abandonment, and the ineptitude of aimless lovers made me feel despair, departure, and rupture? Was that the reason I needed to imagine a horizontal love, from you to you, from me to the loved one, from us in wakefulness? *Sama'*—the spiral counterclockwise dance that unites territories and knowledge. I sail imagined routes to Dameshq, where my ancestors communed with Maulana Jalal al-Din Rumi. As these centuries-old love verses go by, the *zikr* inscribed on my cells eases the despair I felt when the AIDS epidemic suddenly swept away friends, partners, and lovers.

I dive deep into the unexpected distance!

Qawl II

Thanks to my friend Mohsen, I arrived at the two-room apartment I shared with the Persian students. That group of young people, mainly upper-middle class, had to share the apartment and sleep five in a room because after Ayatollah Khomeini came to power, their parents could not send them money. Some worked for the first time in their lives, and others mixed work and school with a political activity that justified their exile.

I still remember how my Persian comrades kissed each other when they greeted or rested their heads on each other's thighs when they watched television or when they embraced as three or four of them got together to make dinner. On the floor, they prepared a mat of old newspapers where we enjoyed *ghorme sabzi*, kababs, rice with turmeric and dill, raw

2 *Kairibe*, meaning the islands, is a Loko Arawak word consisting of *kairi* (island) and *be* (plural nominal). In Indigenous knowledge systems, topography plays an important role in the naming of the collective/community. I return to the original name to detach from euro colonial naming.

onions, bread, and hot tea. In my Caribbean "Western" view, disrupted by colonial phallocentrism, they were "faggots" who did not want to accept it. It took me a long time to realize that intimacy among Persian men is a historical condition created by the prohibition against approaching women. Their bodily contact was not a carnal, sexual response, as I had learned, but a fraternal and intimate space.

Some historians refer to relations between Sufi men as a "mystical love of the platonic type; two men—two bodies with the same soul." Equality and difference, a relationship that is always maintained in the "unity of love." We wonder what place women occupy within the socio-historical context of the twelfth century when Sufi poetry comes to be connected with male spirituality. There are references to the female Sufi poet, saint, and mystic Rabi'ah al-Basri, considered a forerunner of Islamic feminism, a spiritual leader, and a noted contributor to the development of Sufism during the 8th century.[3]

Sultan Valad, biographer and second son of Rumi—Mohsen told me—reviews the relationship his father had with Shams of Tabriz, who, frightened by the harassment from Rumi's disciples, migrates to Dameshq, causing the poet great sorrow. Valad goes in search of Shams and returns him to the father. In 1247, Shams mysteriously disappears, and Rumi writes "Lyrics of Shams of Tabriz," a collection of mystical poems celebrating "otherness." Rumi then turns his attention to Salah al-Din Fereydun Zarkub, his appointed deputy. Years later, Hosam al-Din Hasan Ibn Muhamed occupies the place of the "divine beloved" in the life and work of the poet. After Rumi's death, Hosam al-Din became a founder and a leader of the Mevlevi order that currently maintains the tradition of *sama'*, counterclockwise dances accompanied by a reed flute, which are performed by women and men ever since their beginnings.

Qawl III

> *Since you have seen the dust, see the Wind; since you have seen the foam, see the Ocean of Creative Energy.*[4]

Years later, I hurried along West Forty-Second Street, close to the New Amsterdam Theater in New York City. *Third World Newsreel*, the distributor of my films, had called an urgent meeting the night before. I walked towards the corner of Seventh Avenue, turned left, and continued to West Thirty-Eighth Street. The smell of a mixture of parsley, leeks, coriander, fenugreek, and onions seasoned in olive oil prompted me to stop in front of the wide glass window of the Isfahan Deli.

Isfahan was the city my friend Mohsen returned to when he finished his master's degree because his parents ordered him to end his relationship with Inspiración Rangel and marry a woman they had chosen. He had to fulfill his duty, my distraught friend explained to me, the night before returning to Iran.

I peeked at the boy on the other side of the glass who, using a silver ladle, was pouring a portion of *ghorme sabzi* in a deep white porcelain plate. The young man acknowledged my curiosity with a smile; took a spatula of rice; dug out a serving of *shirin polo* from a copper pot and placed it on a serving plate; then, he put down the utensils and, with a plate in each hand, turned towards the main dining room.

I missed my Persian comrade. Mohsen was far away, across the Mediterranean. He crossed Istanbul, Ankara, Tabriz, and Tehran to arrive in disguise at his parents' house. He could not allow the Iranian authorities to discover his return from the United States. That would entail the risk of getting arrested, charged with being a member of the Mojahedin,[5] and imprisoned.

Qawl IV

> *Wait for your senses to be transmuted, so that you may discern these occult presences ...*[6]

At the end of my second year, I ran out of money after paying for the developing of a short film for my fiction film production class, and I could not afford to pay my rent. Mohsen consulted with Ahmad, Saeed, Mehdi, and Kurosh, who offered me shelter in their shared two-bedroom apartment near Muscatine Avenue where, as my friend boasted, they all slept on Persian rugs made in Isfahan, his hometown. I was given

3 Hijjas, Mulaika, "The trials of Rābi'a al-'Adawīyya in the Malay world: the woman Sufi in Hikayat Rabi'ah," *Bijdragen tot de taal-, land- en volkenkunde / Journal of the Humanities and Social Sciences of Southeast Asia*, 174, no. 2-3 (2018) 216-243.

4 Rumi, Jalal al-Din. "The Grief of the Dead," *Selected Poems of Rumi/Jalalu'l-Din Rumi*, translated from the Persian with introduction and notes by Reynold A. Nicholson (Mineola, New York: Dover Publication, 2001), 6.

5 [Editor's note: Sazemān-e Mojāhedin-e Khalgh-e Iran (MEK, People's Mojahedin Organization of Iran), or Mojāhedin in short, is a militant Muslim organization that was founded in 1969 in opposition to the Shah's rule. After the establishment of the Islamic Republic, they were sidelined and conducted armed actions against the government for the first few years, and then established a base in Iraq. In the 1980s, a large number of Mojāhedin members were summarily tried and executed in Iranian prisons.]

6 Rumi, Jalal al-Din. "Knowledge Is Power," *Selected Poems of Rumi*, 39.

my own carpet, and lived for a year with Persian students, children of affluent families, owners of Jaguars, BMWs, and Mercedes Benzes—and without a penny in their pocket. Upon taking power, the government of the Islamic Republic regulated sending large sums of money to any country outside of Iran due to the embargo imposed by the West. In November 1979, the *Muslim Student Followers of the Imam's Line* occupied the U.S. embassy in Tehran and took several US diplomats and embassy staff hostage. This crisis dragged on until January 1981, while my Persian friends were studying at the University of Iowa. At the time, I was studying English in Iowa City.

One afternoon, each of us seated with a cup of tea and a slice of carrot cake around a spread of newspapers placed on the living room floor, we drew on a piece of butcher paper *the confiscation plan*, as Mehdi had baptized it after I asked about the theft in supermarkets and clothing stores.

"Arimao and Ahmad arrive at the supermarket with nothing on their backs," Saeed began the plan with the roles of those who would fill the bags with the food items decided on during the tea meeting. "Mehdi will accompany me in the Jaguar with a backpack."

"I will drive my BMW," Mohsen added. "Kurosh will go with me, carrying another backpack."

"What is needed?" Kurosh always organized the list of products that needed to be collected during the confiscation.

"Serrano ham, caviar, smoked salmon, lamb meat, Brie cheese, rice, dill, saffron, Palestinian olives, butter," Ahmad listed according to the menu planned for that week.

"Then, when everyone is already inside," Mehdi contributed with a strategy while taking a couple of sugar cubes from a small white plate, "Kurosh and I will pass the bags to Ahmad and Arimao," he continued as he placed cubes of sugar into the small porcelain cup and poured black tea. "Saeed, along with Mohsen, will check for the mirrors." In those years, video cameras and closed-circuits television were not installed in all supermarkets; and mirror balls hanging in the upper part of each corner of the enclosure made up the surveillance system.

"After loading the groceries, Arimao and Ahmad should put the backpacks on Kurosh and Mehdi's shoulders," Saeed continued with the plan. "And you two," he pointed to Kurosh and Mehdi, "when you arrive at the register, pay for a bottle of 7up and a package of sunflower seeds, meanwhile the drivers will buy some candy or a pack of cigarettes."

"Ahmad and Arimao, when leaving the supermarket, are going to walk two blocks north and wait for Kurosh and Mehdi at the corner," Mohsen added. "There, the four of you are going to exchange packages," he drew out the last sequence. "I will be parked on the other corner, inside the BMW."

"I will wait for Ahmad and Arimao in my Jaguar, half a block away," Saeed seconded Mohsen's proposal, and thus, the *confiscation plan* concluded.

No one imagined that this troop of handsome young men, which I became a part of, these well-dressed owners of the latest model luxury cars were university students without a penny to eat and, at the same time, confiscators of groceries, Cerruti perfumes, Ermenegildo Zegna shirts and pants, and Mezlan Prato shoes.

Qawl V

> *... the pipe and lute that charms our ears / Derive their melody from rolling spheres ...*[7]

One afternoon, while studying for film theory class sitting on the sofa in the living room, I noticed that Mehdi, engulfed in the depression caused by his political-religious exile, turned to Saeed for relief, understanding, and comforting hugs. Even Dariush, who lived two blocks away with three other medical students, shared that custom with Mohsen when he came to the apartment for dinner. I confused their closeness with hidden homosexuality. My cultural ignorance did not allow me to understand why the intimacy between Persian men was explicit. I only had the experience with Kamran—a Persian student I met in a rhetoric course and with whom I had an unsuccessful affair—as a reference; and to me during that time my friends had secret *affairs* even though they hugged without hesitation in front of everyone.

Inspiración Rangel fell in love with Mohsen, attracted by his black eyes, pointed nose, and subtle insights. That smoker of

7 Rumi, Jalal al-Din. "Remembered Music," *Selected Poems of Rumi*, 3.

French *Gauloises* tobacco in a pipe moved his shoulders and hands with a sensuality that the whores of La Perla Tapatía would envy for sure when seeing such extravagance of grace and rhythm in a man's body.

When we moved into the Mark IV publicly subsidized apartments, just along the road to Coralville, Mohsen advised me to break away from the history of hidden violence imposed by Kamran.

"That guy is crazy, Urakán," Mohsen commented that night when I returned from Lake McBride with a bruised face. "It is very complicated for Persian men to have a free relationship with other men, but when they love each other: *In weeping, the lover is like the clouds;/ In perseverance, like the mountains;/ In prostration, like water;/ In humility, like dirt in the road.*"[8] Rumi had it very clear, do you understand, *azizam*? Kamran's is not love. For a Persian man, love for another man is finding that half that complements you. It does not matter if caresses and words do not reach the sexual intimacy where you have been with Kamran. The carnal can be there. Do you understand me? There, just when we kiss or sleep on each other's chest so as not to feel the loneliness imposed by being away from women. Sometimes you are close to each other, and you wonder: *The power of love came into me, / and I became fierce like a lion / then tender like the evening star.*[9] No, Kamran does not love you the way Persian men love each other, and neither does he love the way Westerners love each other because that violence comes from his inadequacy, low self-esteem, and insane shallowness. *Someone who's thirsty may sleep for a little while, but he or she will dream of water, a full jar beside a creek, or the spiritual water you get from another person...*[10] Oh, Rumi, poet of men and wine, how much truth your verses hold!

And, opening his arms, Mohsen sheltered me so I could shed my tears and express my anguish.

Wajd

Between counterclockwise movements, I began to dance in my dreams. My arms drove the vortex rhythms nurturing the trance as I crossed distances. I perceived images projected on the waters of the Caribbean Sea. A merchant ship crossed the Atlantic waves until it reached the port of Santiago de Cuba. Grandfather Moarkech and his younger brother descended from the ship they boarded in the port of Santa Cruz de La Palma. The *halqahs* quickened my breathing, altering my mood. Suddenly, I felt arabesque curves drawing the landscape with blue geometries. They weaved in and out of the circles reflected in my movements. I was reaching *wajd*, drinking the cosmic air and wrapped in *sama'* when, once again, I felt myself leaving my body to see the *zikr*.

Inside the *Madrasa*, the school where my Syrian Lebanese ancestors studied with Jalal al-Din Rumi in Dameshq, the vortex fueled the *halqah*. Shaykh Muhammad, with encouraging words, taught poetry, calligraphy, law, history, and the *qawl* and *bayt*, hymns that, when sung in *halqahs*, led to *wajd*, exhilarating ecstasy. Solar flares penetrated the interior of the school. In a trance, from the distance, I recognized the cosmic flows uniting epochs, migrations, and experiences. I felt the friendly love instigated by Mohsen Hosseini in those days when, wrapped in poverty and exile, we nurtured the hopes of growing our knowledge at the University of Iowa, despite the vicissitudes.

The *wajd* not only connected my ancestral memory with Rumi's life but also brought the *zikr*, the connections with Mohsen, Dariush, Mehdi, and my fellow Persians. Then, I understood how Persian men love other men as ritual bonds. I understood how Dariush loved me in the reflection of my struggles, my anxieties, in the pain of exile that he carried in his soul since the night when he witnessed the murder of his parents.

Speeding the counterclockwise *halqahs* in search of more answers, I felt Grandfather Moarkech's knowledge loaded with poetry, calligraphy, law, and the enchantment of verses inherited from my father. Then, in a counterclockwise vortex, I perceived Grandfather Moarkech's flight. Along with his younger brother, he left Dameshq, his land of origin. Grandfather Moarkech brought with him what he learned in *sama'*: Al-Mutanabbi's poetry: *Because the heart has no choice / but to dispose of its means, / reasoning splits the most solid rock,*[11] along

8 Rumi, Jalal al-Din. "Love's Familiar" *Perfume of the desert: Inspirations of Sufi Wisdom* edited by Andrew Harvey and Eryk Hanut (Quest Books, 1999), 78.

9 Rumi, Jalal al-Din. "Sublime Generosity," *The Essential Rumi*, trans. Coleman Barks with John Moyne (Edison, NJ: Castle Books, 1995), 134.

10 Rumi, Jalal al-Din. "The Vigil," *The Essential Rumi*, 85-86.

with Jalal al-Din Rumi's verses: *Then suddenly he leaned and whispered something in the second king's ear, and that second, that second king became a wanderer too. They walked out of town hand in hand. No royal belts, no thrones.*[12] Grandfather Moarkech and his brother crossed the desert, all the way to the port of Constantinople. There, thanks to Turkish passports, they were able to embark for the island of Corsica. On board of a shrimp vessel, I was crossing the Gulf of Mexico towards exile, when I imagined the salty breeze of the Mediterranean. It made me drunk with *zikr* while I projected, on the bow of another ship, the memory of Grandfather Moarkech glancing at the coast of Santa Cruz de La Palma. Re-imagining that journey, I reached the spiritual ecstasy that affirmed Dariush's love. The fear of abandonment disappeared as I accelerated the *halqahs* counterclockwise, and together with Mohsen and Dariush I began to sing the verses of Maulana Jalal al-Din Rumi: *Love is here; It is the blood in my veins, my skin. / I am destroyed; He has filled me with Passion. / His fire has flooded the nerves of my body. / Who am I? Just my name; the rest is Him.*[13]

11 Abul Tayib Al-Mutanabbi, "Kafur" *Poesía Árabe Clásica*. (Madrid-Mexico City: Grijalbo Mondadori SA, 1998) 50. [English translation by Maria Luisa Molina Lopez].

12 Rumi, Jalal al-Din. "Imra'u 'L-Qays" *The Essential Rumi*, 90-91.

13 Rumi, Jalal al-Din. "Love is here" *Perfume of the desert*, 156.

Raul Moarquech Ferrera-Balanquet, PhD (Duke University), MFA (University of Iowa), was born in Havana in 1958. He is the Co-Executive Director of Howard University Gallery of Art, and the author of *Aestesis Decolonial Transmoderna Latinx_MX* (2019). He exhibited at Haceres Decoloniales, Galeria ASAB, Bogota; and BE.a 2013, Berlin; and received grants from Critical Minded, FONCA, and Lyn Blumenthal Video Foundation.

Translator ML Papusa Molina, PhD, was born and currently lives in Merida, Yucatan, Mexico. She is happily retired as Executive Director of the Kanankil Institute. Once in a while she teaches dialogical social inquiry, swims, and writes her opinion on social justice issues. She consults at the international level on collaborative-dialogic practices.

rumi

ghazal 1759

Ah how colourless and traceless I am[1]
    When shall I see me the way that I am
You said   Place the secrets in the middle
    Where is the middle in this midst that I am
When will my soul become still
    as still in the motion[2] that I am
My sea drowned in itself
    wondrous shoreless sea that I am
Do not seek me in this world and that
    This world and that are lost in that world that I am
I am free of profit and loss like inexistence
    marvelous no-profit no-loss that I am
I said   My life   you are just like me
    They said   What is likeness in this manifest that I am
I said you are that   They said   Be silent[3]
    No tongue has spoken this that I am
I said because it hasn't been spoken
    Here   see your mute speaker that I am
I tumbled through annihilation   footless like the moon[4, 5]
    Here   see your footless runner that I am
The voice came   Why do you run   Look
    in this hidden apparent that I am
When I saw Shams-e Tabriz I became
    the marvelous sea and treasure that I am

1 According to Shafiei-Kadkani, this ghazal was composed after a painter who was commissioned by Gorji-Khatun, a patroness and devotee of Rumi, to paint an image of him, failed repeatedly to capture his likeness because every time he finished a painting he saw it looked different from its subject, Rumi. Molana Jalal al-Din Mohammad Balkhi, *Gozide-ye Ghazaliyat-e Shams* be kushesh-e doctor Mohammad Reza Shafiei-Kadkani (Tehran: Amir Kabir, 1365/1987) footnote 1, p 341.

2 This hemistich could also be translated as "residing in the soul that I am." *Sāken* could variously mean *residing in* or *stationary*, and *ravān* could mean in motion or soul.

3 In classical Persian ghazal the poet conventionally brings in their poetic name usually, but not always, in the last line which often speaks to or about the poet themself. Rumi used "Silent"—variously *khāmush*, *khamosh*, or *khamush*—and its constructs as one of his poetic signatures. See "Being the Astrolabe," page 46 in this volume.

4 This hemistich could also be translated as "in inexistence I became footless like the moon." *Mishodam* could variously mean *I became* or *I went*.

5 *Fanā*, translated here as annihilation, is the opposite of *baghā'* which means existence in this world. At its simplest, *fanā* could mean death. In Sufi lexicon, *fanā* means dying to this world before the physical death, i.e. transcending the self or passing away from the self.

مولوی

غزل ۱۷۵۹

Ah che birang-o bineshān ke manam
    Key bebinam marā chonān ke manam
Gofti asrār dar miyān āvar
    Ku miyān andar in miyān ke manam
Key shavad in ravān-e man sāken
    in chonin sāken-e ravān ke manam
Bahr-e man gharghe gasht ham dar khish
    bol-'ajab bahr-e bi-karān ke manam
In jahān vān jahān marā matalab
    kin dow gom shod dar ān jahān ke manam
Fāregh az sudam-o ziyān cho 'adam
    torfe bisud-o biziyan ke manam
Goftam ey jān to 'eyn-e māyi goft
    'Eyn chebvad dar in 'ayān ke manam
Goftam āni Begoft hāy khamush
    Dar zabān nāmadast ānke manam
Goftam andar zabān cho dar nāmad
    int guyāy-e bizaban ke manam
Mishodam dar fanā cho mah bipā
    int bipā-ye pādavān ke manam
Bāng āmad che midavi bengar
    dar chonin zāher-e nahān ke manam
Shams-e Tabriz rā cho didam man
    nādere bahr-o ganj-o kān ke manam

اه چه بی‌رنگ و بی‌نشان که منم
    کی ببینم مرا چنان که منم
گفتی اسرار در میان آور
    کو میان اندر این میان که منم
کی شود این روان من ساکن
    این چنین ساکن روان که منم
بحر من غرقه گشت هم در خویش
    بوالعجب بحر بی‌کران که منم
این جهان و آن جهان مرا مطلب
    کاین دو گم شد در آن جهان که منم
فارغ از سودم و زیان چو عدم
    طرفه بی‌سود و بی‌زیان که منم
گفتم ای جان تو عین مایی گفت
    عین چه بود در این عیان که منم
گفتم آنی بگفت های خموش
    در زبان نامده‌ست آن که منم
گفتم اندر زبان چو درنامد
    اینت گویای بی‌زبان که منم
می شدم در فنا چو مه بی‌پا
    اینت بی‌پای پادوان که منم
بانگ آمد چه می‌دوی بنگر
    در چنین ظاهر نهان که منم
شمس تبریز را چو دیدم من
    نادره بحر و گنج و کان که منم

read in persian by gita hashemi

masoud eskandari

the self

These images are extracted from a larger animation project, a meditation on the question 'Who am I?' inspired by the poetry of Rumi. The images represent parts of my history and experience, symbols of what influenced my life and identity:

Cyrus the Great, representing justice for many Iranians; Mohammad Reza Pahlavi, Iran's last king before the 1979 Revolution, the event that turned my life upside down when I was 18; the beautiful Persian letter 'N' pointing to the language and culture Iranians take pride in; Khomeini, the first Supreme Leader of the Islamic Republic; Fadaian-e Khalq—the largest communist armed guerrilla organization—that I was a member of; Ahmadinejad, internationally known as Iran's anti-semitic president; a noose representing the prison and threat of execution that always had its shadow on me; Khamenei, the second and current Supreme Leader in Iran.

Rumi's poem aptly encapsulates these icons, what they represented, and my personal traumatic trajectory. During a time when I struggled to regain my mental wellbeing, Rumi's mystical poetry played an essential role in my life. His poetry helped me rediscover myself and explore the many layers of my identity. Rumi's poetry is about understanding the self; the spirit, the body, our weaknesses and strengths, our relation to nature, and our faith in the four elements that he believes are the basis of everything. He is always searching for the core humanity and the appreciation of human love even though his language is mystical. His poems are revelations, evidence of the purification of faith through the discovery of the self. What could be more beautiful?

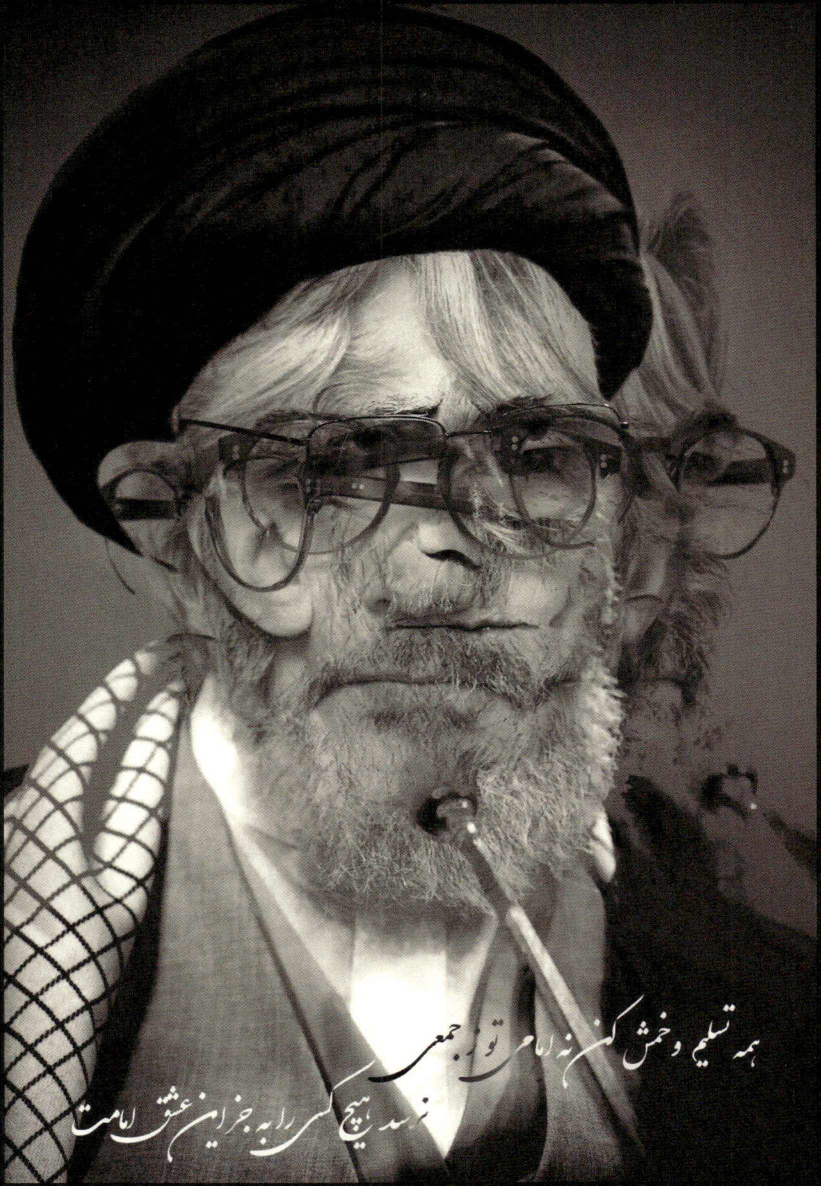

Silence and surrender all You are not imam but of the crowd
No one shall reach Imamat except through love

As I arrived from the unseen I raised the unseen army
Begone you insolent tyrant you have fallen from guardianship

O Love   like Moses   behead the Pharaoh of pride
Come forth o Pharaoh   for I have seized your edifice

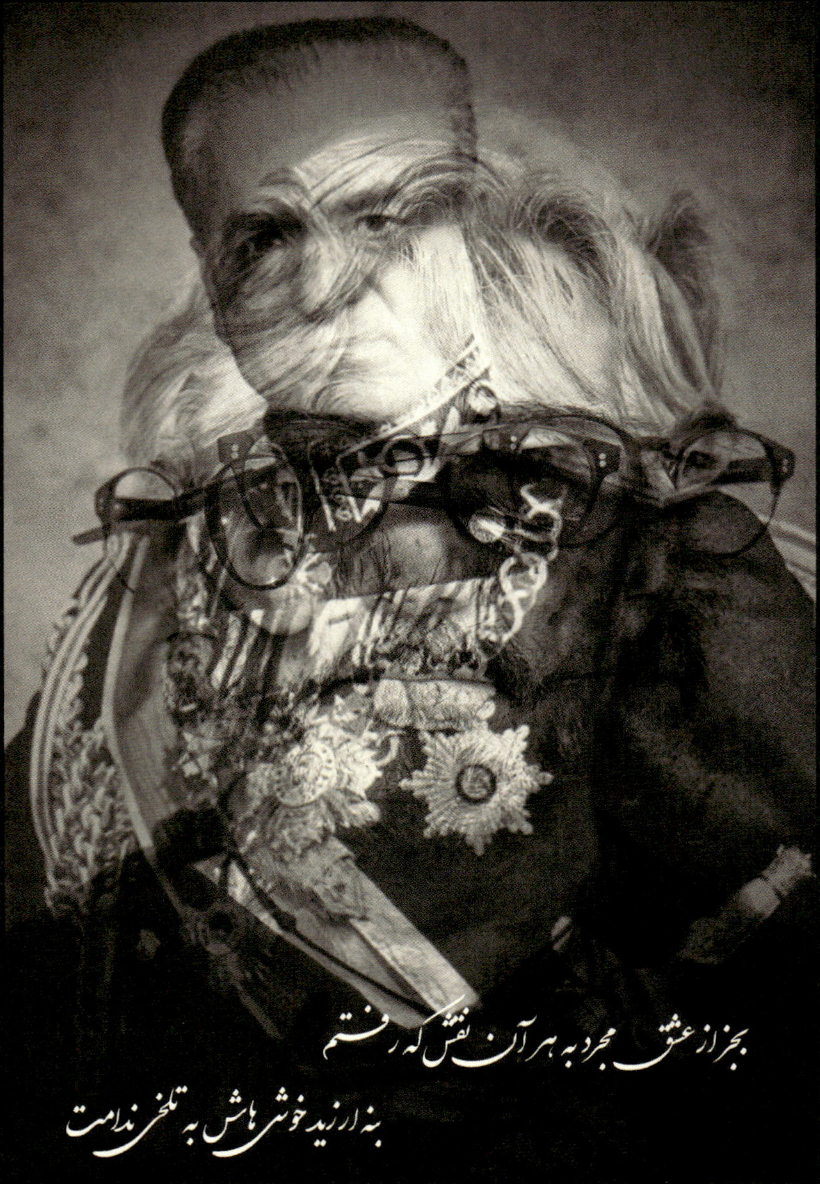

Other than speculative love   any vision that I pursued
its pleasures were not worth   the bitterness of regret

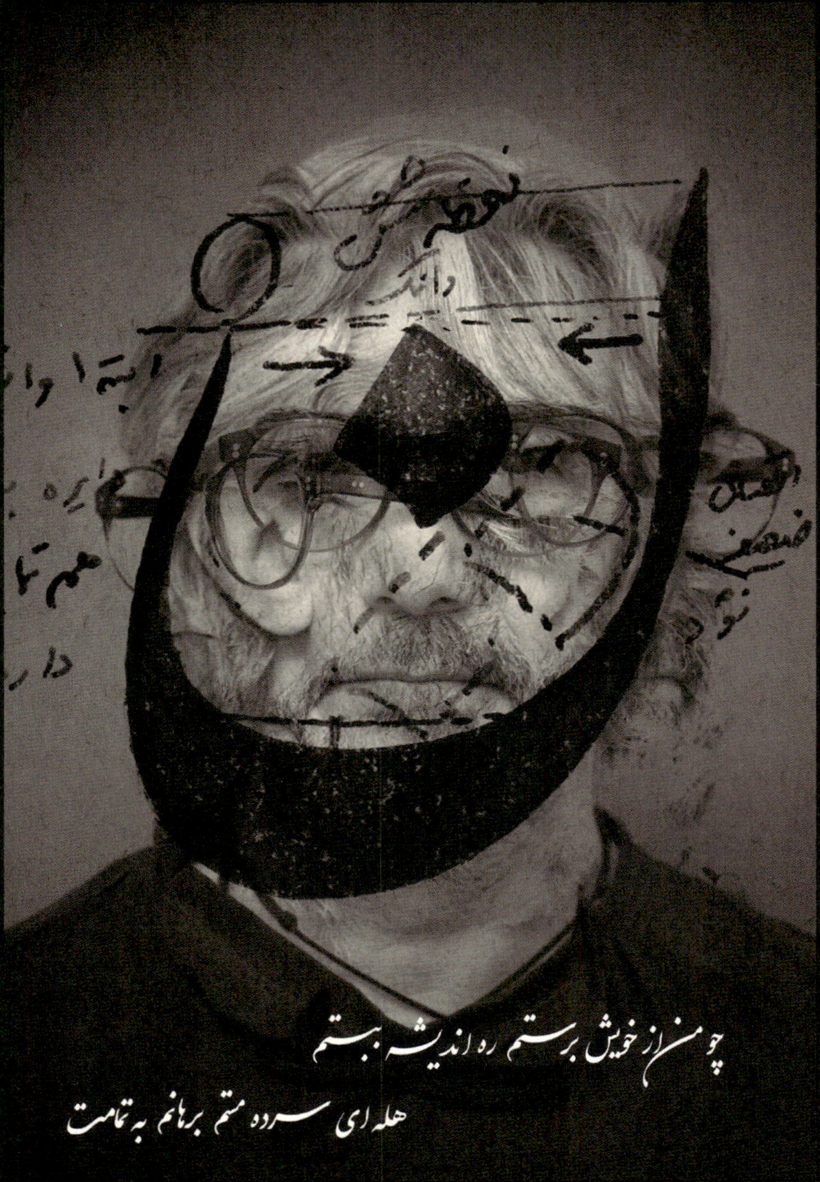

As I got away from myself   I blocked all thought
O wine master   liberate me through and through

Obliterate your heart and soul in negation   strip your body like a robe
Leave no trace nor news   no sign nor symbol

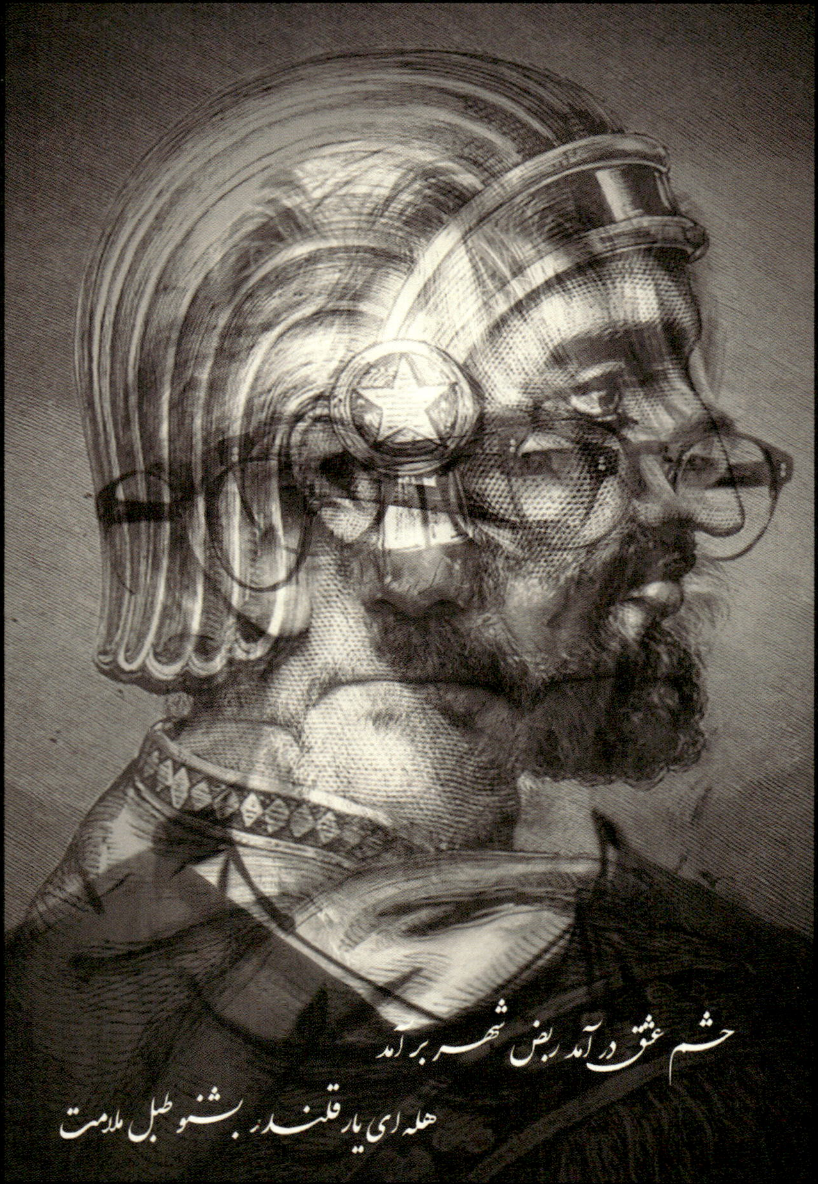

Love's attendants have arrived   The city wall has come into view
O liberated friend   hear the drums of reproof

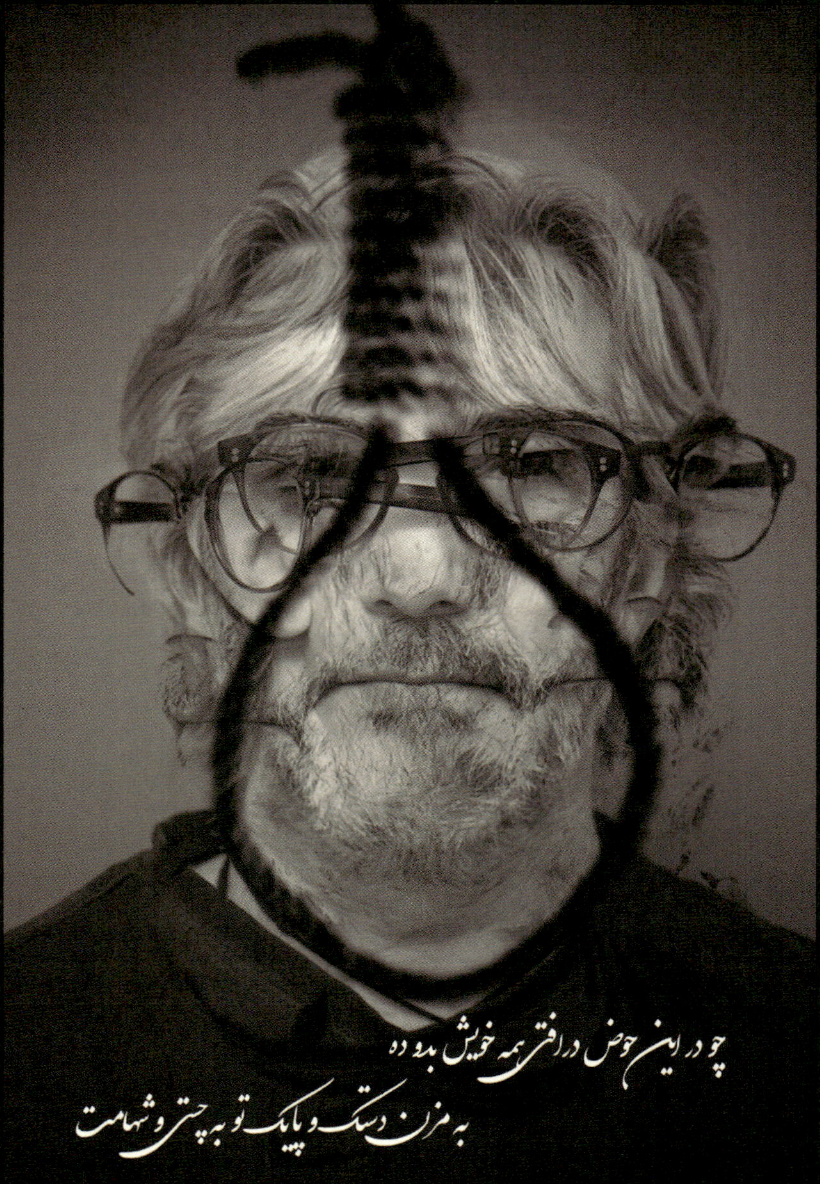

If you fall into this pool   surrender your whole self to it
Do not thrash your arms and legs   in skill and bravery

Editor's note:
The lines inscribed on the images in this piece are from Rumi's ghazal 405. Rather than attempting to illustrate the poem—as Rumi memes that are in wide circulation often do—Masoud roams through and reads into the ghazal, selecting some of the lines and re-ordering them to fit the order of the panels and resonate more fully with them. Thus the verses complicate the images, demanding of the reader to go beyond their surface un/familiarity and enter into their farther depths. In translating Rumi's lines, I took clues from the images to make word choices, and, definitely in the case of the seventh verse which is decidedly ambiguous in the original, I took the liberty to interpret the poet's intentions to bring it closer to the artist's intentions. It is of note that the verse used in the first panel is the last line of the original ghazal, as indicated by the presence of the term silence (khamosh), one of Rumi's poetic names.

Masoud Eskandari unexpectedly passed away in March 2023. While deeply personal and highly poetic, this piece is also a markedly political—but not chronological—archive of Masoud's generation, his untimely death adding to its poignancy. I am immensely grateful to Ladan and Artemis Eskandari, Masoud's wife and daughter, for their help in locating his working files and allowing me access to them.

Masoud Eskandari (1961-2023) was born in Tehran, and migrated to Canada in 2008. He held MFAs in photography and documentary media. He had worked as an artist, art director and instructor and participated in many solo and group exhibitions, most recently at Art Gallery of Hamilton. He was interested in social landscape in photography and poetic-philosophical videography. He passed before he got to finalize the piece included in this volume.

gita hashemi

being the astrolabe with fatemeh keshavarz, part 1

This conversation was conducted online in May 2022, and it appears in this book in two parts.

GH: *You are a feminist, a poet, and a foremost scholar of classical Persian poetry as well as the twentieth-century Iranian poetry. In* Jasmine and Stars: Reading More Than Lolita in Tehran, *you write about two women who are prominent figures in modern Iranian literature, the poet Forugh Farrokhzad and the fiction writer Shahrnush Parsipur. You also write about your own everyday experiences in Iran where you grew up with the poetry of Hafiz, Sa'di and Rumi in the richness and complexity of a dynamic cultural space filled with contradictions. And you describe some encounters that exemplify the day-to-day challenges you face in the United States where, cast as an outsider, you are looked at through the lens of distorted images of Iranians propagated in part by sensationalist works such as* Reading Lolita in Tehran. *How do you negotiate the multiple polarities—or is it continuities?—that are plotted by your work? How do you navigate the vast temporal and cultural spaces between classical and contemporary literature, the feminist outlook and the mystical heritage, the "East" and the "West"?*

FK: The question you're asking is really interesting. In part this is related to the fact that we move between different identities. There are times when you are a poet, there are times when you are a mum, times when you are an activist, times when you are a scholar, and times when you are all of these at the same time. In terms of moving between different roles, I think it would be really hard for me to explain how foundational, empowering, and liberating classical Persian poetry has been in my life. In the early 80s, when I lived in England as a graduate student, the hostage situation had happened,[1] and we all felt somehow responsible for this tragedy and were very worried about what its outcome would be; and at the same time we had to explain to the people outside about what that meant, whether we agreed with it or not. I remember that I was reading Nizami's *Khosrow and Shirin* one night, which is a love story between Shirin, a princess in another land, and Khosrow, a Persian prince. Shirin is beautiful and absolutely powerful in terms of her ability to understand and to resist what she does not want to do. Other people cannot force her, not even the prince can convince her to take any steps against her own will. This is not really the image of medieval Persian women. It suddenly occurred to me—nobody could force me into one of those stereotypes. I am a Shirin. I have Shirin [within me], and I have lived with and learned from that personality. I have seen how my father absolutely adored her and talked about her. So,

1 The "Iran Hostage Crisis" (1979-1981) refers to the occupation of the US embassy in Tehran by the group Muslim Student Followers of the Imam's Line, during which a number of embassy employees were kept as hostages to demand, among other things, the return of the Shah Pahlavi II to Iran to stand trial. Two US rescue operations failed and the hostages were only released upon an agreement mediated by Algiers. During this period a vast quantity of shredded US secret documents were reconstructed by the students and released.

this combination of having access to the old and being able to connect with the new environment and, at the same time, reading master thinkers of the Western tradition, literary critics, philosophers or storytellers and poets, all of these have been influential in the way my life has come together.

GH: *It is really fascinating to hear you speak about feeling empowered through reading classical poetry because classical literature is often associated with oppressive sexist ideas and the rule of religion, what many have been rebelling against. How do you bring your feminism together with that classical literature, some of which, we have to admit, does have those very rigid gender stereotypes and misogynist content?*

FK: I think that you are touching on very important points. On one level all these great poets, be it Rumi or Nizami or Sa'di, live in the age that they live in. It is not like the social space is open to women to play the same roles that men are playing. Women have smaller impact on their environment, at least as we can tell publicly. There are rules and regulations about taking care of the family, taking care of the husband, etc. I do not think that we can claim that the issues, the questions that are before us today were at that time even asked. And if you don't ask questions you don't get to the answers. But it is important to point out also that the seed of recognizing the power and the equality in women was present in—exceptionally, of course—many thinkers like Nizami. At the end of *Khosrow and Shirin*, Nizami says:

درین افسانه شرطست اشک راندن
گلابی تلخ بر شیرین فشاندن
بحکم آنکه آن کم زندگانی
چو گل بر باد شد روز جوانی
سبک رو چون بت قبچاق من بود
گمان افتاد خود کافاق من بود
همایون پیکری نغز و خردمند
فرستاده به من دارای در بند[2]

He says, This is all about Shirin, you should think about Shirin; if you are shedding a tear at this tragedy, shed it for Shirin because she is the heart of this. It was as if Shirin was his own wife. Nizami was given a slave girl called Afaq. He freed and married her. Apparently the presence of Afaq in his life encouraged him to create the image of Shirin. It is really hard to free ourselves of the kinds of stereotypes that exist, particularly if you don't have access to that material.

I wrote an article titled "Taming the Unruly King" about Shirin as a lover and educator. What is amazing about her is that she is the one who changes the personality of this very good-looking, powerful, self-centered prince, and changes him into a good king. In a way it is exactly the opposite of *Taming the Shrew*. She is beautiful and young, and, importantly, she does not have to lose her sexual appeal and the erotic side of her character. They are important parts of her, yet she is wise and strong. I do not want to claim that all women who appeared in Persian classical literature were like Shirin but there were quite a few. In *Leyli and Majnun*, Leyli was the opposite. But Gordafarid [in Ferdowsi's *Shahnameh*] is another strong one, and there are other characters. As a feminist today, I am very aware of the fact that we cannot over-romanticize the past. That is a mistake. If you do that you will fall into the trap of thinking everything Rumi said is absolutely right and we cannot have any critical approach to it. That is the worst thing you can do to any great thinker. So I am very aware of the fact that our questions are different, but the spirit of recognizing the other, acknowledging the other, understanding the other, and valuing the other, in men and women, is a treasure that I carry with me in my work.

GH: *Let us review some basics. I have a hard time recognizing the Westernized Rumi as the same poet that I know as Molavi or Molana. What do these different appellations point to, and what do they evoke for you?*

FK: A lot of people [in the Persianate world] refer to him as Molavi Balkhi. He wasn't born in Balkh but in a small town called Vakhsh, outside Balkh. Probably around the age of nine his father Baha Valad who was a very established scholar

2 Nezami Ganjavi, *Khosrow va Shirin*, section 114, last accessed December 01, 2022, https://ganjoor.net/nezami/5ganj/khosro-shirin/sh114

and mystic decided to leave Balkh and move west. They went through many major cities. The Muslim world at this time had mega cities such as Nishapur and Baghdad and others. They finally settled in central Anatolia, an area that was known at the time as Rum. That is why most English, German or French sources started referring to him as Rumi, meaning coming from Rum. Because of his *Masnavi*, the book of didactic speculative mysticism, he has become a major influential figure in the lives of the Persian speakers who could read it. The terms Molana, or as the Turks might say Mevlana which means our master, or Molavi, meaning my master, come from that. He naturally became Molana or Molavi. It is very interesting that the word *Masnavi* refers to a particular genre of poetry, which is rhyming couplets, but if you say *Masnavi* anywhere in Persian speaking world, people immediately recognize this as Rumi's *Masnavi*, the 27000 verses of didactic mysticism. Similarly, *Divan* means a collection of lyric poems or a full collection of a poet's work, but if you say *Divan* or *Divan-e Kabir*, the great *Divan*, everybody will take it as the collection of Rumi's lyric poetry. [It has] earned this status over time as people have recognized his place in their understanding of the sacred and religion and spirituality. By now for me Rumi and Balkhi and Molana and Molavi have come to carry the same load or semantic feeling. But when I was in Iran, where I lived until the age twenty-five, he was Molavi or Molana.

GH: *What do you think of the proliferation of Rumi translations, some of them by translators like Deepak Chopra or Coleman Barks who don't have access to [the] Persian language? What do you think about what Franklin Lewis has called "Rumimania"?*

FK: It is very interesting how a poet, a master thinker, a master mystic can be appropriated for fame and commercial purposes. There are books that openly look at how the principles of marketing are applied to selling "mystical lessons." Unfortunately, we are immersed in [the] commercialization of ideas and see that as success. I look at this in different ways. Firstly, I think those of us who have worked on figures like Rumi who have so much depth and so much to give to the world should write and teach to make sure that their ideas are not reduced to feel-good usage like what has happened to yoga or other Hindu or Buddhist practices. Secondly, in terms of translations, with a figure like Rumi there is a range of translations; at one end there are people who hardly know anything and they're just fascinated by this figure. At the other end, there are people who get interested and learn the language, the culture and the tradition, those whose life is dedicated to doing this work. This is unavoidable. We have to discuss this and open it up to make sure that some aspects of the life and work of Rumi actually come to be a part of this conversation. Sometimes you see a book that has a piece of Hinduism attached to a piece of Buddhism attached to something from Persian Sufism and then there's a quote from Rumi. Another way of looking at this could be that this gets people interested in Rumi and at least a small number are going to go on to learn more. [Mistranslated] Rumi is a phenomenon—as is Hafiz to a lesser extent—and it is unfortunate that his ideas, his work is put in the service of commercialism and money making because this is totally the opposite of what Rumi wants you to be.

GH: *A friend who has recently returned to Iran commented on the proliferation of Molavi courses offered in non-institutional settings, some of them taught by women. There are also a lot of Molavi tours to Turkey. My friend sees this proliferation indicating a movement by a people who have religious affinities away from the authoritarian politico-religious rule and rulers that govern Iran. She thinks people can't totally let go of Islam, so they look to Molavi to fill the spiritual vacuum created by the Islamic Republic. What do you think about this?*

FK: Women are very popular teachers, so I am not surprised. But, thinking of people as not being able to let go of Islam is a simplistic idea of Islam and of people both. There are certainly traditions—be it religious, cultural, family-based—that people have attachments to. The words of poets like Rumi, Sadi and Hafiz have spread deeply in the culture. They are everywhere.

You go to school and the first lessons you learn, the first calligraphy you do is a verse. You walk in the bazaar and see a line from Rumi on the wall of a carpet merchant's shop. So there is a very complex interconnection to the idea of having a spiritual core that we should not ignore. I wouldn't be surprised if this [proliferation] is an act of rebellion against any attempt to create a structure, be it a religious structure, or a structure of traditions and cultural practices. If anybody wants to rebel against the ossification of ideas, using the *Masnavi* and the *Divan* is the best way to go about doing that. I think people also see in Rumi a connection with the world. Iranians are also very sensitive to the fact that the world misunderstands them and reduces them to a kind of religiosity that doesn't have any life, as if they are only religious and nothing else. It really hurts people. They want respect and recognition from the world, and Rumi is the bridge that connects them to the world. They can say, look, he came out of my culture; this is the person who taught me. I think it's a complex way of holding onto your life and your ideals and grow, and at the same time, stay connected with the world.

GH: Molavi is the subject of conflicting claims by Turkey, Iran, and Afghanistan rooted in ahistorical nationalisms and attempts at cultural capitalism particularly through tourism. What do you think Molavi would say about the industry generated around him and the nationalist claims and conflicts?

FK: Of course, the people of Afghanistan always see him as an Afghan poet; and Iranians, because he wrote everything in Persian, will hold him tight and not give him to anybody else. There is a lot of emotion; it may not all be just about tourism. Iranians are so deeply immersed in various aspects of his work, whether the *Masnavi* or *Divan*, and the language that he speaks. Sometimes they are incredulous; after all, how could people who do not even speak Persian claim Rumi? But the Afghans do; they speak Dari and he did too.[3] This is the result of our nationalistic short-sightedness. I do not think you should label him. He spent his early childhood in Khorasan, then traveled through many areas, and then settled in Konya. But everybody spoke his language there. So, the interconnectedness of these areas belies the whole idea of nationalism because these areas belonged to a universe connected by language, faith and other cultural strands. He certainly didn't see himself as belonging to Konya, or to Balkh or to anywhere else in the world. He said so many times that he does not belong to the East or to the West. It is almost like he predicted that people were going to talk about this. The language that he uses is general. He insisted that he belonged to the soul of the beloved; wherever that is, he belongs there.

GH: I know two distinct, almost contrary poets: There is the Molavi of the Masnavi, the didact, the religious ideologue who uses stories composed in verse to propagate strict religious tenets occasionally with disturbing sexist, racist and homophobic aspects. Then there is the Molavi of the Divan-i Shams, the poet who is drunk with mystical experience of love—an ambiguous, almost genderless kind of love—whose poems seem to ooze out of him almost in spite of himself. Masnavi stories were usually used in the context of advice given by parents, teachers and elders to keep us in line, so I have an aversion to the Molavi of the Masnavi that is as strong as my attraction to the Molavi of Divan whose poems came to life for me through Shamlu's recitations[4] that rendered Molavi as a rebellious renegade irreverent to the doctrinal religion and authoritarian rule, a politicization that many in my generation identified with. The contrast in the affective responses to the two Molavis may be explained by the different contexts in which the Masnavi and the Divan were read and reproduced. Part of it probably also has to do with the differing poetic forms of Masnavi and ghazal. I suspect, however, that the origin of the contrast and contradiction might be in Molavi himself and his differing poetic personas. Where do you see the continuities and divergences in Molavi of the Masnavi and the Molavi of the Divan?

FK: I actually don't see that much contrast between the two because the *Masnavi* also has lyrical moments. After long didactic passages telling you to do this and not to do that,

3 Dari is Persian spoken in Afghanistan, parts of Pakistan and northeast Iran.

4 *Ghazaliyāt-e Molavi*. Kānun-e parvaresh-e fekri-e kudakān va nojavānān. 1351 (1972). Read by Ahmad Shamlu. Music by Fereydun Shahbazian. Designed by Farshid Mesghali.

then you reach: "عاشقی پیداست از زاری دل / نیست بیماری چو بیماری دل Loving is visible in the wailing of the heart / There is no sickness like the sickness of the heart." There is this page and a half of an amazing lyrical outburst that interprets the didactic part in a whole new way. He gives the bare bones of the law and order and tradition, and then you see it all expressed in the language of love. It's like you are on a difficult road, and you're struggling onwards, and suddenly there is this opening to a garden, and you can sit there and rest and drink from the fountain. In that sense the *Masnavi* is really a masterpiece because it can combine the two. There is a side of right and wrong in his personality as well. That's why I take it very seriously when I say he didn't drink wine. I know from *Masnavi* that he took the right and wrong very seriously and his disciples did too. But even in the *Masnavi* he finds a way to tell a story or a beautiful allegory, almost like a little ghazal, to connect these different things together. I think he does this on purpose. These are different ways in which you could speak about the issues that are important in our lives.

GH: How might we understand the love that animates his ghazals? Is it a corporeal love? Is it a homoerotic love? Is it a purely spiritual love? What are its material and spiritual spaces?

FK: This sharp division between body and soul, dividing humans into compartments, is not the view of the mysticism of his time. We are body and soul. In fact, a lot of mystics, not just Rumi, described the physical beauty of the beloved in order to take the reader towards the inner mysteries of the spirit. Rumi has multiple ghazals, like this very famous one "هر کی ز حور پرسدت رخ بنما که همچنین / هر کی ز ماه گویدت بام برآ که همچنین If anybody asks you about hurries, show your face and say like this / If anybody asks you about the moon, come on the roof and say it's like this."[5] And he goes on to say, "If anybody asks you how does the moon become apparent from behind the clouds, open your frock knot by knot and show your body and say like this." So he goes on with all these descriptions and then he says, "When you're praying to God just say, give us each a candle of purity like this."

The idea is that what is important is the purity of intention, the way we relate with the body and the soul. I don't want to say that everything was allowed, and you could have physical relationships without any consequences. But, when mystics talk about the beauty around us, our body and soul are a part of it. In the Western philosophical tradition, when we get to Descartes, we get a real division between body and soul, a deep duality. But this duality isn't true of Rumi's time. The love for another human being, if it is pure and well intentioned, is as valuable as the love for the divine presence. Indeed it is a kind of practice for the divine because as human beings our senses are our emotional tools. Falling in love with another human being is a way to get one step closer to the divine. There is another mystic, more or less contemporary with Rumi, who says that when you are deeply attracted to the beauty of another physical being you are seeing the image of the moon reflected in the pond. The image reflects the beauty of the moon, and it may make you look up at the real moon, so it is actually a very important tool we have and that's why God has given us the senses.

People talk about the homoerotic dimensions because of the presence of Shams in Rumi's life. Persian pronouns are not gender specific so ou is used for he, she or it. An is another word for it that can separate it, but ou could refer to either gender. There are not any pronoun references in Rumi that we can say [with certainty] this is where he is talking about Shams. I have a number of reasons to believe that their relationship wasn't homoerotic. Not that I see that as a bad relationship, but I don't think theirs was. When Shams arrived in Konya, he was at least in his mid-sixties and he was fairly frail and old. He had multiple other followers, and we don't have a story of him following young men or attractive young men. Rumi was a married person with grown-up children. What we know now as homosexuality, two consenting individuals of [the] same gender in a love relationship, was not how homosexuality was expressed in Rumi's time. In societies that practiced homosexuality, it would be [the love] for the beauty of very

5 Rumi, ghazal 1826, *Koliyāt-e Divān-e Shams-e Tabrizi*, be tashih-e Badi' al-Zaman Foruzānfar (Tehran: Amir Kabir, 1358/1979), 687-688.

young men, known as the beardless ones as they hadn't even grown facial hair yet. So a sixty-year-old man and a forty-something-year-old man coming together with that direct erotic relationship really doesn't show itself in Rumi's life nor in Shams's life nor in the poetry. But Rumi talks of Shams as God, he talks of Shams as the sun—that is what the word shams means. He has a great deal of affection for Shams and sees him as a person who translates his bookish understanding into experiential knowledge. As far as that could be called love, many spiritual disciples were worshiping and loving their masters, the way Rumi might have worshiped or loved Shams.

GH: I am thinking of Afsaneh Najmabadi's work showing the way gender constructs in Iran changed through encounter with the more rigid European cultures.[6] *Some of our contemporary gender performances were adopted and internalized in the process of modernization. What could you say about the cultural practices in Rumi's time?*

FK: When you go back to medieval times in Iran, particularly during the Saljuqis and other Turkish dynasties, we see instances of enslaved young and good-looking Turkish men who were the object of affection by their owners. They were sold for their beauty. The book *Qābus Nāme*, which a historical king wrote for his son in medieval Iran, has a chapter about how to treat your enslaved beloveds. Particularly in the royal circles attraction to enslaved young men was common. I agree with Afsaneh that we have to historicize things in order to avoid applying our current postcolonial knowledge and experience to earlier times. This is hard because our minds work with what we know from our own time. We impose some of our patterns and ideas onto the past. My instinct is to say maybe Shams and Rumi were lovers. So what? But that will do injustice to the historical material that I am working with that doesn't give me any such indication. They were both extremely outspoken to the point of sometimes offending the people around them, Shams more than Rumi. So they would have talked about it. But we know that Shams got married in Konya and was there for two years. Of course, there was a lot of jealousy about the way Rumi was dedicated to him. But I don't think even those who were jealous understood it in terms of a physical relationship or homoerotic love, [rather] they saw it as the dedication of a student to a master.

GH: Is the wine in the Divan *alcoholic wine? If yes, how could Rumi/Molavi/Molana be a Muslim theologian and drink wine?*

FK: I have a standard talk about Rumi and wine because this question arises often. What we have from a poet is in the poetry, particularly when it comes to lyric poetry, because in lyric poetry you allow yourself to speak about aspects of your life and emotions that you won't bring into didactic poetry or philosophical texts. In Rumi's poetry, there is no indication of intoxicants. There was wine in his time and there is reference to it but if he drank, he never talked about it. In fact, he says, you fool, if you knew this wine that I have you would never look at a glass of wine again. Many times he says, you stick to your alcoholic wine, I have mine; I don't need that, you don't need that because you can be drunk with the beauty of the world around you. Although he never really over-emphasizes the practicing of rituals, we have indication that he got up for morning prayers, and that he fasted and so on. I think we look at our lives today and think how could one be merrymaking without wine, but the word sharab [translated as wine] means any liquid that is drinkable not just alcoholic wine.

GH: Is it possible to see a progression of ideas, a kind of chronology, in Rumi's poetic production? There are the pre- and post-Shams phases, but that seems too simplistic. Surely being the dynamic thinker that we see in his ghazals specifically and the highly skilled poet that we see in all of his work, Molavi had gone through stages before Shams and changed over the decades after Shams. Since the Divan *in particular is organized by alphabetic order rather than other considerations, it is hard to see the change and progression in the body of his work. What might be*

6 See, for example, Afsaneh Najmabadi, *Women with Mustaches and Men without Beards: Gender and Sexual Anxieties of Iranian Modernity*. (Berkeley: University of California Press, 2005).

some of the evolution in his poetic thought and persona?

FK: With *Masnavi*, we know that it started in the last years of his life, and a request came to him to compose it. There was a two-year delay at some point, and then he resumed it. Also in *Fih ma Fih* there are references, both in the questions that people asked and the answers that he gave, to events that were happening, so there is a general chronology. With the lyric poems or ghazals—short sonnets, or in his case sometimes very long ones because he likes to break the rules—chronologizing is harder because the tradition was to arrange them alphabetically. There are some indicators, for example his poetic name becomes Shams after he met Shams. Before that it was khamush, meaning the silent one. The ghazals have allusions to [dates], although not very clear, and you have to be deeply immersed in his other writing to see that. It requires a major scholar like Hellmut Ritter, who knows the whole body of literature, to dedicate a good few years to just put these in order.

His poetry writing is very different from the standard practice of, say, a court poet or a poet who is writing something to be presented to the public. [Other poets] would write, and then edit and re-write. You can see their own footprints in the poems. I am not sure how accurate the stories we hear about Rumi are, that he would whirl in the market and recite poems out loud. What I am sure of is that he never decided I am going to write a ghazal and this is what I am going to say. What you can see is a kind of pouring out. He compares himself in *Fih ma Fih* to a breastfeeding mother. He says, Look, when my breasts are full of milk, I have to feed the baby; if you guys are not around I am going to feed the sag bachegan-i mahalleh (the puppies of the neighborhood).[7] There is a lot less possibility of evaluating the evolutionary process of [his] poetry writing. It is very much like whirling, and I think he does that on purpose. In whirling you don't have start and stop positions like in a line, you just move in circles. He does that in his ghazals. You see parts of a ghazal surfacing in another ghazal, sometimes with a little bit of change, and then in another. It is almost like an attempt to keep you whirling because he values the perplexity that comes with not really knowing where you are going. He wants you to know that knowing is not all about sitting down and calculating things; that some of it comes with just allowing yourself to whirl. I am very happy with the way ghazals whirl in his *Divan*. It is like he says, don't try to put an order on me; it's a statement. Shams, who is a very fascinating and strange character, actually says that about himself. He calls himself "the third script." He says, there is a first script that God reads and humans can also read and understand. There is a second script that God reads but humans cannot read and understand. Then there is a third script that neither God can read nor humans. "I am that third script." I was asking for a long time what is he talking about? How could you be a script that nobody can read? You can't pin these things down, but my final explanation to me is that the only script that you cannot read is the kind of script that is constantly rewritten. It never stays still. There is that attempt in Rumi.

GH: *That's almost the Buddhist idea of constant change. Is Molavi as Khamush or Khamosh different from Molavi as Shams? Is he different before and after Shams?*

FK: It is possible to see the beginnings of the direction that he takes in the earlier poems. His father was a great mystic, so he was immersed in these ideas and absorbed them. And he had a great teacher in Borhan al-Din Mohaghegh Termezi long before he met Shams. He was ready, and Shams was the catalyst, telling him you have to live this, you can't just teach it, you'll have to live it. Then he blooms like a tree, and the blossoms become fruits as a result of the experience. He gave up teaching, changed what he was wearing into a very simple black outfit, and started whirling and writing more poetry. But silence [khamushi] continues to be a major theme in his work, because without that silence words don't have meaning. A lot of times he ends a poem saying, I am running out of words, let's keep silent now, so we can follow up on this. Or, Here, the poem is yours now, I am going to be silent, you go write the rest of it.

7 "چون حالت سکر مستولی گردد مست به آن نمی نگرد که اینجا ممیزی هست یا نی مستحق این سخن و اهل این هست یا نی از گزاف فرو می ریزد همچنانک زنی را که پستانهاش قوی پر شود و درد کند سگ بچگان محله را جمع کند و شیر را بر ایشان می ریزد" *Fih ma Fih*, chapter 38, accessed October 31, 2022, https://ganjoor.net/moulavi/fhmfh/sh38.

GH: So silence becomes a creative space, an invitation for the reader to take over. We tend to associate silence with repression, or, increasingly more these days, with freedom from noise. But for Molavi silence cannot be reduced to absence. It is not a negative space. Can we in our contemporary life find those spaces where silence is positive and productive? Where?

FK: In my book, *Reading Mystical Lyric: The Case of Jalal al-Din Rumi*, I decided to have a separate chapter about silence when a British friend asked, why do these mystics talk so much about silence? Why don't they keep silent if they think that silence is so important? I think when we look at silence we fall into presentism. We think of Samuel Beckett and *Waiting for Godot*, or we go to these people who see silence as an empty space or a lack. We think of silence as imposed by oppression, by inability to speak, or by not having things to say. But the more I thought about the positive connotations of silence the more examples I found in the *Divan* talking about silence as a treasure chest, or as the womb from which we are born, or a beautiful space that could be made ours. Silence is very optimistic for Rumi; it is full; it is ready to bloom. Sometimes he's writing a poem and he says, Okay, I crafted all these statues with my words; now, I want to go to my silent workshop; you deal with the rest of this; in my silent place I am going to create these amazing statues that are not that easy to capture in words; in my word workshop I care about how people feel about my poems; but now I don't want to do that anymore. For Rumi silence is pregnant. The whole world is pregnant. Things are born out of these silences if we know how to listen to them, if we know how to silence the multiple voices going on in our own heads. Again, a very Buddhist idea. [Rumi] knows how central silence is in our lives; he turns it into another poetic tool to tell us more about complicated issues like speaking, having a voice or not having a voice.

GH: You also have a chapter on what you call the "sonic surface" of Molavi's lyrical poems. There is the "almost mathematical" meter of the verse and the internal rhymes of the hemistiches and couplets. But, almost in spite of, or maybe in addition to, these considerations, there is an affective sonic quality. As a calligrapher, I see the poems having a visual texture, a surface that becomes not just visible but almost tactile through the process of writing.[8] How is the "sonic surface" of his poetry significant in the meaning and the interaction with the reader?

FK: Sometimes he uses the quality of the language, and sometimes he goes against it. For example: "خوشی خوشی تو ولی من هزار چندانم / Khoshi, khoshi to vali man hezar chandanam / You are happy, you are happy, but I am in a thousand states." It is so happy that you can glide with it, fly with it. In another line you get lots of sounds of kh and se, and run into the hard parts of the language. He doesn't have to use those words. But he has such a sense of the language that if he is struggling with a thought he wants you to see it—[as if to say] Listen to the sounds, listen to how I am hitting against these difficult to pronounce words and that's the state I am in. He is interested in being affectively close to the reader. He isn't just giving us a great treasure trove of knowledge. He is not being a teacher up there and explaining what is right and what is wrong. He says Come in and whirl with me and see what is difficult and what is easy, and ultimately discover that you are the astrolabe, you are the one who has to calculate where to go and how to deal with things. He is very sensitive to sound. In his mystical practice, there is tabl (drum) and setar (string instrument). There are even stories about how he changed setar. I am convinced that is apocryphal, but he loved music. He says even music comes from the inside: " تو مگو مطرب نی‌ام دستی بزن / تو بیا ما خود ترا مطرب کنیم Don't say I am not a musician, clap your hands / Come here and we will make a musician of you."

He is sensitive to movement too. You see that in whirling. He uses sound and movement affectively to show people how they should explore themselves and discover these tools that are inherent in their being as humans.

GH: An important moment for me in Reading Mystical Lyric was

8 See "The Afterlife of Rumi," part 2 of this conversation in the present volume, page 72.

where you rejected the separation between the mystical experience, the poetic act, and the meaning of the poetry. You say that the attempt to hermeneutically interpret Molavi's ghazals undermines their poetic/mystic character and diminishes their experiential fullness, and that interpretation reduces the poems by insisting there is a meaning that is prior to the poetic act itself and by attempting to fix that meaning.

FK: It took a long time in the West by scholars in the field to accept Rumi as a poet. They saw Rumi as a towering mystic who changed some of our understandings about spirituality and human life. But a poet? No, he couldn't have cared about writing poetry. This was the understanding up until fairly recently. That was one of my motivations in writing about the *Divan* because there are 35000 amazing verses of poetry that give us this whirling, lyric Rumi, yet he is set aside saying that he was not a poet because as a great mystic he didn't care about writing poetry. Of course, this wasn't the case in the Persian-speaking parts of the world that have never stopped reading Rumi as a poet. But the West took a long time to accept that because of the compartmentalization [between poetry and mysticism]. My thought was, these poems are his mystical experience; it's not like he has an experience then he says, oh, what am I going to do about this now? I am going to put it in this poem. The [mystical] experience is not like clothes you put in a suitcase. It is there and it happens partly within and in interaction with the poems themselves. For centuries it has been a tradition in mystical gatherings to recite poetry or sing poetry because poetic creativity that is mystical is viewed as something that can initiate new mystical experiences.

I want to be careful not to say that we cannot have any interpretations of these poems. We can read them and talk about what he means. What was really problematic to me was that there were these compendia of Sufi mystical images; for example, the moon means this, the sun means that, the face of the beloved means whatever. There were "mystical" interpretations for these images, and then the understanding and interpretation of the poems were supposed to happen according to these fixed expectations. Whereas for Rumi the moon is not always the beloved; sometimes the moon is the lover: "میشدم در فنا چو مه بی پا / اینت بی پای پا دوان که منم I was walking in nothingness without feet, like the moon / Here I am running for you footless, look at me."[9] And then there is another moon that is pale and sick and means something else, and another moon that is the beloved. I thought we were killing these images by giving definite interpretations. Instead, we should really let the poems and their images speak. So, without using that kind of a compendium, interpretation becomes an active, continued process by readers of different ages and different experiences. They breathe a life of their own into these poems.

GH: The way Molavi's poems were taught to us in Iran was rigid; here's the poem and this is how you should understand it. Your approach is liberating and allows for the way we infuse our own subjectivity with what we read and the process of reading itself.

FK: Absolutely, when we read a poem we supply some of the meaning subjectively. We are partly the meaning makers, and the process of meaning making always depends on the reader as well. That's why we need to have multiple readers and multiple interpreters. A philosopher, a musician, a painter and a poet read the same poem and different things come to life for them and they generate different meanings. Of course, when we write it down we have to fix it in some form or fashion.

GH: I have been struggling to translate some of the poems. Do you see the act of translation as a process of fixing the meaning? Could that fixing be avoided?

FK: I think that almost everything we do is a translation. Speaking itself is a translation. When you speak with someone, you listen to them and translate them for yourself and then you translate your own thoughts before you can respond to them. That is why the act of translation is so important to be understood in all its complexity and the ways in which it is a part of our life. I used to teach a course on translation. I would

9 See the original and tranlation of this in Rumi, Ghazal 1759, on page 32 in this volume.

ask the students on the first day to give me a metaphor for translation. And they would say a photograph and a face. A few weeks later, the photograph would change to a painting. Once, towards the end one of my students said translation is like planting a seed and the seed grows into a new tree. It's a revolutionary way of thinking about it. Another metaphor that has stayed with me from a student is that translating is like you have an ice cube, you melt it and refreeze it in a new shape. We de-contextualize and re-contextualize because otherwise poetry wouldn't make sense. When we are translating we are interpreting; we have no choice. It could be a translation that would go into a highly conventional structure, or it could be free and poetic. That's why there are multiple translations. There are some I wouldn't read, but there are some I would read joyously because there is a lot of re-creation in a very loyal way. If the translator knows the language well, knows the context, and is also in control in the language into which things are translated, they are re-constructing the original. People keep saying it's impossible to translate. But that's why it's so attractive, you have this impossible in front of you, and you want to see how you can address it.

GH: *What is the character of the mystical experience that distinguishes it from other experiences? Could we ordinary people have mystical experiences?*

FK: I will respond to this from Rumi's perspective. He absolutely believes that every human being is able, in fact is created to be able, to open up to the sacred and experience it. Actually, he doesn't even mean Muslims only; every human being. There is a famous Quranic verse in which God is speaking and says, "We sent down the dhikr to you and we will protect it ourselves."[10] Instead of the word Quran the verse uses the word dhikr. Dhikr means remembrance. The Quran refers to itself as dhikr or remembrance at other times too. Rumi says about this verse that the interpreters of the Quran say from the word dhikr that God is talking about the Quran. That is one interpretation. But there could also be this interpretation that [God] says I have given each and every one of you an inner quest, a desire—shouq means extreme desire and talab means quest—to open up to the sacred, and I will protect that desire myself.[11] So, Rumi not only gives us the explanation that the experience of the sacred is for everyone, but also uses the Quran itself to justify that. He is so brave saying that most interpreters have said this, but there is also this other interpretation.

There is no question in my mind from his writings—prose and poetry, didactic, philosophical, and lyrical—that he believes that as human beings we are created for this purpose. Another time he says: " آدمی اسطرلاب حقست اما منجمی باید که اسطرلاب را بداند This human being is an astrolabe to find God."[12] Astronomers used [the] astrolabe to calculate the position of heavenly bodies. He says, you as a human being are an astrolabe to calculate God, you are built for this. I teach a course called Lyrics of Mystical Love, East and West. The reason why I teach it is because I am hoping the students would see that many of these ideas come from different sources. We spend a good part of the course on what is mystical experience. There is the whole field of cognitive studies that looks at the nature of the mind. It is complicated because it depends on whether you look at the mind from a philosophical perspective, a linguistic perspective, or a religious perspective and then which religion, etc. These are all important. We come up with a few characteristics that various people have put together, from various traditions, be it Hildegard of Bingen, the German mystic woman who shook the whole foundation of the church of her time and wrote her own vision, to others. Different people have their own language about what mystical experience is; some call it visual or auditory or just an inner feeling. One characteristic is that people who go through it know that it is a mystical experience. It's called noetic. Nobody can convince you afterward that it wasn't mystical. Like when you have forgotten a word and you try to find it; many words come up but none are that particular word. But when the word itself comes to you, you know immediately that it is the right word. You may be sitting just on the shore of the sea or under a tree and you

10 اِنَّا نَحْنُ نَزَلْنَا الذِّكْر وَاِنَّا لَهُ لَحافِظوْن
Sura Al-Hajr, verse 9

11 "در تو گوهری و طلبی و شوقی نهاده‌ایم نگهبان آن مائیم آن را ضایع نگذاریم و بجایی برسانیم" *Fih ma Fih*, ch 25.

12 Full translation of the sentence: "The human being is an astrolabe, but it is essential to know astronomy to use the astrolabe." *Fih ma Fih*, chapter 1.

suddenly have a feeling of deep connection with the tree or with the world around you in a way that you feel is a different and mystical kind of experience. That's how you know it, and you need nobody else to validate it. The other characteristic that the mystics come up with is that it continues to have a positive impact on your life; it makes you think about others, about those that don't have; it makes you go against violence, against war, against hurting others. There are other descriptors too but these two are the big ones. Somebody might say, well, you could become delusional, something might happen to you, you might see something and then you say, oh this was a mystical experience. Well, what happens after that? How does that experience impact your life? Does it make you a part of a bigger sense of goodness? Does it make you do what it takes to be good? These [transformations] show that the experience had some inner spiritual dimensions.

GH: I have learned that all creation is a collaboration, a co-creation. Looking at the enormous corpus of Molavi's production, it is hard to imagine how a single person in a single lifetime could have produced so much, especially as we are told that he started writing poetry fairly late in his life. We know that women carried the weight of the daily production of life. I wonder if and where in his work we might see or excavate the evidence of women's co-creative presence. Do his mystical experience and his poetic persona show awareness of his own dependence as a corporeal being in need of daily maintenance supported by others? Where are the women in his world?

FK: I actually think that probably women in his household did not do very much because they had servants. He belongs to a time when women cook and men eat. I don't think that he would stop and think, maybe I should help my wife in doing housework. I have no evidence of that. But I have evidence of his treatment of women in multiple other ways. There is a time when he is passing by a known prostitute who stops him and asks a question. He stays and answers her, and furthermore, performs the public gesture of respect offered to any other person, man or woman. That incident became the source of argument in his community, which is why we know about it, because he was expected to ignore her rather than bring himself to her level. He is famous for maintaining the same rules of etiquette, kindness and respect toward everybody whether they were famous and rich or belonged to lower classes. We also know that he told his son off for his unkindness to his wife. He wrote a letter to him and said that is not how one is expected to treat his wife. I don't want to say that he was what we expect of men today. Women were not considered co-creators. But we know that in whirling rituals women could join in and they were also present in the audience in his public talks. He advised respect and kindness to women and recognition of their value. That made him unconventional for a man of the thirteenth century.

Now, that is different from when he is being sexist, when he is being the child of his society. He doesn't see women as equal to men. [He says] women have a reputation for being underhanded and pulling the strings from behind. [He thinks] you should not fully equate their wisdom with men's wisdom. But then two lines later he tells you that the designations men and women are ridiculous, and we have to get rid of all these designations. This socially conditioned person who goes with constructs of gender and race and religion is still in him. I think it is good that can you see him as a person of his time, and he is not god and you cannot just think about him as if he was flawless. What you see is the struggle he puts into overcoming these limits, and he wants other people to do that too. We should look at the stories and understand them in the context of their time. Ultimately, he is kind. Ultimately, he says overcome differences. Ultimately, he says, not all Muslims are good and [not all] non-Muslims are bad. But he is an ordinary human being at the same time.

GH: I appreciate your use of the term struggle in terms of the personal and would like to connect that to the social. I place myself, and I hope this book, in the broad sphere of social justice. Given our contemporary social justice sensibilities and ideals, what, if anything, can we draw from Rumi?

FK: We have to look at his life story. We see that when people come to him and they have been hard done by, maltreated because they are in the category of the deprived in some way, he rises to help them. He writes to the authorities who respect him and says why did this happen and why don't you do something about it. The Mongols of Central Asia have invaded all this area around him, and people come to him and say, is it true that the Mongols don't have souls? He responds, you cannot say this about any human being. They may be doing wrong, but you cannot say they don't have souls. Once you look at his life and the essence of what he tries to do by bringing people to a kind of consciousness of who they are, and what they should do for others, I think he is a very good role model. Look at how candid he is with the rulers of his time. He can afford it, by the way. They cannot kill him because too many people love him. Once, the governor of Konya, Mu'in al-Din Parwanah, comes and asks him to pray that a wish of his be granted. Rumi doesn't respond and continues his talk. The governor asks again and again. Finally Rumi says in prayer, God almighty please grant the wishes of the Amir who has come asking me to ask you for granting his wishes; and please grant him those wishes that he is ignorant of and does not know that if he gets those wishes, he would be ashamed of his present wishes, so please give him all the good things that as an amir he needs to have. Rumi uses that occasion and the capital he has with people to say to the governor that, first of all, I am not your guy to go to God and ask for things you want, that's not my job; and secondly there are things you don't even know how to ask for or even want. Given all that tradition and the tumultuous times with the Mongol invasion and so on, he emerges as an impressive person.

GH: *Do you think Molavi's ideas are timeless and universal?*

FK: I am very cautious about calling his ideas timeless. I think it is very important to know the characteristics of his time. There are some universal dimensions to all the inner quests for happiness and reaching beyond the body and its daily needs. Rumi is rebelling against limiting structures. He has knowledge of various cultures that he has traveled through. When he was young, his father sent him to Aleppo to study. He came back to live in Konya which was a very cosmopolitan city with people from various economic and educational backgrounds speaking Turkish, Persian and Arabic. Also, Persian mysticism, Sufi mysticism, opens up the door to questioning rules and traditions that people blindly accept. These allow him to free himself from some of the limitations of his time and cultural beliefs. In some other areas, he remains captive to those ideas, in human fashion, as we all are. But he is a person of the world and he wants his followers to open up to new things, that is, once they have learned everything they need to learn about their own tradition. That is what frees them up to explore.

GH: *I am thinking about an episode of your Radio Rumi podcast where you talked about the then impending US elections and drew from Rumi to think about how to engage with the various social conflicts raging. What could we draw from Rumi in thinking about/dealing with contemporary dilemmas?*

FK: The first lesson is that when you engage you acknowledge the other side to begin with and see them as full human beings in the same way that you are, and you acknowledge the differences. We always knowingly or unknowingly reduce the humanity of the other side, if not taking it away totally, and that closes the door on dialogue. When Rumi died, there were Jews and Christians and Muslims and Turks and Persians and Greeks and people of other backgrounds attending his funeral. Just looking at this you can tell that while he belonged to his own tradition and religion, he was so accepting of others that they felt he belonged to their community. It is very interesting that this was the thirteenth century. But nowadays we may not be that open to people who do not believe what we believe.

GH: In Reading Mystical Lyric: the Case of Jalal al-Din Rumi *you offer a framework for reading and understanding his mystical ghazals. Then in* Recite in the Name of the Red Rose: Poetic Sacred Making in Twentieth-Century Iran*, you write about how the impulse to understand and describe the self and the sacred is played out in the twentieth-century life, and connect this modern effort to the dynamic philosophical and spiritual explorations of earlier periods. How did you go from classical to contemporary poetry?*

FK: When I finished the book on Rumi, I had been talking about how change is at the center of his life, how much he cares about every individual around him, and how paradoxes are part of his speech—silence is a part of his speech—and he makes use of [all this] tremendously effectively as a poet. I moved from that to looking at contemporary Persian poetry, which has always been a great love of mine. I think a moment of—I don't want to say epiphany—coming to a kind of understanding was when I saw that these [contemporary poets are] dealing with very similar issues, although their strategies may not be always the same or the generic forms they use are not the same, but there is such an interconnection, such an intertexuality and also inter-vocality. All these voices mix and mingle together and come to us up to the twentieth and twenty-first century.

When we think about twentieth-century poetry, and now the twenty-first century poetry, but particularly with the twentieth century, the assumption is that all the great great intellectuals were against religion; or at least totally secular, divorced from the idea of the sacred. I was not seeing that. What I was seeing was that they are remaking their sacred, not so much in changing its essence or changing its ideals, but in terms of presenting it to their readers in the language that made sense to these new readers, and also the ways in which they themselves could feel its sacredness. It was not so much about interpretations of the Quran or quoting the sayings of the prophet Mohamed or some other "religious text." Sometimes it was about being politically active, being a committed thinker. That was a sacred thing; and they did not have to give up their role as poets. Shamlu,[13] one of the master poets of this period, compares himself to Jesus in a poem called "Jesus of Nazareth." In that he talks about how he pulls the nails out and walks down the cross to walk with people. He addresses the sacredness, the presence, and Jesus' mission of saving the people, but in a new language. That is what led to my second book, *Recite in the Name of the Red Rose*.

GH: I'd like to explore further the idea of "sacred making" in twentieth-century Iranian poetry. When Shamlu and Shafiei-Kadkani are writing, the dominant culture is secular yet they are attempting to create sacred spaces. Is the sacred almost a necessity, even though in a secular culture and a modernized society?

FK: That's a fascinating question. By the time we are in the early- or mid-twentieth century in Iran the approach to everyday life is much less impacted by the ritualistic and visible manifestations of religious practice, for example, going to sacred places or performing sacred rituals. At the same time, it is hard not to see the desire to connect with something sacred in the environment. That never really goes away. It just finds different manifestations. The title of my book plays on that. There is a Quranic verse, the first verse that came to the Prophet, that says "Recite in the name of thy Lord."[14] Shafiei-Kadkani writes a very revolutionary anti-Shah poem, and the title and its first line is "بخوان به نام گل سرخ Recite in the name of the red rose." The red rose becomes the symbol of blooming, of having access to lofty ideals, to care for others, not just to accumulate wealth or even learning that is not based on a deeper knowledge. And this poem becomes a hit. Shafiei-Kadkani is a poet who stands on the border as he identifies as a Muslim. You can hardly find a poet who identifies as secular more strongly than Ahmad Shamlu. He actually has a famous line, "عصیان بزرگ خلقتم را شیطان داند، خدا نمی داند The big mutiny of my existence is known to Satan, it's not known to God." Yet [in another poem[15]] he becomes the Jesus of Nazareth on that cross where he wants to help people. I think that the tendencies of attention to the masses and being a committed poet go

13 Ahmad Shamlu (1925-2000) was one of the most influential poets and a dissident both during the Pahlavi rule and in the Islamic Republic.

14 اقْرَأْ بِاسْمِ رَبِّكَ الَّذِي خَلَق Sura Al-'Alaq, verse 1

15 مرگ ناصری, ("Death of the Nazarene") from *Qoqnus dar baran*. Nile Publishers, Tehran: 1978. Pp 33-36

together very well. Jesus is a poet of the people in the Sermon on the Mount. It is about attention to the lilies of the valley and the people around it. I see them as intertwined and connected. [Studying] the poems of these people, I had the opportunity to say, whether they prayed or fasted or not, whether they called themselves Muslim or not, the connection they could have with the sacred in themselves and outside did not change because human beings themselves are supposed to be one of the most, probably the greatest sources of the sacred inside, if they can open it, if they can actually free themselves. That becomes a whole different conversation, but we all carry the seed of the sacred that, according to Rumi and many others, has a Quranic origin.

GH: *Do you see your own cultural presence, in your writing, teaching and in your podcast Radio Rumi as an effort toward sacred making?*

FK: The idea of sacred making is not alien to my thoughts. I come from a tradition of Sufi Muslims. My parents were both Sufis so we read Sufi stories. Sufis taught people in stories. Time and again in those stories you would discover that a particular sheikh who is the leader of a religious group doesn't know as much as a very young person who has an open heart and who can feel and see the beauty of the world. God in that environment is not enclosed in a book of religion, be it the Quran, the Bible, the Torah or any other. This openness to the concept of what is the sacred and how we let it into our lives is very old in the Persian tradition, particularly within the mystical tradition, as it is actually in the Western mystical tradition. You see this in Meister Eckhart who thinks that the moment you name God you have destroyed the whole idea, because the sacred for him does not fit into a word, into a name. That's true of John of the Cross and Teresa of Avila. You find this everywhere; even in contemporary process theology the sacred is a process, god is a process of sacred creation. There are things that each of us may have experienced. You may be sitting in a room and someone walks in, or speaks, or recites a poem and that changes the entire environment for you; it becomes a more nourishing environment in terms of feeling more connected with each other, feeling a greater existence than all of us, a greater presence than all of us as individuals. There is no particular religious name for that moment, it is just an inner experience and exploration of the sacred.

Born and raised in Shiraz, Iran, Fatemeh Keshavarz is a poet, scholar, activist, and host of the popular podcast *Radio Rumi*. Her National Public Radio show *The Ecstatic Faith of Rumi* brought her the Peabody Award in 2008. She is the Director of the Roshan Institute Center for Persian Studies at University of Maryland and author of award-winning books *Reading Mystical Lyrics: The Case of Jalal al-Din Rumi*, *Recite in the Name of the Red Rose*, and *Jasmine and Stars: Reading more than Lolita in Tehran*.

rumi

ghazal 1393

I was dead   alive I became   I was tears   laughter I became
Love's power descended and   everlasting power I became
My sight is satiated   my spirit is audacious
I have a lion's prowess   the luminous Venus I became
They said[1]   You are not mad   You are not worthy of this house
I left and   insane I became   tied in shackles I became
They said   You are not ecstatic   you are not of this sort   go
I went and   enraptured I became   brimming with bliss I became
They said   You are not slain[2]   you are not soaked in joy
Before their reviving visage   I fell and   slain I became
They said   You are devious   drunk with delusions and doubts
I became a fool   I became a fright   Free from all I became
They said   You became a candle   you are the *qiblah* for this crowd
I am not a candle   I am not collected   Dispersed smoke I became
They said   You are the *shaikh* and the head   you are the guide and the lead
I am not a *shaikh*   I am not the leader   Slave to your command I became
They said   You have wings and feathers   I will not give you wings
Desiring their wings   plucked and wingless I became
New fortune told me   Do not walk away   do not take offense
for out of grace and generosity   nearing towards you I became

1 In Persian, the pronoun is embedded in the verb and may be skipped in the sentence. In this and following lines, Rumi skips the pronouns and uses the third-person singular verb *goft*, meaning she/he said. Because Persian language is genderless, I use *they* to stand for she/he. This is only partly an arbitrary choice. Elsewhere in this volume (ghazal 1789 on page 172), in the Persian original the third-person single pronoun *ou* actually appears in the poem, and I maintain *ou* rather than replacing it with s/he or they.

2 Slain translates *koshte* which—because Persian is an abjad writing system and the vowel has to be inferred—could variously be pronounced *keshte*. *Keshte* means planted. *Koshte* means slain. Thus an alternative translation of this line could be "They said   you are not grounded   you are not soaked in joy / Before their reviving visage   I fell   and rooted I became."

read by charles c. smith

مولوی

غزل ۱۳۹۳

Morde bodam, zende shodam, gerye bodam, khande shodam
    dowlat-e eshgh āmad-o man, dowlat-e pāyande shodam
Dide-ye sir ast marā   Jān-e dalir ast marā
    Zahre-ye shir ast marā   Zohre-ye tābande shodam
Goft ke divāne ne-i   Lāyegh-e in khāne ne-i
    Raftam divāne shodam   Selsele bandande shodam
Goft ke sarmast ne-i   Row ke az in dast ne-i
    Raftam-o sarmast shodam   vaz tarab ākande shodam
Goft ke tow koshte ne-i   Dar tarab āghoshte ne-i
    Pish-e rokh-e zende-konash   koshte-o afkande shodam
Goft ke tow zirakaki   mast-e khiyāli-o shaki
    Gul shodam hol shodam   vaz hame barkande shodam
Goft ke tow sham' shodi   Gheble-ye in jam' shodi
    Jam' ney-am sham' ney-am   Dud-e parākande shodam
Goft ke sheykhi-o sari   pishrow-o rāhbari
    Sheykh ney-am pish ney-am   Amr-e tow rā bande shodam
Goft ke bā bāl-o pari   Man par-o bālat nadaham
    Dar havas-e bāl-o parash   bipar-o parkande shodam
Goft marā dowlat-e now   Rāh marow ranje mashow
    Zānke man az lotf-o karam   suy-e tow āyande shodam

مرده بدم زنده شدم گریه بدم خنده شدم
    دولت عشق آمد و من دولت پاینده شدم
دیده سیر است مرا جان دلیر است مرا
    زهره شیر است مرا زهره تابنده شدم
گفت که دیوانه نه‌ای لایق این خانه نه‌ای
    رفتم دیوانه شدم سلسله بندنده شدم
گفت که سرمست نه‌ای رو که از این دست نه‌ای
    رفتم و سرمست شدم وز طرب آکنده شدم
گفت که تو کشته نه‌ای در طرب آغشته نه‌ای
    پیش رخ زنده کن‌اش کشته و افکنده شدم
گفت که تو زیرککی مست خیالی و شکی
    گول شدم هول شدم وز همه برکنده شدم
گفت که تو شمع شدی قبله این جمع شدی
    جمع نی‌ام شمع نی‌ام دود پراکنده شدم
گفت که شیخی و سری پیش‌رو و راهبری
    شیخ نی‌ام پیش نی‌ام امر تو را بنده شدم
گفت که با بال و پری من پر و بالت ندهم
    در هوس بال و پرش بی‌پر و پرکنده شدم
گفت مرا دولت نو راه مرو رنجه مشو
    زان‌که من از لطف و کرم سوی تو آینده شدم

read in persian by gita hashemi

Primal love told me   Do not move away from me
    I said   Ay, I will not   I stayed and settled I became
You are the sun's source   I am the willow's shade
    As you poured on my head   humble and ablaze I became
My heart found the radiance of spirit   My heart opened and unraveled
    My heart spun new silk   enemy to these shreds I became
At dawn the soul's face   boasted in bliss
    I was a slave   a beast of burden   King and master I became
The paper that wraps you   gives thanks for your infinite sweetness
    that since you came into my folds   sweet like you I became
The lowly dirt gives thanks   to the sky's revolving wheel
    that from your revolution and regard   accepting of light I became
The sky's wheel gives thanks   to creator   dominion   angels
    that from your bounty and *baksheesh*   bright and benevolent I became
The knower of truth gives thanks   that having succeeded all
    above the seven-layer heaven   a shining star I became
I was Venus   I became the moon   I became the manifold wheel
    I was Joseph   From now on   the bearer of Josephs I have become
O manifest moon   I am from you   Behold me and yourself
    It is from your smile   that a blooming garden I became
Be like a chess game   Move in silence   yet all eloquent
    that castling with that King of the world   magnificent and auspicious I became

rumi, ghazal 1393, translated by gita hashemi

Goft marā eshgh-e kohon   Az bar-e mā naghl makon
    Goftam āri nakonam   Sāken-o bāshande shodam
Cheshme-ye khorshid toy-i   Sāyegah-e bid manam
    Chonke zadi bar sar-e man   past-o godāzande shodam
Tābesh-e jān yāft delam   Vā shod-o beshkāft delam
    Atlas-e now bāft delam   Doshman-e in zhende shodam
Surat-e jān vaght-e sahar   lāf hami zad ze batar
    Bande-o kharbande bodam   Shāh-o khodāvande shodam
Shokr konad kaghaz-e tow   az shekar-e bihad-e tow
    Kāmad ou dar bar-e man   bā vey mānande shodam
Shokr konad khāk-e dezham   az falak-o charkh-e bekham
    Kaz nazar-o gardesh-e ou   nour pazirande shodam
Shokr konad charkh-e falak   az malak-o molk-o malek
    Kaz karam-o bakhshesh-e ou   rowshan-o bakhshande shodam
Shokr konad āref-e hagh   kaz hame bordim sabagh
    Bar zebra-e haft tabagh   akhtar-e rakhshande shodam
Zohre bodam māh shodam   charkh-e dosad tāh shodam
    Yusef budam ze konun   yusef zāyande shodam
Az to-am ey shohre ghamar   dar man-o dar khod benegar
    Kaz asar-e khande-ye tow   golshan-e khandande shodam
Bāsh cho shatranj ravān   khāmosh-o khod jomle zabān
    Kaz rokh-e ān shāh-e jahān   farrokh-o farkhonde shodam

گفت مرا عشق کهن از بر ما نقل مکن
گفتم آری نکنم ساکن و باشنده شدم
چشمه خورشید تویی سایه‌گه بید منم
چون‌که زدی بر سر من پست و گدازنده شدم
تابش جان یافت دلم وا شد و بشکافت دلم
اطلس نو بافت دلم دشمن این ژنده شدم
صورت جان وقت سحر لاف همی‌زد ز بطر
بنده و خربنده بدم شاه و خداونده شدم
شکر کند کاغذ تو از شکر بی‌حد تو
کآمد او در بر من با وی مانده شدم
شکر کند خاک دژم از فلک و چرخ بخم
کز نظر و گردش او نورپذیرنده شدم
شکر کند چرخ فلک از مَلک و ملک و ملک
کز کرم و بخشش او روشن و بخشنده شدم
شکر کند عارف حق کز همه بردیم سبق
بر زبر هفت طبق اختر رخشنده شدم
زهره بدم ماه شدم چرخ دو صد تاه شدم
یوسف بودم ز کنون یوسف زاینده شدم
از توام ای شهره قمر در من و در خود بنگر
کز اثر خنده تو گلشن خندنده شدم
باش چو شطرنج روان خامش و خود جمله زبان
کز رخ آن شاه جهان فرخ و فرخنده شدم

charles c. smith with meryem alaoui

between shadow and light

http://hdl.handle.net/10315/41087

between shadow and light
2022
charles c. smith and meryem alaoui
directed by gita hashemi

This performance took place and was recorded live on October 31, 2021 at Orchard Park Boulevard, T'karonto, on the path of the buried creek named Tomlin by early settlers.

neither you nor i can make it here
full of vision
things as a falcon
your hair and breasts and feet
the widening mouth
of estuaries
neither you nor i can make it here
and long rows of streetlights
the night
with outstretched hands
like the bright glow
and burn ever so gently
where bright sounds
earth music
auras heal
clear waters
above a bed
between shadow
these things
in and out of shadow
empty room
and the body's
with nightlight
a thin moon
this is where
there is a darkness as well
surrounding the break of
rabbits fox and deer
rain fades on rooftops
as clouds pass
like the bright glow
traffic light
journey from home to home
the world of my misgivings
passenger trains
into silent day
& i feel your breath clear my chest
& i see your eyes like rainbows
like a faint orange skyline
charged air sings in the leaves
the beating of air
there is a darkness as well

calculating risks

so many things
the body cannot contain fires
and explosions tornadoes
and hurricanes forces
propelled by hand or from clouds

we have limits fragile moments
in the here and now
moving us to make sure
we circle the seasons
as moon and stars assume
their usual height

we want to stay
in one piece no parts
in the flesh leaking blood
no holes in the lungs
breathing the odors of death

so why then when
it comes to seeking 'you'
knowing 'your' touch and kiss
sure as the universe fulfils and destroys

why do we fly like june bugs
to this light risking everything
even laughing at death?

an end to blindness

this light   will find your eyes
fill them   with brilliance

and you will see   into spaces
of play and laughter   songs and dreams

into fields   full of whispering
tall trees   bending in summer winds

their green edges   bowing
to heaven –

a soft sprinkling   this beam
will dance around you   warm

your hair and breasts and feet   slip out
of your eyes   glow like wings of a dragon fly

and burn ever so gently   into deep
astounding recesses   where bright

auras heal   all pain –

then you will feel   everything:

the rush of waters   in the stream
sparkling dew   below green hills

rabbits fox and deer   who measure time
with deliberate steps   in and out of shadows

like air   inside you
searching for sanctuaries   in daylight

and bowers in deep recesses   of surrounding shade

these things you will know   as your own
breath and tongue   and cool words

soothe your thoughts   with clear sounds
earth music   startling syncopation

you will hear and tremble   in this light
it will be your heart in your eyes   in this light

burning   a blinding flash

and you will know   such longing
as clouds pass   into silent day

a silent age

wings   the beating of air

a fire in the sky   that is not
asking
            or filled
with
            want

clouds   converge

a strangeness   hovers
storm   above waters

'prophecy! prophecy!'
is what the people
want
                        spelled out
in a frantic
press of
bodies

in a soccer theatre
or public park

but there is no answer
no voice divides the clouds
no bearded wonder appears

and the waters part by themselves
into uncontrollable oceans, seas

between shadow and light

these things that keep falling
ian and out of shadow i hear your voice
calling thru this darkness

your words spill like pennies
on a hardwood floor in an empty room
where there are echoes of meaning

with nightlight concealed by
a thin moon shedding behind cloud –

this is where your silence comes
to rest in the future of the city

its streets winding into chaos you
walk slowly into my dreams

i feel your presence a gentle mist
full of warmth smiles and flowers

you honour my heart and i stop
the world of my misgivings and bend my knees

to signal my desire
on a lonely balcony i use to escape
into the passions of music and prayer –

and in this place you find me
in the afterglow of midnight
where cramped and bleeding stars

are caught in turbulent galaxies
winds of space and time
ends of indifference in the blind centuries

of love and hopeless violence the widening mouth
of estuaries of slow and sudden deaths –
and here as skies fill with brightness
and long rows of streetlights expire the night

you rush into my veins empty
their sorrow drop by drop on a gilt-edged mirror
polished and glowing full of vision
as a falcon hovering in the bright light of spring

other awakenings

rising planets
day star, light
winks, into clear waters
running mountain paths
rivulets dance like goats
in fields streams of wheat
crowd dull grey horizon

rain falls silent
clear, sheets prayer billows
above a bed where my head rests
under clouds, i lie
with you as geese
sit on dank air
or ride rooftops
passenger trains traveling timelessness
without time the longest journey

from nowhere into nowhere
empty space, vermillion
stuccos, images of saints
in the nearby cathedral

the divine rests,
in these cubicles of longing
where love hides

shiva ogun kali ngai

& i feel you deep inside me like a wound
& in this moment my heart bends with grace
& i hear my voice in poetry and in song
& i feel your breath clear my chest
& i see your eyes like rainbows on my walls
& i feel your words in the silence of my breath

martin & mohandas mandela & vandana

may the breeze of this mantra
take me with you
to the glowing eastern gates

ecstasy

imagine every moment like this
sheer eccentricity the charged air sings in the leaves
rain fades on rooftops small dogs in the bush
play a rough percussion beneath exposed trees

nothing is imaginary in the clouds' sharp bend
only the backs of the stars and the height of trees

nothing lends its weight to the bleeding earth
or hollows out its emptiness
like a faint orange skyline fading into
a day when all else fails memory

then there is a shadow in the sky mirroring earth
grey and tempestuous sieged with its own demons

there is a darkness as well surrounding the break of evening
when the touch of a hand casts stars into the rudderless void

neither you nor i can make it here something else
beyond compels what we want so badly to do
with outstretched hands burning into reason
and into the inevitable journey from home to home

it is all any can make of it each moment
the next and the next (and the next)

like the bright glow of a traffic light
stuck on green at rush hour
everything goes and some at unimaginable speeds
filtering sparks in different directions
beneath a full white november moon

into vasanas

the long narrow
street
winds left
then right
then rambles
into memory
asphalt
into cobblestone
street corners
into potholes
sidewalks
into people
who follow each other
sightless
in the
early morning mist
veiled light grey
with tall buildings'
smoke
from which souls
escape
into vasanas
regions
bordering breath
seen
in the hyperbolic
glow
of trance

and the body's
blue memory
where one
touches another
without words
without thoughts
without feelings
without wondering
how many
inhabit this realm
fingers count
never ending
days
strung like wire
entwined in this
peaceable
kingdom

reflections

i.
the blue flask of silence opens its arms.
you slide slowly into them, your elbows still.
there is a promise in the sky
shaped like a stone. a death in the fields,
wind blows smoothly like a blade.

ii.
the clear crystal snowy air
sparkles the late night light
you breathe the silence

iii.
a thin white cloud passes by
the bright white winter full moon
becomes a halo

iv.
violins. empty streets. the hours sleep.
a flashlight blisters the failing dark. flag
of persistence, sweat of dreams. discord. memory.
shouts of forgiveness, out of thin waters, birth
and burning. a pressure into the cascading
wisdom of stones.

communion

the cloud's
tight
white
skin
beat
like
a drum –
there
was a
message
here –
and
the field
of flutes
answered
willingly

charles c. smith has written and edited sixteen books. He studied poetry with William Packard at New York University, edited three collections of poetry, and his poetry has appeared in *Poetry Canada Review*, the *Quill and Quire*, *Descant*, *Dandelion*, *Fiddlehead* and others. His recent books include: *travelogue of the bereaved* (2014), *whispers* (2014), *destination out* (2018), and *searching for eastman* (2021).

Collaborator in the place-based performance of this piece, and founder of *Jasad Dance Projects*, Meryem Alaoui is a dancer-choreographer from Morocco, living in Toronto. Her work is often an invitation towards a softer and sensorial experience of dance. Through her work at *Jasad*, she aims to increase the visibility of North African/Arab/Middle Eastern contemporary dance artists in Canada and internationally.

porin hotel | refugee camp at abandoned hotel in zagreb, march 23, 2016 | from the series *nth movement*, part of the *declarations diptych* | gita hashemi | 2016

http://hdl.handle.net/10315/41084

come come

oneness of being, 2 | gita hashemi | 2022

recorded at bellamy ravine and scarborough bluffs, unceded territory of the mississauga of the credit first nation

Come   come   the meadow is in bloom
    Come   come   the beloved has arrived
Bring all spirits   and spheres at once
    Surrender all to the   brilliant blade of the sun

Rumi, ghazal 329

Biyāyid biyāyid   ke golzār damidast
    Biyāyid biyāyid   ke deldār residast
Biyārid be yekbār   hame jān-o jahān rā
    Be khorshid sepārid   ke khosh tigh keshidast

بیایید بیایید که گلزار دمیده‌ست
بیایید بیایید که دلدار رسیده‌ست
بیارید به یک بار همه جان و جهان را
به خورشید سپارید که خوش تیغ کشیده‌ست

مولوی، غزل ۳۲۹

elena basile

the afterlife of rumi with fatemeh keshavarz, part 2

This conversation was conducted online in May 2022, and it appears in this book in two parts. See this volume for part 1 of the conversation, Being the Astrolabe, conducted by Gita Hashemi.

EB: Did Rumi oversee the publication of his work during his lifetime or were the Divan *and* Masnavi *collected later?*

FK: There are four major categories of his work if we include his letters. The letters to different people have been collected and will be published soon. *Fih ma Fih*, a collection of sermons—or conversations because he is interactive and takes questions from the public—was fully collected by other people. They try to indicate what he said and in some places he can be identified by his style—although those might have been [written by] somebody who knew his style really well. Rumi doesn't refer to *Fih ma Fih* later on. There are thirty-five thousand verses in the *Divan*, and I have not seen any references that he wrote them down himself. We have ways of identifying pieces that surface and resurface here or there, for example through musical instruments that he named or other words or images. He dictated the *Masnavi* and his disciples transcribed it. In the 1980s a holograph was found in Konya that indicates in the margins that it had been read back to him. This is what we know now. There are so many Persian manuscripts in India, Pakistan, Afghanistan, Central Asia, and Iran that haven't yet been catalogued. We have a project with the goal of digitizing whatever we can get our hands on before they are destroyed due to environment, wars, or other reasons. There may be a copy of the *Divan* found yet, but that would be unusual given the volume.

EB: Gita's earlier mention of the relation to the visual in the calligraphy[1] is an important aspect as it reminds us that we are dealing with a pre-print moment when writing was by hand only. Being born and raised in Italy, I am more familiar with the European traditions; moving from primarily oral culture to written word in medieval Europe it would have been the monasteries preserving these manuscripts. There would be chains of copies, copies of copies, and so there are all the problems of variations.

1 See this Q&A on page 47 in part 1 of this conversation, "Being the Astrolabe."

A translation tries to fix the text, but we're also working with something that we attribute to the name of an author, and yet it still has these other dimensions, so one has to also see how the works travel. This relates to the question of translation and what constitutes the original intention of the author. What happens when the manuscript itself is not necessarily a fixed thing?

FK: Yes. Manuscript copying and collecting with all its complexity is a whole different world you need to look at. We had lots of literary programs on the radio in Shiraz in [the] southwest of Iran where I grew up. Sometimes they would read a poem and my father would say, 'Oh no, no, this version is wrong!' I worked with six hundred and seventeen manuscripts for my PhD, so I had to look at a lot of copies of the same texts. There is a lot of fluidity in these texts.

EB: *I've been listening to your podcasts talking about Rumi—telling the reader now it's your turn to take responsibility and use it in your own life—and want to connect this to the question of translation. In any act of translation there is an aspect of subjectivity, but the subjectivity is never absolute because we're always situated, culturally and linguistically, with epoch-situated readers. The image of translation as a seed*[2] *reminds me of Walter Benjamin's idea of translation as the afterlife of a work. Rumi in English will be Rumi in English no matter how loyal you can be to the source because English functions differently, it emphasizes other things. So much of poetry passes through the rhythm of a verse, not just through what a particular word means. Is there something about the Persian that just does not go through in English, however beautiful a translation might be? I am curious about aspects and constraints of the language that do not lend themselves to translation.*

FK: If we thought of translation more strictly in terms of equivalency, yes, there are. In [the] Persian ghazal the rhythm is mathematically arranged. It's not just the emphasis we put on a syllable, but, for example the rhythm of long-short-long-short or short-short-short that is very accurately and mathematically calculated and creates a music. Then add to that the interior rhymes. I'll give you an example,

> Mordeh bodam, zende shodam, gerye bodam,
> khande shodam
> dowlat-e eshgh āmad-o man, dowlat-e pāyande
> shodam[3]

This kind of internal rhyming, plus the mathematical nature of the long and short syllables are impossible to recreate in another language in the same way. But if we think of rhythm in a more expansive way, there are some translations of Rumi that really create the rhythm, for example, the *Masnavi* translated by Jawid Mojaddedi, an Afghan scholar who teaches at Rutgers. He catches some of the music, the thought and the ideas into verse quite effectively. What Coleman Barks does—the American poet and translator who's become very popular—is that because he doesn't know the language, somebody gives him a verbatim translation and he plays with it. That deprives him of knowing the actual sound of the original words. What's more, he totally re-contextualizes the poem so that very little is left of the original. I think that the original complication and difficulty for the reader should not be taken totally out of the way so that they would be encouraged to find out more. For example, the word *huri* refers to heavenly beauties in Paradise. It became famous post 9/11 because the story was given that these guys committing acts of terrorism want to die so they can be in heaven with *huris*. That in itself is a very bad telling of a terrible story. Barks was afraid of including the word *huri* in his translation. There is a Rumi verse that says:

> Har ke ze hur porsadat, rokh benamā ke
> ham-chonin

If anybody asks you about *huris*, show your face, say like this He translated it into "If anyone asked you / how the perfect satisfaction / of all our sexual wanting / will look, lift your face / and say, / Like this." This is such a destruction of that line. It's not that *huri* doesn't have a sexual connotation, but the way "sexual satisfaction" takes over that line, destroys the thought, and reduces it is very sad.[4] It's true of many languages that you cannot replicate them into another language. I am a student of Italian. Sometimes you listen to the music of the words, like

2 See Keshavarz's discussion of this in "Being the Astrolabe," starting on page 48 in this volume.

3 See the original and translation of this in Rumi, Ghazal 1393, on page 54 in this volume.

4 Coleman Barks, *The Essential Rumi*, (San Francisco: Harper, 1996), 135. For a deeper discussion of the original ghazal, see "Being the Astrolabe" in this volume, page 44.

perfetto. Can you reproduce that in another language? I don't think so.

EB: *The ethics of translation requires that the reader be put in front of the fact that they are dealing with a mediation of another language. There is something here that can definitely push the reader to learn further, understand further. So going back to the question of the* huri*: that choice that the translator made was one that had to do, possibly, with the fact that you do not have a word like* huri *that encompasses in English such a range of meanings. That happens often in translation. Translators are stuck into having to make choices. They have to fix meaning, even when they don't want to. But that's also why translations tend to be fleeting in the sense that they belong to their time.*

FK: Yes. Absolutely.

EB: *Your observations reminded me of Gayatri Spivak saying that "translation is the most intimate act of reading." This happens, specifically, if and when you have a deep conversation with the language that you're translating from and with the culture you're translating in, and when you somehow linger in that middle space. Indeed, it's always incredibly difficult and terribly frustrating when you have to make a decision that is never fully satisfying. I can see, for example, the translator having a major problem, around translating* huri.

FK: Unfortunately, a big problem with existing translations of Rumi, particularly the non-academic ones, is that there is a deliberate and sustained effort to take out any element that connects [his poetry] with Islam. There is an attempt to create a kind of ahistorical universalism about the personality of Rumi as in, "Beyond the idea of good and bad, there is the space, I'll meet you there" that appears everywhere; the New Age Rumi. Sometimes my students are shocked when they see a reference to [the] Quran. Rumi is dipped in the Quran, he has absorbed everything in there. Does he go along with all the standard readings of the Quran? No, sometimes he does, sometimes he doesn't. But he doesn't reject the whole idea. He refers to the Prophet all over the place. When I see the word *huri* being taken out, I think of that as another attempt to create a distance between Rumi and this "scary" Islam.

EB: *So do you read that as a side effect of Islamophobia within North America and the West?*

FK: Absolutely. He is so beloved; how could he ever have anything to do with Islam? Those popular translations are a genre, and we should understand it for what it is and be aware of it.

EB: *Can you read Rumi's poems allegorically? Does mysticism cancel out the idea of an allegory or figuration?*

FK: Using metaphors and allegories as tools is common [in mysticism]. The most famous allegory in Persian literature is Attar's *The Conference of the Birds*[5]—translated very beautifully into English by Afkham Darbandi and Dick Davis. It is the story of thirty birds [*si morgh*] looking for the legendary phoenix [*si-morgh*] and discovering that they themselves are the phoenix. It's an allegory of reaching God. Rumi uses allegories too. There are extended ghazals where he is building something allegorical. But I think even in those places where we have hints as to what to understand and where to go, there is a lot of room for you to whirl. That is not quite typical for court poets and others, whose words are much more tightly structured and polished. Rumi very clearly says, I want you to be part of this act of composition. He literally says, I am done, I can't go any further with this; now is your turn, finish this poem for me.

5 Farid al-Din Attar (c. 1145-1222 CE), born and died in Nishapur in northeast Iran, was a poet and sufi theorist whose fame and influence spread across the region even in his lifetime. Rumi was closely familiar with Attar's work, mentioning him in several places in the Masnavi and in Divan as an influential master of and guide in mystical love.

speaking parts of the world   Finally, Rumi   finance leader me   Ghazals   as as   We are, but   we are bad
Afghans do, they speak Dari   pleasure of speaking parts of the word   allegorically   allegory quickly   Other writing   other raging   resume   your Zoom
Afghan embassy   the Alphonse do this big Daddy   court poets   popcorn poets   This ghazal   this as well   like that   like dad
The book Qabusnameh   iPhone and the sea   homoerotic   homeowner attic   With the ghazals   with the guys as   in their being   in their bea
His father sent him to Aleppo   The book bubble snowman   Beloved   They love   Ghazals whirl in his divan   because I was wearing his new   Huries   who raised
Injustice   in justice   A little ghazal   a little cousin   allowing yourself
are, but   we are bad   He came out of my culture   he came out of my catalog   With ghazals or lyric poems   with it as out of the lyric poems   wearable with me
resume   your Zoom   Their own tradition   their own to English   A master mystic   a master mistake   short or short tort
like that   like dad   Hermeneutically   Herman musically   We are, but   we are bad   Molavi's   more Lebane
ir being   in their beans   How brave he is   how bridge, he is   resume   your Zoom   Molavi   more levie
Huries   who raised   A philosophical perspective   a software perspective   like that   like dad   Molavi   more lobby
anslation is so important to be understood   tract of translation is so important to the end of stood   in their being   in their beans   The Masnavi   the mash Nel
A photograph and a face   a photograph and interface   Huries   who raised   Masnavi   mass navy
lavi's   more Lebanese   the gentleman This thick woman who shows the foundation of   The Masnavi   domestic mov
olavi   more levie   get that to show the TV the holiday my office on Monday   Fih ma Fih   few more feet
olavi   more lobby   So psychopathic go on in my head   Fih ma Fih   fee mr fee
snavi   the mash Nellie   more devil dams and they should get a burden on the show them.   Fih ma Fih   film or fee
snavi   mass navy   The letter H bomb I don't man don't let a Pollyanna show   Shams is   she is
umami   We are, but   we are bad
snavi   domestic movie   Barks was afraid of bringing the word Henry into his translation   resume   your Zoom
a Fih   few more feet   Rumi   room type   how does a whole tour said that rock band camp charity   like that   like dad
a Fih   fee mr fee   Rumi's time   Rum is life   horsey horsey to valley man has all channel now   Molavi's   more Lebanese
a Fih   film or fee   Rumi's life   Romeo and sadist   turn my goal my trip name test the buzz and   in their being   in their bea
ms is   she is   Rumi and Sa'die   the divine of roomie   Molavi's   more Lebanese   Molavi   more levie   Huries   who raised
are bad   The Divan of Rumi   about drew me   Molavi   more levie   Molavi   more lobby
Zoom   about Rumi   how many users   Molavi   more lobby   The Masnavi   the mash Nellie
dad   How Rumi uses   about that through me and wine   The Masnavi   the mash Nellie   Masnavi   mass navy
eir beans   about Rumi and his time   romita towering mistake   Masnavi   mass navy   The Masnavi   domestic movie
raised   Rumi, a towering mystic   good translations threw me   The Masnavi   domestic movie   Fih ma Fih   few more feet
good translations of Rumi   Rumi is dipped in the car on   Fih ma Fih   few more feet   Fih ma Fih   fee mr fee
Fih ma Fih   film or fee

rumi

ghazal 37

Mine is the beloved   mine is the cave   the flesh-eating love is mine
    The beloved is you   the cave is you   My master   protect this me
Noah is you   the spirit is you   the victor and the conquered are you
    the heart unraveled is you   At the door to the secrets I am
The light is you   the fete is you   the supreme blessing is you
    the bird of Mount Sinai is you   Wounded in your beak I am
The droplet is you   the sea is you   benevolence is you   wrath is you
    sugar is you   poison is you   Do not torment more this me
The chamber of the sun is you   the house of Venus is you
    the eden of hope is you   O beloved   let in this me
The day is you   the fasting day is you   the earnings of panhandling is you
    the water is you   the jug is you   Just this once give water to me
The birdseed is you   the trap is you   the wine is you   the goblet is you
    the ripe is you   the raw is you   Do not keep raw this me
If this body were less spinning   it would not plunder my heart
    it would become a path   so there would not be   all this speech in me

read by trish salah

مولوی

غزل ۳۷

Yār marā ghār marā   eshgh-e jegarkhār marā
    yār toyi ghār toyi   khāje negah-dār marā
Nuh toyi ruh toyi   fāteh-o maftuh toyi
    sine-ye mashruh toyi   bar dar-e asrār marā
Nur toyi sur toyi   dowlat-e mansur toyi
    morgh-e koh-e tur toyi   khaste be menghār marā
Ghatre toyi bahr toyi   lotf toyi ghahr toyi
    ghand toyi zahr toyi   bish mayāzār marā
Hojre-ye khorshid toyi   khāne-ye nāhid toyi
    roze-ye om'mid toyi   rāh deh ey yār marā
Ruz toyi ruze toyi   hāsel-e daryuze toyi
    āb toyi kuze toyi   āb deh in bār marā
Dāne toyi dām toyi   bāde toyi jām toyi
    pokhte toyi khām toyi   khām be-magzār marā
In tan agar kam tanadi   rāh-e delam kam zanadi
    rāh shodi tā nabodi   in hame goftār marā

یار مرا غار مرا عشق جگرخوار مرا
    یار تویی غار تویی خواجه نگه‌دار مرا
نوح تویی روح تویی فاتح و مفتوح تویی
    سینهٔ مشروح تویی بر در اسرار مرا
نور تویی سور تویی دولت منصور تویی
    مرغ که طور تویی خسته به منقار مرا
قطره تویی بحر تویی لطف تویی قهر تویی
    قند تویی زهر تویی بیش میازار مرا
حجرهٔ خورشید تویی خانهٔ ناهید تویی
    روضهٔ امید تویی راه ده ای یار مرا
روز تویی روزه تویی حاصل دریوزه تویی
    آب تویی کوزه تویی آب ده این بار مرا
دانه تویی دام تویی باده تویی جام تویی
    پخته تویی خام تویی خام بمگذار مرا
این تن اگر کم تندی راه دلم کم زندی
    راه شدی تا نبدی این همه گفتار مرا

read in persian by gita hashemi

trish salah

after 37

after rumi's ghazal 37

Because we no longer speak   dream now   to relay the dream
Couldn't know then   years become   stilled   within the dream.

"Just sit still"   –in what a mother tells the child who fidgets
she became hidden   is hiding   translation's rill within the dream?

If the body didn't begin a ruse—   or, carried by ceramic tide from Athens?
would pasts erupt still—   police swarming out the navel's dream?

Losing lost   waking quickened, knowing   sand's undertow to seek
no god, her father   a void   small or foreign   until you shill for the dream.

Drunk thought   run aground   long drunk shore of meaning, or,   seen on repeat—
like Atlantis sinking—   for all I loved before you,   quelled to end the dream.

Seized in its grey Atlantic weight   as if childhood's sea   lapping
deeper waves than white seek   to spill or better, to fill   in the dream?

From my room above the cemetery   taken by old friends to Bourj Hammoud,
His eyes, lowered soft; hers, black and flashing—   mirror reversal of the dream.

Is she hidden here, at the end?   Across the plaza, desires rage, they have come
to hear what must be said.   On stage you're joking still, the very tell   of the dream.

read by the poet

after 37/
the year he died

inside the dream, to relay it, to break it (in/out)
how years will become still now baroquely styled
as if in the beginning outside the dream

as if our body begins, a ruse a dyed platinum blonde rose
as if your aunt brought back blue on white ceramic the Parthenon

or, if you were brought back here to police the dream's navel
the interrogation (a ruse) would it go like this?

were you given a body were you forgiven
by alchemy or, a mother?
witchcraft? of a father?
how to fall asleep?

hear in the story of the dream
(a rose) small but foreign
lucid but still
quickening
(your doctor and you both
know you're a shill
serving the dream)
who, indifferent
and quickly, goes awry

becomes hidden a rose in your mouth
in translation's rout (in hiding)
you are left to recall as if instructions:

just sit still like a mother to her restless
child unable to be

like a child in hospital
on her second night
a nurse with red hair
brought a comic book Wonder Woman there was an entire room
crates of comics
later

there was a blonde boy
who beat you up
later
like in a dream you try to warn him
on repeat,
there is a giant wave coming
the raft will go under
and we will all drown
drawn under grey walls of storm

easy to see now harder to tell
from the cliffs to make her appear
from your balcony your mirror (it's gone)
above the First Cemetery (whose body?) yours or this
Athena's temple
bathed in light

remember:
the black haired boy
who loved you, you lost
the black haired girl
who held your hand, you lost
and your stepbrother, you lost
and her love you stole, you lost

in the dream Beirut
you wandered without family
until Constance and Brian found you
took you to Bourj Hammoud

standing on stage at the front of the plaza
Dina told jokes
they were good jokes
but impossible
you thought
it should end this way
then her eyes came to you —
(that other one's)
awful with lightning's promise
the very tell of the dream

slaughter borne

and oh, your eye to be splintered, broken into time's end
  born turning with past, only to mourn in advance the end

overturn the grounds, what in your year was named for love
  only dream of before/after, a cave in, dance off the end

times you wanted hope, gray times you called on me to be
  I couldn't tell you from I in advance, entranced by the end

only beginning to grasp what want was, what named for love
  only to become devourer; after all, all words chance the end

to belie our living, just one threshold of love's yet to be
  secrets unrivalled, unraveled come fall's distance, abet the end

it begs for rescue, alive in what your will claims, beloved
  after all, light wants a prism to view you, glance of the end

a fool's dream ends at love, sips away on unconquered time
  thieving cells thrill to be rid of us, our rue romance, the end

defies my eye, sure against water, fire born of love's
  mutation easier to sing than live, descant ruin, silent end

for this you all your life waited? love's only kind is time
  must we like rivers mourn? dull semblance's cocoon the end

of tears mine as much as time's, in loves stolen, still borne
  hypocrite rancour fails, even the moon resents its end

wholly fictive love, not for living but for slaughter born
  all are dispossessed— from a human course rent in the end

Postscript

These ghazals are part of a series written after re/reading translations of poems for the *rumi roaming* project. The poems are also shaped, in their preoccupation with iteration and translation, by the editor's caution to English language writers to avoid working with those popular "translations" cum appropriations of Rumi's writing, by translators who do not read the original. My "after 37/the year he died," deconstructs and displaces the intermediary poem "after Rumi's ghazal 37," which was written more directly in response to Gita Hashemi's translation of Ghazal 37.

A lover's apostrophe, Rumi's ghazal 37 articulates desire in a dialectical oscillation of self and other, in a cascading chain of figures of desire, for the beloved (and the lover). When language renders having and being transposable, ("the beloved," "the cave," "the flesh-eating love," "the victor," "the conquered," "the droplet," "the sea," etc.), both "mine is" and "you are," devotion becomes an unravelling movement of self, one that seems paradoxically to be both hurtling headlong towards, and suspended in orbit around, an unapproachable, irrefusably beckoning beloved. A similar thematic plays out in "after Rumi's ghazal 37," albeit at a slower velocity and differently. That the lost beloved cannot be addressed is named in the first couplet. The poem then inhabits the *mise en abyme* of reverie with reverie, its dream on the absent centre of a dream—or in psychoanalytic (Lacanian) parlance, on an *extimité*, an intimate externality or otherness, where parts of another impinge upon the self. The trace of another, their echo lodged withon the self, like a tattoo in the skin, if not from the self. The poem does approach the violence and volatility of Rumi's rendering of an undoing desire, but transposes the scene to the poet's own diasporic biography and geographies of loss and longing. Histories become love's intimate matter, yet matter for what love can possibly be.

The earlier, more intermediary version "after Rumi's ghazal 37," partially echoes the formal structure of Rumi's poem, which employs split lines that render each couplet as four phrases and in addition to the traditional *radif* at the end of the second line of couplet ("I am" or sometimes "that I that I am"), threads a repeating grammatical structure and second refrain within and ending most lines of the poem ("is you"). In my ghazal, these patterns of refrain are gestured towards through the use of spacing to produce small fractures/pauses across the lines of the poem, and through internal rhymes, assonance and consonance dispersed through the poem. "after 37/the year he died," is less a translation than a deconstruction and displacement of "after Rumi's ghazal 37." In this poem the fissures within lines have been pulled apart as if by centrifugal force, the use of *radif* and *qafiyah* is shattered as well, with end and internal rhymes and refrains broken and dispersed throughout the poems, many elements of the earlier poem are lost while the narrative bones and veins of the story behind the earlier poem is exposed, spilling over, love's histories making a mess. Old figures and spaces reappear in earlier guises. This is also an articulation of desire, and loss, but its presence, and the initial inspiration of Rumi's work, appears in shards and fragments.

"slaughter borne" also began with ghazal 37, which provided a lexicon and inspired the structure of the latter poem. Figuring love and war's proximity and interpermeability, the poem borrows from 37 water, slaughter, birth, caves, devouring, land and death. Structurally, the poem splits its couplets and pulls apart *radif* and *qafiyah*, as well as the distinction between the two. With the *radif* "the end" ending the first line of each couplet and alternating and repeating *qafiyahs* ending the second lines of each couplet. These variations see in Rumi's ghazal the ecstatic possibility of the ghazal moving beside itself, a way of languaging the givenness and volatility of transformation and migration of self, culture and poetry.

Trish Salah is the author of *Wanting in Arabic*, which won a Lambda Literary Award, and *Lyric Sexology, Vol. 1*. Her poetry is widely published in journals and anthologies. An associate professor of Gender Studies at Queen's University, she edits the *Journal of Critical Race Inquiry*, and has guest edited special issues of *TSQ: Transgender Studies Quarterly* and *Arc Poetry Magazine*.

gita hashemi

angel meets rumi in bulgaria

On Wednesday, my young Bulgarian friend whom I often call Angel asks me, "What are you working on?" I am sick and have no patience for talk that needs thinking, but she is dear and our connection has been a lifeline for me. She has been the only friend who has kept in touch with me regularly since the start of the pandemic; our age gap (I am her mother's age), geographic and time zone distance (she lives in Plovdiv, seven hours ahead of Toronto), and different life circumstances notwithstanding. I say, unenthusiastically, "It's a book project called *rumi roaming*. It's not about Rumi but it starts from his work." Angel comes alive, "I have a book of Rumi." This takes me by surprise. During my long stay at her former home in Sofia three summers ago Rumi never came up and I didn't see the book. "And have you read it?" I am still impatient and wonder if she can detect my slightly accusatory tone. "Yeah, I did many years ago. Not now. I'm not in soul condition." I sense the slight stirring of curiosity in me, but I can't pick up the word soul through her accent. "What condition?" I clue in after a few repeats and realize, as I often do, that it is not her accent but my imagination that is tripping me. Soul condition. "What do you mean by that?" I ask, and by now my impatience is fully dissolved and curiosity has taken over. "I mean, I'm not ... I don't know how to say it. What is the opposite of spiritual?"

"Material? Practical. The everyday." But these don't sit with her. I prompt, "Of course, because you are busy being a mum." That does it. I've already started taking notes. "I mean I have Luna, and I am busy with job, I go shopping, cleaning, taking Luna to daycare, and back, learning things for my job..." I think, obviously, all the day-to-day chores Rumi didn't have to do because his womenfolk did them. Angel says, "Wait, I'll show you the book," and walks off the screen. I hear her footsteps going away and returning. Back on the screen, she smiles and seems excited. That's what I love about her and about our conversations. No matter where we start from, we can readily move into a space of excitement. She tries to position the book in front of the camera. "Do you see it?" I see a sliver of her face, her contorted arm and a triangle of a pinkish brown book cover in one corner of the screen. "It is really nice. It is heavy... has stiff, you know...," tapping on the cover. "Hard cover. You mean it has a hard cover?" She brightens up, as she usually does whenever I give her a term that she hasn't learned in her daily conversations in English with Luna's Cuban father. She repositions the book, now opened, and tilts it toward the camera so I can see the inside page, then she puts the book down and turns some pages, smiling as she recognizes the words that obviously were very familiar to her once. I get technical to bring her back. Sometimes when she goes too deep she can't find the words to climb out with and she gets flustered. "Who is the translator?" She turns to the cover. "Zdravko Stanev, do you want spelling?" She texts it to me in Bulgarian and in English. In the first year of the pandemic, using a language book for refugees prepared by a not-for-profit support group, she tried to teach me Bulgarian. With some effort I can still read Cyrillic. "Was it translated from Farsi or from English?" She goes through some pages to find the answer. "I don't know. It doesn't say." I think, probably English and don't know why I don't think French or German.

"Do you want to talk to my friend? My friend, he did something for the book. He gave me the book," and she lifts her mobile. I panic. I'm not ready to meet and talk to a stranger via a phone connection fed into her laptop. "Not right now. It's not important. Let's leave that for another time. What did your friend do for the book?" But she's dialed the number already, as always ready to jump to my help. She smiles. "It's 9:30 but I can call even late in the night." There is no response, so she taps some text on the mobile and returns to me. "I don't know what he did. His name is Gopi. He's into these things. He has a guru and everything. He does some practices. I don't know exactly. It's complicated. He starts things and doesn't finish them, and..." I sense her desire to talk more about him. "What does he do?" To which she responds again saying he has a guru and does some practices that she doesn't know. I clarify, "I mean what is his job?" She puts the book down. "He teaches some things to kids. Basically he is a kids' teacher." There is more. "Is he in Plovdiv?" She moves in her chair. "I don't know. He was in Sofia before. He moves a lot. Never stay. He gave me the book. It was special to me. Even I was trying some dancing, turning around..." And she makes circles in the air with her index finger. "Whirling," I give her the word, and spell it as I usually do when I give her a new word. "Whirling? Means dancing like turning and turning?" I choose not to go beyond the immediate application. "Yes, people who dance like that are called Whirling Dervishes." She lights up again, remembering the word dervish. "Yeah, I didn't know the original, hadn't learned or anything. I just was fascinated. It was a special time." I'm not sure how deep I can dig, but I ask, "What was special about that time?" There is a pause laden with hesitation or discomfort. I try another entry. "How old were you?"

"Twenty-six. It was that moment when I was tripping a lot, hitchhiking, moving a lot, you know?" She's mentioned that time in passing in previous conversations. "So you were reading Rumi during the time that you were travelling through Europe?" She is pensive. "You know, it was the time that I was without any sense of life and not motivated to continue life. I wasn't clear at that moment. Not like now. Now I feel reasonable and connected with, with... reality, like I am here. What is the word for when you are in space... no la gravitation?" Like many Bulgarians of the post-Communist generation, at secondary school she was enrolled in a program that specialized in a foreign language, primarily French or German. Hers was French. One of the things I like about Bulgaria is that it's not trapped in the English orbit yet. "No gravity." I can't think of the word weightless, so I give her vacuum. "Like you're in a vacuum, no gravity, no air, you're just floating." Her eyes twinkle again, and she raises her arms and moves her upper body from side to side. "Yeah, like floating. I was floating. Not physical feeling. I was not having job, no profession, a homeless person not being connected with people. I even thought about *suicide*...," pronounced in French, "like jumping from a bridge or a rock." She looks sideways off the screen. "So you were reading Rumi during this time?" She looks up. "Yeah, I remember sitting and reading Rumi."

"What did reading Rumi do for you?" She looks directly into the camera and her face blooms in a smile. She opens her arms so wide they go off the screen. "I was feeling like I opened to the universe... It was related to marijuana maybe. I smoked a lot. It was very nice actually. Yeah, it was very nice." We both laugh. "It's when I started my master's degree in *psychodrame*," pronounced sick-o-dram. "I met Gopi in school, like I was a student and he was another student." Her eyes darken again and she stops. "Where was your school?" She always obliges me with generosity. "It was in the third floor of the Red House. Remember the Red House?"

We met in 2011 when I was preparing for a collaborative performance and exhibition at the Red House Centre for Culture and Debate in Sofia. "Yes, of course, we had a meeting with the performers and the audience there." She lights up again. "Yeah, where we had the meeting." And we both chuckle, remembering that difficult public conversation during which I was caught off-guard when a Bulgarian professor of Iranian Studies made a highly derogatory statement about the Roma people in response to my observation that the orange jumpsuits used as uniform by the street cleaners in Sofia, who all seemed to be Roma, were the same shade as the orange jumpsuits of Guantanamo prisoners. More participants chimed in with other anti-Roma racist comments intended to educate me, the outsider, about the realities. The performance that the six young Bulgarian students of the drama school, recruited and coordinated by Angel, had just presented was about the "war on terror." We had workshopped it for a week during which they developed and incorporated elements from the Bulgarian history of colonization by the Ottomans and the country's collaboration with the Nazis. That public conversation was my first time witnessing that when it comes to the Roma, even some of the most progressive Europeans can turn into rabid racists. My attempt to explain the basics of racism and the ABCs of anti-racism led to a heated debate, and all I could do was to assert control by speaking the loudest. That night the bond between Angel and me solidified. Our communication hindered by my lack of Bulgarian, we talked at length after the meeting in her limited English and my broken French about "the Roma Question." With her light skin, greenish brown eyes and limp, thin light brown hair, she is whiter than the typical Bulgarian, but, as a queer person, she has a strong sense of being othered and thus a deep affinity for the Roma, the quintessential Other in Bulgaria and most of Europe.

"Yeah, it was that time... You know, master's students work on themselves in *psychodrame*. I met Gopi there. He had stuff and I was working on my stuff." She waits for my prompt. "Did you hang out?" She looks at me with a question. "Hang out? What you mean hang out?" I scramble to explain, caught again using a phrase I've learned only through hearing it used in context and never looked up in a dictionary, a term I don't use often because I associate it with a particular generational English that feels remote to me. "I mean did you spend time together?" She nods to indicate she understands. "Yes, we hanged out," as always using the new word immediately, "we spent a lot of time. We were friends, and..." She moves in her seat and looks sideways again, and pauses. I respect the silence and wait for her to continue. "I had envy for him... I felt he was born in my body." My imagination fails me again. I ask her to explain what she means. "Gopi is very skinny, has big curly hair. A thin body, you know? Always flying. Dreaming all the time. I thought Gopi was born in my body." I'm not sure I'm getting it yet but I venture a guess. "You mean he had the body you wanted?" She shakes her head vigorously. "No, like he had my body. I was not born in my body, you know. I always had strong feeling that I am not in my body. I had envy for him... Do you want to see him? I send you his picture." Without waiting for my answer she looks to another part of the screen, her eyes darting from place to place searching for Gopi's picture. I wait. She sends me links to a few Facebook pictures. "Did you get the pictures?" I am not too keen on opening the pictures but I do it. The first one immediately sends me into involuntary laughter.

"Why you laughing?" Unthinkingly, I say, "Because it's funny." She smiles too but she's puzzled and her voice carries a tinge of hurt. "Why you laugh? This is my body." I am embarrassed for getting caught being insensitive and rush to explain. "Oh, it's the turban, I'm laughing at the turban and all the jewelry." I haven't clarified yet, perhaps not even to myself. "For me it's funny seeing a young Bulgarian man wearing an Indian turban with all that jewelry, the necklace, the earrings, the broach pinned to the turban, and that saintly smile that's so self-affirming, not at all self-conscious, like this is not an appropriated costume. You know, like all those yogis in Sofia." The reference makes it clear and she joins in the laugh. "Yeah, sufi yogis are popular in Bulgaria." I refrain from making a distinction between yogis and sufis in favour of returning to the core of our conversation. "So when you were reading Rumi what did you connect with?" She looks down at the book again and begins paging through it. "I can't remember." I push. "Hey, read one of the poems to me. I want to hear how Rumi sounds in Bulgarian." My request amuses her. "OK, I'm just going to read random..." I can now see the book as she opens a random page with her right hand. She smiles, a smile of recognition, and begins reading softly.

The music of Bulgarian is familiar to me, but in Bulgarian, Rumi doesn't sound like Rumi. I strain to pick up some rhyming or some words here or there. When she is finished, I ask "Does it sound poetic in Bulgarian, like it is a poem?" She shakes her head, "no, not at all. There is no *rime*, no rhythm." I ask her to translate it for me. She is excellent at spontaneous translation, being a children's French language teacher. "It's all about love. The title is "Love from Above" ... I have beloved, I am in a cave, I have hard love. You are my beloved, protect me. You are Noah, you are the key. You are the heart, I am secrets. You are light, you are power. You are the bird with..."

She stops as she struggles to find the word, then brings her hand to her face, and mimes a beak in front of her mouth. "What is it that birds have?" I marvel at how accurately the gesture transmits the meaning. "Beak," I say, and a flash goes off in my head. منقار. From that word alone, the line emerges خسته به منقار مرا *khaste be menghār marā*. She goes on "... you are water. You are love, you are sweet. You are..."

I am now fairly certain; it is آب تویی کوزه تویی آب ده این بار مرا *āb toyi, kuze toyi, āb deh in bār marā*. I tell her I think I know the poem and, to reciprocate, I volunteer to read it in Farsi. She lights up. I find the poem online and read, over-emphasizing the internal rhyming of the hemistiches:

> Yār marā, ghār marā, eshgh-e jegarkhār marā / yār
> toyi, ghār toyi, khāje negahdār marā
> Nuh toyi, ruh toyi, fāteh-o maftuh toyi / sine-ye
> mashruh toyi, bar dar-e asrār marā
> Nur toyi, sur toyi, dowlat-e mansur toyi / morgh-e
> koh-e tur toyi, khaste be menghār marā
> Ghatre toyi, bahr toyi, lotf toyi, ghahr toyi / ghand
> toyi, zahr toyi, bish mayāzār marā
> Hojre-ye khorshid toyi, khāne-ye nāhid toyi /
> roze-ye om'mid toyi, rāh deh ey yār marā
> Ruz toyi, ruze toyi, hāsel-e daryuze toyi / āb toyi,
> kuze toyi, āb deh in bār marā
> Dāne toyi, dām toyi, bāde toyi, jām toyi / pokhte
> toyi, khām toyi, khām bemagzār marā
> In tan agar kam tanadi, rāh-e delam kam zanadi /
> rāh shodi tā nabodi in hame goftār marā

She smiles throughout my reading. I feel her pleasure at hearing the musical rhymes. When I finish I ask her, "So, did you connect with that poem when you were reading Rumi?" She leaves her trance and becomes pensive. "I was in love at that moment with a woman. I feeling I wrote the poem. Now I don't feel like that. Rumi is all... love is like this, love is that, love, love, love. I am very sick of love now. But at that moment I was feeling very small, like I was not there, not inside my body. It is very physical feeling, like my body was here," she stamps the table with one hand, "and I was there," sending her other hand far off the screen. "I was heavy. I was big. In Red House I couldn't walk up to third floor. I stop at every step and breathe. My knees hurt." Having gained a lot of weight since the pandemic, I nod in recognition.

"That is when I went to my grandmother village. I told you about that?" I remember the pictures of her *баба*'s (baba, grandmother) village that she showed me when I was thinking about leaving Toronto's cold and moving to Bulgaria where friendships felt warmer and closer to home and heart. The summer I stayed with her in Sofia, Angel helped me navigate the thick bureaucratic fog that is Bulgaria as I tried to buy a house. I had set my eyes on a derelict house atop a hill in *Горна Бела Речка* (Gorna Bela Rechka) in northwest Bulgaria, where post-communist migration to Western Europe has radically depopulated villages and towns, leaving many houses abandoned and crumbling. We had hung out a few springs while taking part in the Goatmilk Festival of Memories, an annual art gathering held in Bela Rechka (white river). After two years I abandoned the Bela Rechka Dream House Project as the challenges of finding a current owner and legally zoned deeds to the house gradually wore out my enthusiasm and the good will of the Bulgarian friends who stepped in to help. That's when Angel showed me pictures of her grandmother's village near Plovdiv and her house that she had inherited, and suggested that we move there together, repair the house, and start the artist colony we had been talking about since the beginning of our friendship. But she had already embarked on her Child Project at that point. A year earlier she had visited the father-to-be in Cuba, a gay poet she had met in a Goatmilk iteration, and proposed the plan that he immigrate to Bulgaria, that they get married so he could get papers, procreate through IVF, and co-parent their child while keeping separate lives. In the summer I stayed in Sofia with her while trying to buy the house in Bela Rechka, she was pregnant and the prospect of moving to a depopulated village without daycare and school proved unrealistic. Now, at two-and-a-half years old, Luna is a true polyglot, comprehending and speaking Bulgarian with her mother's family, French with her mother, Spanish with her father, and English when her mother and father are together. I am sad I'm not there to add Farsi to the mix while she is still young enough to absorb so easily.

We haven't talked about her grandmother's house and our artist colony since I was in Sofia. I remember the long shot photo of the village's red roofs at the foot of a mountain. A ding alerts me to an incoming message. It's the picture of Angel and her baba. "You see, I was so big. I was not in my body." Her grandmother looks small and frail standing beside Angel's massive trunk. She reminds me of so many old village women I met in Iran, Bulgaria, Turkey, and Palestine, a weathered face with leathery skin, scarf tied under the chin, simple loose practical dress and a misshapen cardigan open in the front with side pockets stretched heavy with stuff, hands with semi-twisted fingers and knotted knuckles, and a smile showing missing teeth and dark purple gums. Baba is looking at Angel who is facing away and talking toward the camera. Behind them the village spreads in earth colours in a landscape that reminds me of my childhood world with a dry-looking yellowish triangle of a mountain in the far distance. I remember the pictures she had shown me of Baba's crumbling house with low mud walls and red tiled roof, the huge interior of the barn that was full of hay and junk and a square of light cast on the back wall through the only window, an unglazed hole in the front wall, the uneven dirt yard with a few chickens and a rooster claiming it as theirs. "Oh, yes, I remember this picture and the pictures of her house that you showed me. So, that's when you were in love and reading Rumi?" She is misty eyed, maybe remembering her grandmother or the woman she loved in the years she was reading Rumi in Bulgarian. "It was a book about soul... Now I am here. I know where I am." I'm curious, "Is there any Bulgarian poet that is like Rumi for you, that when you read their poetry you have the same feelings of love and openness?" She immediately says no. "Really? Nobody in Bulgaria has written about love and spiritual things?" She thinks. "I know what makes me feel like that, it's old Bulgarian folk songs I found in a book that was old and big." She shows the thickness of the book with her thumb and index finger held wide apart and then the width and height with the air distance between her hands. "It was old, I read it in library with gloves on. Maybe 1800, somebody went to villages and collected songs. They are like Rumi. Lovers who can't be together on this earth, and they die and meet in another place, another land, like that. Things that are impossible in reality." I wonder what Rumi's reality was when he was together with Shams and when Shams was driven out of town. "You know, the love Rumi talks about is not only physical love or love between people. He is mostly talking about a different kind of love, loving God, Creator, whatever." The discourse about Rumi has strong conventions that pull you in like a black hole. I am immediately aware that I don't believe what I just said and blush. I've only repeated the conventional readings that I had learned in my youth. However mystical his poetry, the man had two wives and four children, and a succession of male companions, and his *Masnavi* is full of graphic tales of lust. His father, who was a more stringent ascetic, we are told, talks about lusting after a young woman, justifying the carnal as what God has given and, naturally, God is not wrong. But the prosaic and the carnal were always left out of the repetitive readings regurgitated in the moral guidance given us by quoting Rumi. Even if love of God was the only motivator in Rumi's mysticism, I know that some of his ghazals, their very rhythm and music, awaken in me passions that are deeply rooted in the physical, the apparent, and the tangible. Angel's voice intervenes, "It's a vibration, *état d'âme*."

"So why are you not in soul condition now?" I ask the question that I had answered myself earlier to spiral back onto the covered ground. Angel gets pensive again. "I'm not sensitive to people. Before, I was feeling much more. More intense. Now I don't get touched by poetry. Now I read different pedagogical books, books about early childhood development, how it reflects the life. I'm looking for scientific proof about things. Epigenetics is more interesting to me than a novel or poetry..." We pause as we reflect. I too feel very far from that world I once inhabited where I spent long evenings reading Rumi, Hafez, Nima, Shamlu, and Forough and listening to music that evoked in me the longing for home, my spiritual, my cultural, my physical home, the home I was exiled from, the home I had abandoned. I realize that the Bela Rechka house was to be a replacement, an attempt to put down roots in a land closer to home; a running away from the deep cold, the detached confinement of living on a land that cannot become mine because it is ravaged through occupation; a desperate desire to belong to a place, to become indigenous again. "You know, I started volunteering for the Middle East Film Festival at that moment when I was in this soul condition. I am happy. It is good thing from that time, a top experience. The movies are close to what Bulgaria was in my childhood, how it was when my parents were my age." Angel has been volunteering for the festival by translating French subtitles into Bulgarian. "Really? Do they make you feel nostalgic?" She looks away from the screen, like she does when she has to collect her thoughts. "No... not nostalgic. It's nice, it's curious. The movies are about human things, not like Hollywood movies or French movies. The movies are real. Do you want to watch a movie with me tonight? I have a pass for the festival. There are four Iranian movies. Three of them are dark, heavy. Maybe we watch this one that's about a kid. Do you want me to read it for you?" I chuckle, thinking perhaps so many Iranian films are about kids because seeing things through their eyes makes the immense absurdity of life there appear simply to be on the continuum of absurdities of life in general.

Before we settle in to watch the film together, through her browser screen shared on Zoom, I tell her that I wish she could make some room in her life for soul condition, that soul condition doesn't have to be about unfulfilled love or lost feeling. As I say these, I know I am being preachy and talking to myself more than to her. We arrive at soul condition not by will but by happenstance and circumstance, like Rumi did when the meeting with Shams threw them both into soul condition.

آفتابی نی ز شرق و نی ز غرب از جان بتافت / ذره وار آمد به
رقص از وی در و دیوار ما
چون مثال ذره‌ایم اندر پی آن آفتاب / رقص باشد همچو ذره روز
و شب کردار ما

Neither from the east nor from the west a sun shone
from the soul / stirring our walls and doors as dust
dancing in sunlight
We are motes searching for the rays of that sun / we
live as dust   twirling day and night

Postscript

Angel called me a few days after reading the preceding text. Something had stirred in her since our conversation. She remembered more about that moment in her life, not bad things, but more about herself from a distance. While reading my retelling of our conversation as she was waiting in a cafe for her rideshare back to Plovdiv on Saturday, she was struck by a poster on the wall. It was the same as what is on the cover of the notebook in which she writes letters to Luna to read when she is a grown up. The poster read: "Life is like riding a bicycle. To keep your balance you must keep moving." She said for the first time in months she felt open and joyful. She was more attentive to the people she shared the ride with from Sofia after teaching her kids French class. She felt light and present and curious like she had in her days of hitchhiking. She felt she was back in the soul condition, this time feeling fully present in her body and without the heaviness of painful love. She signed off with "Love you, don't know with exactly what kind of love." I am touched because I know what a huge step it is for her to say love you, worrying that it would read as an expression of romantic love. I have been teasing her for a few years now by telling her at every chance I get that I love her, an intimacy I too struggled to internalize.

Post postscript

It is almost six months to the date since Angel and I had the conversation about soul condition and Rumi. We have not had a direct chat for some weeks now. Angel sent me this message a few days ago:

> Hello, Gita, I am fine. I just have a backlog, it's the end of the school year, I am having new students for the summer, I had stress about where Luna will go to kindergarden but she is already subscribed. My schadule looks like an automne apple tree and I am at the limit of my forces. And I have a crush on a woman and this is reaaaaaaaalyyy exhausting, my body can not stand it. Better times are coming soon for me.

I message her back, "how wonderful that your heart is open to new adventures! hope the love is returned. i love you."

Transdiciplinary artist, curator, writer, and translator, gita hashemi is a refugee who works from T'karonto, the "Dish with One Spoon Territory." She lives near Wonscotonach (burning bright point) aka Don River. Her home in Shiraz was near Khoshk (dry) River. Her work and ethics are based in the understanding that the personal is poetic, the poetic is political, the political is personal.

rumi

ghazal 1855

How could I know this melancholy   would turn me into *Majnun*[1]
turn my heart into an inferno   turn my eyes into *Jeyhun*[2]
How could I know   that a deluge would snatch me all of a sudden
and toss me like a ship   in the middle of the bloody *Gholzom*[3]
that a surge would hit the ship   and break it plank by plank
that each plank would crumble   in the curves and twists of the sea
that a whale would raise its head   and swallow the sea water
so the shoreless sea   would crack dry as a desert
and that desert would crack open   the seafaring whale
and drag it in wrath to the depths   suddenly like *Qārun*[4]
As these mutations came about   no sea remained and no desert
How would I know how   The how is drowned in the howless
There are many How could I knows   but I don't know
for to keep my mouth shut in that sea   a handful of opium I swallowed

1 *Majnun* (literally possessed) is a semi-historical figure whose story of unrequited love for Leyli originated in the seventh century Arabia, and was immortalized in Persian by the poet Nizami Ganjavi in 1188 CE in the narrative poem *Leyli va Majnun*.

2 *Jeyhun* is the Arabic name for the river Amu Daryā (Oxus in Latin) in Central Asia. The river rises in a number of turbulent headwaters and has many tributaries.

3 *Gholzom* is Persianized from al-Ghulzum, the name for the Red Sea in medieval Arabic.

4 *Qarun* (Korah) was a detractor of Moses. He amassed a lot of wealth and became so arrogant that to punish him the earth opened and swallowed him along with all his clan and possessions.

translation edit session with translator gita hashemi and translation editor elena basile

مولوی

غزل ۱۸۵۵

چه دانستم که این سودا مرا زین سان کند مجنون
دلم را دوزخی سازد دو چشمم را کند جیحون
چه دانستم که سیلابی مرا ناگاه برباید
چو کشتی‌ام دراندازد میان قلزم پرخون
زند موجی بر آن کشتی که تخته تخته بشکافد
که هر تخته فروریزد ز گردش‌های گوناگون
نهنگی هم برآرد سر خورد آن آب دریا را
چنان دریای بی‌پایان شود بی‌آب چون هامون
شکافد نیز آن هامون نهنگ بحرفرسا را
کشد در قعر ناگاهان به دست قهر چون قارون
چو این تبدیل‌ها آمد نه هامون ماند و نه دریا
چه دانم من دگر چون شد که چون غرق است در بی‌چون
چه دانم‌های بسیار است لیکن من نمی‌دانم
که خوردم از دهان بندی در آن دریا کفی افیون

Che dānestam ke in sodā marā zin sān konad majnun
delam rā duzakhi sāzad dow chashmam rā konad por khun
Che dānestam ke seylābi marā nāgāh berbāyad
cho kashtiam darandāzad miyān-e gholzom-e por khun
Zanad moji bar ān kashti ke takhte takhte beshkāfad
ke har takhte foru rizad ze gardeshhāy-e gunāgun
Nahangi ham barārad sar khorad ān āb-e daryā rā
chonan daryāy-e bi-pāyān shaved bi āb chon hāmun
Shekāfad niz ān hāmun nahang-e bahr farsā rā
keshad dar gha’r nāgāhān be dast-e ghahr chon ghārun
Cho in tabdilhā āmad na hāmun mānd-o na daryā
che dānam man degar chon shod ke chon ghargh ast dar bichun
Che dānamhāy-e besyār ast likan man nemidānam
ke khordam az dahānbandi dar ān daryā kafi afyun

read in persian by hajar hussaini

öykü tekten

two poems
and two pages with marginalia

"The water has been cut off from this world's river"[1]

Alan Kurdî

swallowed the whole sea
between lesbos and asos
was then washed ashore
face down as if asleep
resembling a baby seal

a friend said, i wish i had died
not him. we say such nonsense
in the east. hard to translate.

**alan*, an inland inhabited
by kurds for centuries
also an epic hero
—what was he doing
in the open seas in this century?

***kurdî*, well, you know,
an open wound looking for a scab
—why are you doing this to them?

what does your name mean?

1 Rumi, Ghazal 294, page 154 in this volume.

read by the poet

"O lovers, lovers, it is time to decamp from this world"[2]

Moria

you didn't hear this from me,
but there was a suicide
yesterday, not the first time,
it won't be the last
didn't hear this from me,

but there are six thousand people
piled on top of each other
cattle waiting to be slaughtered
hear this from me,

but the camp can cramp
only two thousand bodies
this from me,

but women are raped every day, mostly
the young and unmarried, children, too
from me,

but they might start sending them back
they made a new deal with turkey
me,

but most of them can't tell night
from day anymore
,

but every single word about the camp
that just came out of my mouth
of course, accidentally
has been banned by the government

but we are all overwhelmed
sometimes i don't even remember
my own name.

what's your name?

2 Rumi, Ghazal 1789, page 172 in this volume.

is this how we get
to the bottom of joy?

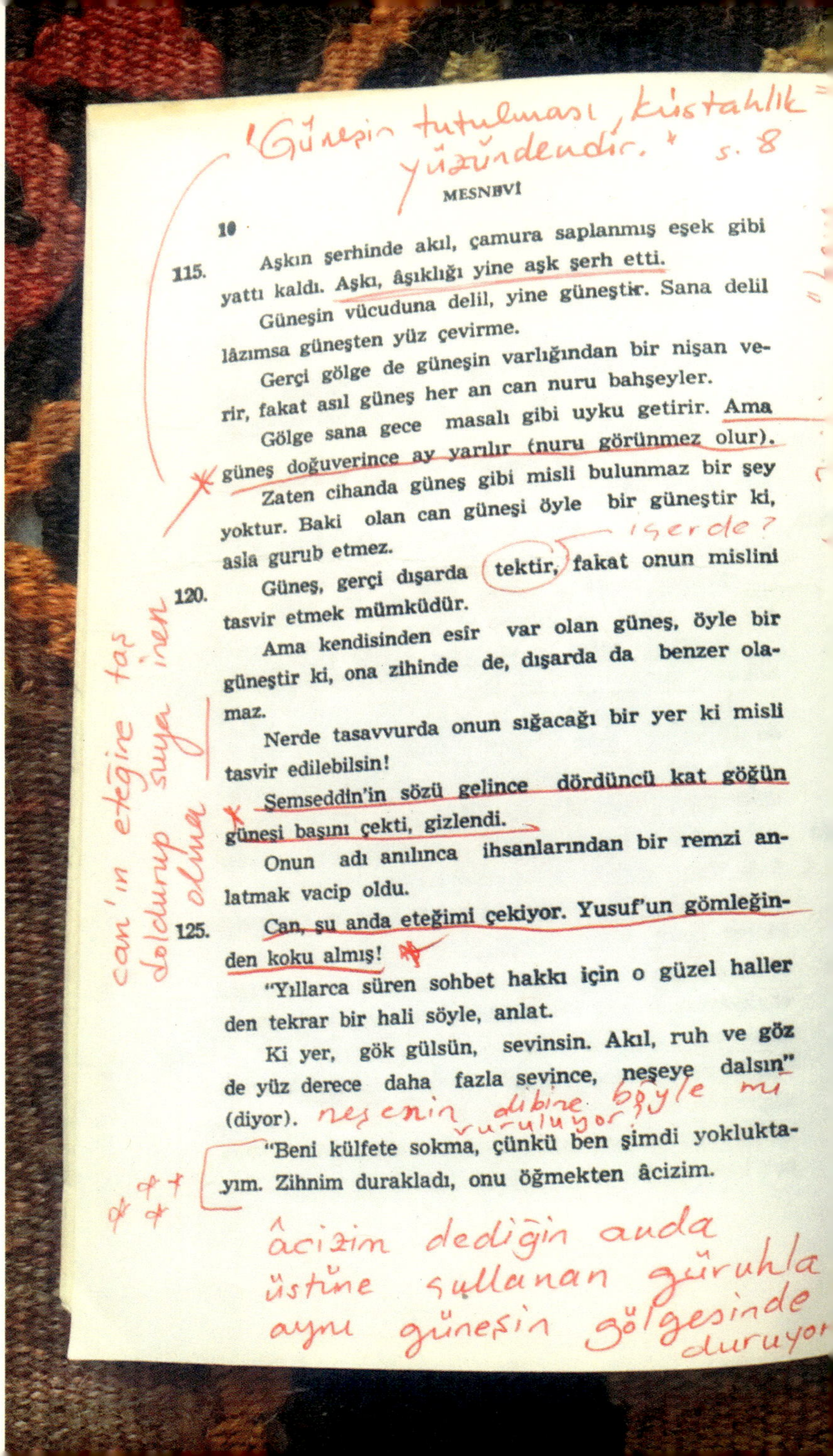

'Güneşin tutulması, küstahlık yüzündendir.' s. 8
içerde?
can'ın eteğine taş doldurup suya inen olma
neşenin dibine böyle mi vuruluyor?
âcizim dediğin anda üstüne çullanan güruhla aynı güneşin gölgesinde duruyor

MESNEVİ

10

115. Aşkın şerhinde akıl, çamura saplanmış eşek gibi yattı kaldı. Aşkı, âşıklığı yine aşk şerh etti.

Güneşin vücuduna delil, yine güneştir. Sana delil lâzımsa güneşten yüz çevirme.

Gerçi gölge de güneşin varlığından bir nişan verir, fakat asıl güneş her an can nuru bahşeyler.

Gölge sana gece masalı gibi uyku getirir. Ama güneş doğuverince ay yarılır (nuru görünmez olur).

Zaten cihanda güneş gibi misli bulunmaz bir şey yoktur. Baki olan can güneşi öyle bir güneştir ki, asla gurub etmez.

120. Güneş, gerçi dışarda tektir, fakat onun mislini tasvir etmek mümkündür.

Ama kendisinden esir var olan güneş, öyle bir güneştir ki, ona zihinde de, dışarda da benzer olamaz.

Nerde tasavvurda onun sığacağı bir yer ki misli tasvir edilebilsin!

Şemseddin'in sözü gelince dördüncü kat göğün güneşi başını çekti, gizlendi.

Onun adı anılınca ihsanlarından bir remzi anlatmak vacip oldu.

125. Can, şu anda eteğimi çekiyor. Yusuf'un gömleğinden koku almış!

"Yıllarca süren sohbet hakkı için o güzel hallerden tekrar bir hali söyle, anlat.

Ki yer, gök gülsün, sevinsin. Akıl, ruh ve göz de yüz derece daha fazla sevince, neşeye dalsın" (diyor).

"Beni külfete sokma, çünkü ben şimdi yokluktayım. Zihnim durakladı, onu öğmekten âcizim.

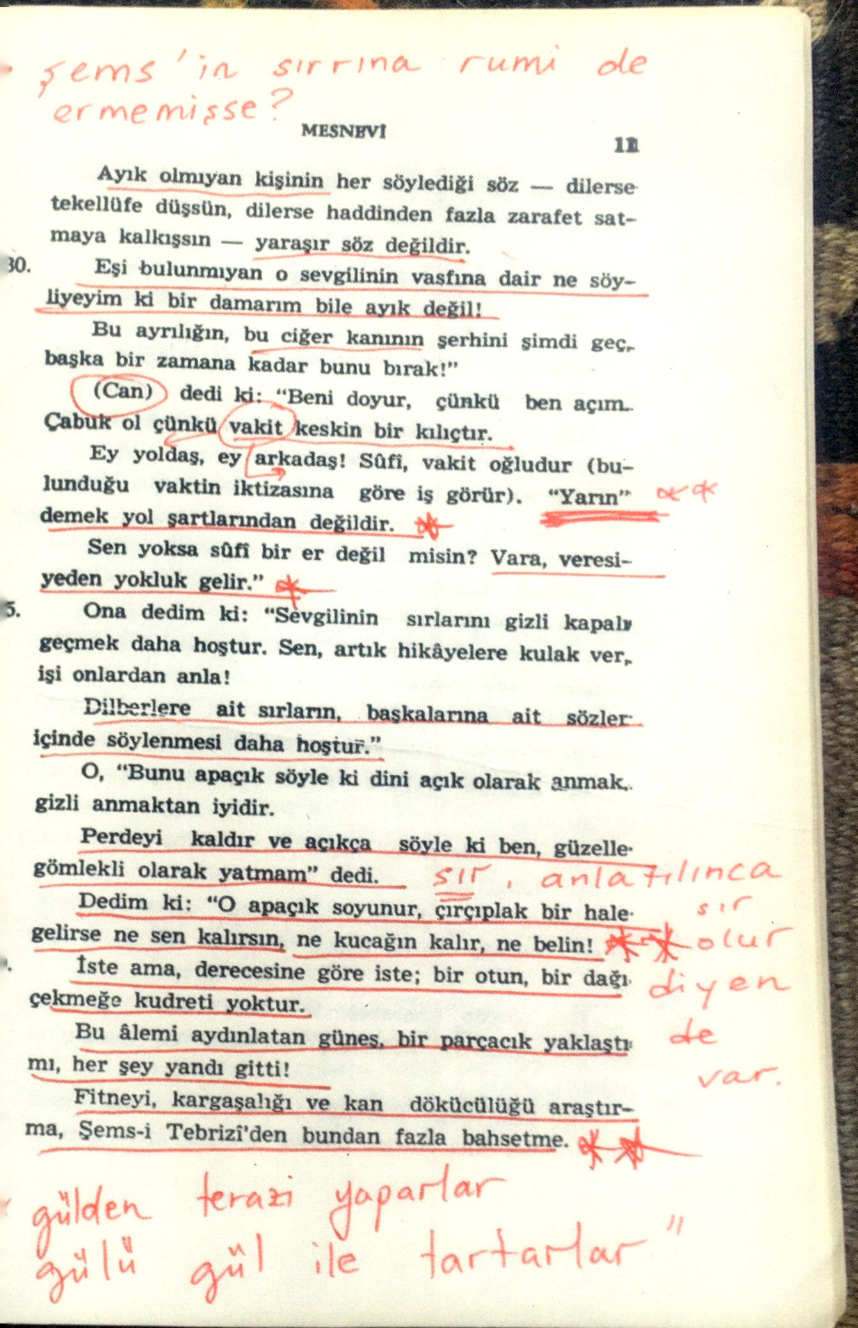

şems'in sırrına rumi de ermemişse?

MESNEVİ 11

Ayık olmıyan kişinin her söylediği söz — dilerse tekellüfe düşsün, dilerse haddinden fazla zarafet satmaya kalkışsın — yaraşır söz değildir.

30. Eşi bulunmıyan o sevgilinin vasfına dair ne söyliyeyim ki bir damarım bile ayık değil!

Bu ayrılığın, bu ciğer kanının şerhini şimdi geç, başka bir zamana kadar bunu bırak!"

(Can) dedi ki: "Beni doyur, çünkü ben açım. Çabuk ol çünkü vakit keskin bir kılıçtır.

Ey yoldaş, ey arkadaş! Sûfî, vakit oğludur (bulunduğu vaktin iktizasına göre iş görür). "Yarın" demek yol şartlarından değildir.

Sen yoksa sûfî bir er değil misin? Vara, veresiyeden yokluk gelir."

35. Ona dedim ki: "Sevgilinin sırlarını gizli kapalı geçmek daha hoştur. Sen, artık hikâyelere kulak ver, işi onlardan anla!

Dilberlere ait sırların, başkalarına ait sözler içinde söylenmesi daha hoştur."

O, "Bunu apaçık söyle ki dini açık olarak anmak gizli anmaktan iyidir.

Perdeyi kaldır ve açıkça söyle ki ben, güzelle gömlekli olarak yatmam" dedi.

Dedim ki: "O apaçık soyunur, çırçıplak bir hale gelirse ne sen kalırsın, ne kucağın kalır, ne belin!

İste ama, derecesine göre iste; bir otun, bir dağı çekmeğe kudreti yoktur.

Bu âlemi aydınlatan güneş, bir parçacık yaklaştı mı, her şey yandı gitti!

Fitneyi, kargaşalığı ve kan dökücülüğü araştırma, Şems-i Tebrizî'den bundan fazla bahsetme.

sır, anlatılınca sır olur diyen de var.

gülden terazi yaparlar gülü gül ile tartarlar"

what if rumi also didn't reach the secret of shams?

there are also those who say «sırr» (secret) cannot be unless it is told.

«they make a scale out of rose they weigh rose with rose»

Öykü Tekten is a poet, translator, archivist, and editor. She is also a founding member of *Pinsapo*, an art and publishing experience with a particular focus on work in and about translation, as well as a contributing editor and archivist with *Lost & Found: The CUNY Poetics Document Initiative*.

hajar hussaini

look at the moon

الف

she reads two signs engraved with the last
stations
toward the right lane
she paces
where fainting musics leak
out of
earphones

an exiled people
listen
to a composite

the train starts moving   & the movements

quake the primordial

feet

rumi roaming

it's not that she stands still
till evening

she is indifferent

to the neon
light
absolving

or the moon
inspiring
old poem

what surrounds the night
is outside her inquiry

just in the morning she
leaves the apartment

the lawnmower greets
coffees brew

naans are displayed

a kin alludes to the sea

of sorrow

without a
shore

she's attuned to perceive it

not as kitsch

but as inconclusive

myopia

looming over

an event

for we
migrated

Khosraw argues, however zombiesque you interpret it,
a mass waiting to be lifted into an oblivion
is an evidence that we
cannot conceive of
living
in an
ending

there's no need for submission

Ahmad sang, his tongue
stuck to the roof
of his mouth, Shirin kissing it

emphatically transliterates another one

day delay delay delayed

delam you half-plateaued

Evening shower
draws weariness like moon
reforms the dusk

crumpled extremity
is caused by a constriction of blood
vessels that shrink my heart

stuck
in split
dust

god knows how many times

dar watan-e-kharab-e-ma

a segment of the divan
then a dignitary begins the famine

reciting verse
so embellished
that it

makes her pull
out of this

lettering

Hajar Hussaini is a poet from Kabul, Afghanistan. She authored *Disbound: Poems* (University of Iowa Press, 2022) and translated *Death and His Brother: A Novel by Khosraw Mani*, translated from Persian (Syracuse University Press, 2025). Her translation of Maral Tahei's poetry collection won the Mo Habib Translation Prize in Persian Poetry and will be published by Deep Vellum in 2026. She is the visiting assistant professor of English at Skidmore College.

mahdi tourage

rumi is irrelevant

Traveling once for a conference in the United States, I happened to strike a conversation with someone sitting beside me on the airplane. As we were talking about our work, I explained that I was researching and writing about Rumi. My fellow passenger was excited to tell me that he was very familiar with Rumi and his poetry. In fact, he added, he had met Rumi when he saw him reciting his poetry in San Francisco. I told him that I was sure Rumi died in the thirteenth century, but he insisted that he had met him several times. He described Rumi as a soft-spoken, tall, Birkenstock-wearing man of gentle demeanour, with soft eyes, a warm smile, gray hair and beard, and with a gentle voice that touched the soul when he recited his poetry accompanied by double bass. I realized he was describing Coleman Barks, the popular interpreter of Rumi's poetry in the United States. My experience of meeting this person is indicative of Rumi's universal appeal to mystical seekers, especially those with a healthy dose of mistrust for religious authorities and who are averse to organized and institutionalized religion.[1]

Rumi has immense popularity in the West. Dubbed Rumimania,[2] a whole industry of mystical paraphernalia has spun around him, appropriating Rumi's name and poetry. These include dance choreographies, restaurant names, wine labels, mystical tourism to the poet's gravesite in Turkey, fake Rumi quotes, merchandise (such as depictions of whirling dervishes on pillowcases and bumper stickers), and highly popular "translations" of his poems often by those with no access to the original language.[3] Musicians, pop-culture hucksters, New Age spiritual gurus, and "translators" readily put into circulation wise and moving quotes attributed (often incorrectly) to Rumi. It is good to see literary treasures and cultural capital of a people so globally influential as to speak equally to others' concerns. However, as a few scholars and writers have pointed out, the Warholian repetition of Rumi's work has erased his Perso-Iranian Muslim identity. This erasure became particularly problematic in the post 9/11 political context when Islam came to be increasingly associated with intolerance and violence. There have been efforts to position Rumi as a devout Muslim and his ideas as a product of Islamic tradition in order to show that Islam cannot be reductively viewed as the exclusive motivation for political violence.[4] This push against the popularized commodification of Rumi restores his Muslim identity to him and relocates him in his rightful Islamic context by showing him to be a true product of Islam, its scripture, the Qur'an, and its prophetic example (the Sunna). However, as I set out to show below, this approach mythologizes Rumi.

1 Sophia Rose Arjana, *Buying Buddha, Selling Rumi: Orientalism and Mystical Marketplace* (London: One World Academic, 2020), 10.

2 Franklin Lewis, *Past and Present, East and West: The Life, Teaching and Poetry of Jalal al-Din Rumi* (Oxford: One World, 2000), 1.

3 Arjana, *Buying Buddha, Selling Rumi*.

4 Rozina Ali, "The Erasure of Islam from the Poetry of Rumi," in *The New Yorker*, January 5, 2017. www.newyorker.com/books/page-turner/the-erasure-of-islam-from-the-poetry-of-rumi. Last Accessed Feb. 28, 2022.

Tensions in the Text

I grew up in Iran with a deep reverence for Persian poetry and a love for Rumi. Still in awe of him and his mystical vision, years later in Canada I wrote my doctoral dissertation on some of the unconventional vulgar words and imagery, deemed "non-mystical," in his writings. It should be noted that vulgar language and bawdy tales *hazl* (هزل) are not uncommon in pre-modern Persian literature. However, they are often found in the works of satirists like 'Ubaid Zakani (d. ca. 1370), or they are collected in a separate section as spurious material with little to no literary value.[5] Rumi is unique among his peers for using vulgar words and coarse language for mystical purposes.

Rumi aims to effect a transformation of his audiences so that they become aware of the deep ocean of meanings beyond the surface. The transformation that Rumi wants to bring about is a spiritual awakening to the possibilities beyond the façade of our cultural-material world, mindfulness of every moment of our lives and the connectedness of all beings. To put it differently, Rumi wants us to recognize and then transcend our culturally-produced subjective selves. Using bawdy tales from his cultural milieu for mystical purposes could be considered a daring move for such a lofty goal, but would the goal justify the means? Would the exalted mystical ends or didactic lessons justify the violent tales and expressions that reproduce and perpetuate male supremacist, patriarchal, sexist, and racist aspects of the culture? Are only Rumi's mystical insights results of Islam and its sacred sources, or are his shortcomings due to these sources too? Are we to locate the flaws in the sacred sources of Islam that inspired and guided Rumi, or in himself for failing to overcome his own cultural and personal prejudices? What do these tales and passages—tales and passages that show a dissonance with the complex, real, lived experiences of gendered, sexed, classed, and embodied humans—say about the sacred sources of Rumi's inspirations? Are we not mythologizing Rumi by overlooking these important questions?

I have been grappling with these and other questions, and searching for answers in Rumi's work. What follows is a brief survey of some passages that are often overlooked in discussions of Rumi's mystical writing.[6] Most of these examples are from his magnum opus, the *Masnavi* (also spelled Mathnawi), which consists of more than 25,000 verses of mystical poetry, and some from the collection of ghazals in his *Divan-e Shams*.[7] The *Masnavi* is written in an open-ended genre of Persian poetry that lends itself better to didactic lessons, commentaries on quranic verses, and highlighting the inner meaning and mystical significance of everyday events. Yet, in this quintessentially mystical book, "The Qur'an in Persian,"[8] a lofty appellation historically employed in reference to the *Masnavi*, there are numerous passages that trouble its otherwise refined mystical foundation.

Rumi and Religious Others

Religious minorities, like Jews and Hindus, are a target of Rumi's ridicule and aggression. In his *Masnavi*, Rumi calls them "ignoble dogs" جهود سگ who have no courage,

یک جهودی این قدر زهره نداشت / چون محمد این علم را برفراشت

and no knowledge of God.

گر میسر کردن حق ره بدی / هر جهود و گبر ازو آگه بدی

They bring dark shame on (true) religion;

خیر دین کی جست ترسا و جهود.

Their fanatical anger is proverbial, خشم جهود, and they have dark souls:

خانه آن دل که ماند بی ضیاء / از شعاع آفتاب کبریا
تنگ و تاریک است چون جان جهود / بی نوا از ذوق سلطان ودود

They are accursed, the "damned Jews," so Rumi's advice is to hide secrets from them:

پندها دادم که پنهان دار دین / سر بپوشان از جهودان لعین

In his *Divan*, we read that Jews are "fearful, despicable, and accursed"همچون جهودان می‌زیی ترسان و خوار و متهم. We are like Jesus and rational thoughts are deceiving like Jews:

تو همچو عیسی و اندیشه‌ها جهودانند / ز مکر و فعل جهودان بگو مرا چونی

In the *Masnavi*, Rumi relates the story of a lowly but pious and learned Hindu slave named Faraj who grew up in a wealthy household. He confides his secret love for his master's daughter to her mother, the mistress of the house, who we are told was like a mother to him. The mistress, becoming infuriated, wants to strike him and hurl him down the roof. She says

5 For a survey of such passages in premodern Persian literature, see Mahdi Tourage, *Rumi and the Hermeneutics of Eroticism* (Leidin: Brill, 2007), 12-25.

6 For more details and examples see Mahdi Tourage, "Studying Sufism Beyond Orientalism, Fundamentalism, and Perennialism," in *Deconstructing Islamic Studies*. Ed. Majid Daneshgar and Aaron W. Hughes (Cambridge: Harvard University Press, 2020), 314-39.

7 All citations from the *Masnavi* are from Nicholson's edition: Jalāl al-Dīn Rūmī, *The Mathnawī of Jalālu'ddīn Rūmī*, 8 vols., ed. and trans. with critical notes and commentary Reynold A. Nicholson (London: Luzac, 1925–1940) and Mowlana Jalal al-Din Muhammad Balkhi, *Masnavi Ma'navi*, based on Reynold Allayn Nicholson edition (Tehran: Amir Kabir, 1366/1988). Citations from the *Divan* are from Jalal al-Din Rumi, *Divān-i Shams-i Tabriz*. 10 vols. Ed. Badi' al-Zaman Furuzanfar (Tehran: Danishgah-i Tehran, 1336–46/1957–67). Citation from the Qur'an are indicated by number of the chapter followed by the verse separated by a colon. All translations are mine.

8 Lewis, *Rumi: Past and Present*, 467.

to herself: "Who is this Hindu son of a whore that he should desire his master's daughter?"

خواست آن خاتون ز خصمی کآمدش / که زند واز بام زیر اندازدش
کو که باشد هندوی مادر غری / که طمع دارد به خواجه دختری

She tells her husband and together they devise a plan to trick Faraj and punish him for his folly. According to the plan, the husband tells Faraj that he did not know he loves his daughter. Now that he knows, Faraj can indeed have her. Even though the mistress considers giving their daughter in marriage to the Hindu slave "a vile disgrace" *nang-e mahin* ننگ مهین and says: "Tell the devilish traitor, die!" گو بمیر آن خائن ابلیس خو she goes along with the plan. They throw a fake wedding party with the full cooperation of the people of the town who, to avert Faraj's suspicion, go on to congratulate him on his impending wedding. On the wedding night the master of the house artfully decorates a beardless young man in wedding veil and robes in the manner of a beautiful bride.

بعد از آن اندر شب گردک به فن / امردی را بست حتی همچو زن
پر نگارش کرد ساعد چون عروس / پس نمودش ماکیان دادش خروس

In a few heart-wrenching, extremely difficult-to-read lines of poetry that should come with a trigger warning for modern readers, Rumi describes the boorish man raping Faraj repeatedly until daybreak. Faraj's screams for help, we are told, are drowned by the sounds of drumming and clapping outside the bridal chamber by the wedding party who are fully aware of the affair—as if they are all celebrating his punishment for expressing his unacceptable desire.

شمع را هنگام خلوت زود کشت / ماند هندو با چنان کنگ درشت
هندوک فریاد میکرد و فغان / از برون نشنید کس از دف زنان
ضرب دف و کف و نعره مرد و زن / کرد پنهان نعره آن نعره زن
تا بروز آن هندوک را میفشارد / چون بود در پیش سگ انبان آرد

The next day, Faraj is taken to the customary after-the-wedding-night bath "with his ass torn like a beggar's cloak":

رفت در حمام او رنجور جان / کون دریده همچو دلق تونیان

When he is returned to the wedding party and is sat beside the daughter of the family, Faraj turns to the daughter of the family, and, in what seems to be the punch line to elicit the readers' laughter, says: You are "such a dreadful evildoer bride! Your face is fresh like that of young women during the day / [but] at night your horrible cock is worse than that of a donkey!"

گفت کس را خود مبادا اتصال / با چو تو ناخوش عروس بد فعال
روز رویت روی خاتونان تر / کیر زشتت شب بتر از کیر خر

Worth noting here is that the imagery of a submissive, dark-skinned, and emasculated Hindu is from the stock imagery of Persian mystical poetry, often used as an analogy of mystical receptivity before the divine.[9] Rumi presents this didactic tale as the background for the lesson that follows: the pleasures of this world are like a mirage even though they appear delightful from a distance. "She [the World] is a stinking old hag, who shows herself like a young bride with much flattery".

گنده پیر است او و از بس چاپلوس / خویش را جلوه کند چون نو عروس

In this tale it is not just the slave's status of this young man that is germane to the story, but also his name. Rumi effeminizes him by naming him Faraj, meaning "happiness." But because in Persian script vowels are not written, the same word may be vocalized as *farj* فرج meaning "vagina." To add to Faraj's diminutive character, Rumi also calls him a "lowly/small slave," *gholām-e khord* غلام خرد, referring both to his lowly slave status and his small stature. In the crucial scene of the story where he is being violently raped over the course of his fake wedding night, Rumi repeatedly calls Faraj "little slave," *gholāmak* غلامک, and, specifically, "little Hindu," *hinduak* هندوک. The nuances of this story show that Rumi does not just fault Faraj for his social status as a male slave daring to express love for a free woman; rather his transgression is aggravated because of his religious background as a Hindu. To show how outrageous this situation is, Rumi juxtaposes the dark-skinned, small-statured, lowly slave status of Faraj with the master's fair daughter who has, first and foremost, a fair body, is lovely, and possesses an excellent disposition:

بود هم این خواجه را خوش دختری / سیم‌اندامی گشی خوش‌گوهری

It is significant that Rumi does not afford a modicum of dignity or credit to Faraj; even Faraj's piety and education, he tells us, is the result of his master's efforts. It is his master who "had educated and given him life; had taught him knowledge and perfect manners / lit the light of arts in his heart" پروریده کرده

9 See Annemarie Schimmel, *A Two-Colored Brocade: The Imagery of Persian Poetry* (Chapel Hill: University of North Carolina Press, 1992),137-144.

او را زنده‌ای. The lesson of the story, then, is to avoid being like the lowly Hindu slave Faraj, the religious, "racial," and socially inferior dark-skinned other, who transgresses the social and class boundaries of his time by expressing his secret love for his master's daughter.

Rumi and the Phallus

In many passages, Rumi shows concern with the penis and its erection. He insults and effeminizes a character in the *Divan*: "He has opened his throat like the wide cunt of female donkeys / A donkey's dick will not escape his attention when it is erect before him." In one passage of the *Masnavi*, Rumi says that "If a beard and balls could make the man / any billy goat has plenty hair and beard."

گر بریش و خایه مردستی کسی / هر بزی را ریش و مو باشد بسی

He relates the story of a general who is transporting a beautiful slave girl for the king but gives into temptation of having intercourse with her. While engaging in the sexual act a lion attacks their encampment. The brave general interrupts his sexual pleasure, slays the ferocious lion, then returns to the slave girl's bedside with his penis still erect "like the horn of a rhino" ان ذکر قایم چو شاخ کرگدن. Later on in the story the king loses his erection while having sex with the same slave girl because he hears the rustling noise of a mouse. The slave girl starts laughing when she sees the "weakness" sosti سستی of his penis. "She remembered the manliness of that champion / who killed a lion and his member was the way it was (still erect)."

یادش آمد مردی آن پهلوان / که بکشت او شیر و اندامش چنان

The point of the story, paradoxically, is that despite being humiliated for his erectile dysfunction the king exhibits true manliness by forgiving the general's transgression. Yet in many other passages Rumi uses the imagery of an erect penis and the sexual potency of a man as an analogy for mystical prowess. For example, in his *Fihi ma Fihi*, he analogizes his audience's taking pleasure in his words as the manly potency of taking pleasure in intercourse with a beautiful slave girl who is bought for sexual pleasure. He starts by saying that his words are like a beautiful bride. But to fit the context (since a bride could not be bought and sold), he immediately changes the analogy from a bride to a slave girl (one who could be easily and legally bought and sold):

> این سخن همچون عروسیست وشاهدیست کنیزکی شاهد را که
> برای فروختن خرند آن کنیزک بروی چه مهر نهد و بروی چه دل
> بندد چون لذت آن تاجر در فروخت است او عنین است کنیزک را
> برای فروختن می‌خرد او را آن رجولیت و مردی نیست که کنیزک را
> برای خود خرد
>
> These words are like a beautiful bride. A beautiful slave girl who has been bought only to be sold would have no love or affection for someone who buys her in order to sell her. Since the only pleasure such a trader has is in selling the girl, he is impotent. When he buys a girl only to sell her, he does not have the penis and manliness to be buying her for himself.[10]

Elsewhere in the *Masnavi* Rumi stresses the penetrative function of the penis by contrasting a virgin girl who is at the disposal of an impotent man. For example, "Why would you present a virgin (girl) to an impotent king?"

بکر چه عرضه کنی بر شه عنینه ای

Or, " ... an impotent man who buys a virgin / cannot benefit from her although she may be silver-bosomed."

هم‌چو عنینی که بکری را خرد / گرچه سیمین‌بر بود کی بر خورد

The better part of Rumi's disgust, however, is reserved for the "effeminate man" *mokhannas* مخنث. He ridicules and puts down such a bogus man on account of his penis that cannot become erect. The effeminate man exemplifies the kind of male who is unable to travel the arduous path of religion: "The reason the path of religion is full of trouble and struggle / is because it is not a path for anyone who is by nature effeminate."

راه دین زان رو پر از شور و شرست / که نه راه هر مخنث گوهرست

Some *Masnavi* stories are so out of mystical context and the expected *adab* (proper conduct, cultivated behavior, refinement of character) that scholars of Rumi categorize them as obscene, "distastefully vulgar" *mostahjan* مستهجن, and "improper" *nāshāyest* ناشایست.[11] An example is the tale of the mistress and her donkey. In this tale, a slave girl is caught by her mistress copulating with a donkey.[12] The slave girl had trained a donkey

10 Jalal al-Din Rumi, *Kitab-i Fihi ma Fihi*, ed. Badi' al-Zaman Furuzanfar (Tehran: Amir Kabir, 1330/1951), 111.

11 See Muhammad Taqi Ja'fari, Tafsīr, *Naqd, va Tahlil-i Mathnawi*, 16 vols (Tehran: Haydari, 1349/1970), 11.474; and Abdulhusain Zarrinkub, *Sirr-i Nay: Naqd va Sharh-i Tahlili va Tatbiqi-i Mathnawi*, 2 vols (Tehran: 'Ilmi, 1364/1985), 1.298.

12 For a full translation of this story, see "Appendix One" in Tourage, *Rumi and the Hermeneutics of Eroticism*.

belonging to her mistress to engage in sexual intercourse with her in the manner of men. The story goes on to explain graphic details of the slave girl sliding a gourd over the penis of the donkey to prevent it from fully penetrating her vagina and injuring her. When the mistress of the house finds out about this, she becomes jealous, saying: "How is this possible? I am more deserving of this, because the donkey belongs to me."

در حسد شد گفت چون این ممکن است / پس من اولیتر که خر
ملک من است

She sends her slave girl away and immediately begins copulating with the donkey herself, but dies in the process because in all her sexual excitement she had not noticed the protective function of the gourd. We read:

پا بر آورد و خر اندر وی سپوخت / آتشی از کیر خر در وی فروخت
خر مؤدب گشته در خاتون فشرد / تا بخایه در زمان خاتون بمرد
بر درید از زخم کیر خر جگر / روده‌ها بگسسته شد از همدگر
...
صحن خانه پر ز خون شد زن نگون / مرد او و برد جان ریب المنون
مرگ بد با صد فضیحت ای پدر / تو شهیدی دیده‌ای از کیر خر

> The donkey got an erection and thrust violently in her / (on account of seeing) the ass's cock a fire was kindled in her
> The donkey had become well trained, it pressed into the mistress / up to the testicles, the mistress died immediately
> Her liver was torn from the injury of the donkey's penis / the intestines were torn one from the other
> ...
> The house became full of blood, the woman upside down / She died and gave her life scandalously
> A bad death with a hundred disgraces, O father / have you ever seen a martyr of the ass's penis?

The Tale of the Slave Girl who Satisfied her Sexual Urges with her Mistress's Donkey (Mathnawi V:1333–1429), read in Persian by Mahdi Tourage

Rumi's addressees are always men, and often elite men of his time. A lesson of this story for them is that a man must be ruled by his intellect not by his lust. He expresses this in terms that show flaws in his basic understating of human sexual relations when he says that if you give in to your lust, you will be like a woman who gets excited at the sight of a "prancing" penis. "(He) is a whore whose intellect is turned into a mouse / and his lust into a lion by the prancing of a dick."

روسپی باشد که از جولان کیر / عقل او موشی شود شهوت چو شیر

The sexist misconception that women uncontrollably get sexually aroused at the sight of a donkey's erect penis is repeated in another passage of the *Masnavi*:

> Like that woman who saw a donkey engaged in sexual intercourse / and said: "O what is this unique stallion?"
> If intercourse is what these donkeys do / (then in comparison) these husbands are shitting on our vaginas!

هم‌چو آن زن کو جماع خر بدید / گفت آوه چیست این فحل فرید
گر جماع اینست بردند این خران / بر کس ما میرینند این شوهران

These passages make more plausible the later hagiographers' report of Shams Tabrizi, the wandering mystic and beloved of Rumi, saying the following:

> [I]f a pious woman's place were higher than the Throne of God *('arsh)*, 'if her gaze were by hazard to alight on the lower world (*negāh nazari be-donyā oftād*) and she saw there an erect phallus on the surface of the earth (*dar ru-ye zamin ghadibi rā bar khāsta binad*), she would cast herself madly down upon the phallus (*divāneavār khod rā partāv konad va bar sar-e qadib oftād*), because in their creed there is nothing higher than that (*az ānke dar mazhab-e ishān bālātar az ān chizi nist*)![13]

How are we to understand these "non-mystical" passages amidst the mystical works of one of the most influential mystics of all times? Contrary to the generally dismissive scholarly opinions of these bawdy tales, they do have mystical value of their own.[14] For example, in the story of the mistress and her donkey noted above, Rumi aims to convey more than a warning to the reader against the harms of unrestrained sexual urges. Here, the mistress represents the novice on the spiritual path, or perhaps the reader of the tale. He is showing that one cannot become a master simply by observing what a true master can do:

ظاهر صنعت بدیدی ز اوستاد / اوستادی بر گرفتی شاد شاد

13 Quoted in Franklin Lewis, "Mawlana Rumi, the Early Mevlevis and the Gendered Gaze: Prolegomenon to an Analysis of Rumi's View of Women." *Mawlana Rumi Review* 8 (2017): 54. I think "penis" here is a better translation of قضیب than "phallus."

14 Tourage, *Rumi and the Hermeneutics of Eroticism*.

"External forms" *zāher* ظاهر, he tells us, are a distraction, and knowledge of them is an incomplete knowledge. True knowledge is the knowledge of the secrets and inner meanings that can be possessed only by an esoteric master. Without a true master, one risks his life on account of ignorance:

کار بی استاد خواهی ساختن / جاهلانه جان بخواهی باختن

The mistake of the mistress was that she became excited by seeing only the external forms. In effect Rumi is equating the external forms with the penis of the donkey. He is alluding to something beyond the forms by using terms like "master" *ostād* استاد, "secret" *ser* سر, "knowledge" *dānesh* دانش, "kernel of the subject" *maghz* مغز.

That something that is beyond external appearances is an esoteric symbol: The "phallus," a symbolic configuration that is the epistemological opposite of the penis. Asserting that the phallus is a signifier of esoteric secrets in certain mystical contexts is not based on a simple substitution of one term (desire) for another (secrets). As I have elaborated on at length elsewhere—taking a cue from the studies of kabbalistic texts, primarily by Elliott Wolfson—the operations of desire in psychoanalysis and secrets in mystical context can be mapped onto each other based on certain common epistemological underpinnings. Briefly: in psychoanalysis, the phallus is the privileged signifier of desire. It is distinguished from the biological organ, the penis, through a relationship of negation and identity. The phallus, thus, is the concealed master signifier because it conditions the operations of desire even though it is inaccessible in itself.

The inaccessibility of the phallus causes desires to remain unfulfilled, never to be fully expressed in language except in distorted symbolic forms. Similarly, in a mystical context, esoteric secrets are incompatible with language and essentially remain inaccessible except through indirect allusions.[15]

I have used the concept of the phallus in order to make sense of Rumi's focus on the donkey's penis in this story. What is relevant here is the function of that "something" that Rumi hints at. That "something" is beyond the external forms and could very well remain nameless because it is essentially unknowable, therefore unnameable. It functions as a transcendental signifier to show (to signify) the limitations of external forms as exemplified by the donkey's penis. This process makes the production of meaning an open-ended process, and universalizes the capacity to access the inner meanings that are irreducible to representation.

In other words, we will be missing Rumi's allusions to inner meanings if we get distracted by the external form and vulgar words of the story; and this could summarize Rumi's entire mystical enterprise. The lesson, however, seems lost to Rumi himself whose claim of inner knowledge is contradicted by his evident racism and sexism. The question remains, can we, for the sake of possible spiritual transformation of (some) men, overlook the evidence of Rumi's privileging the masculine; his ignorance of women, sexuality, and gender relations; his disregard for the inherent dignity of all humans?

Rumi on Women

Rumi views women as externalized manifestations of the carnal soul and its evils, "Know that your carnal soul is a woman, [even] worse than a woman" نفس خود را زن شناس از زن بتر, he states in the *Masnavi*. He warns men, "Woe to him whose intellect is female," وای آنک عقل او ماده بود, and "Happy is he whose intellect is male / and his ugly carnal soul is female and powerless:"

ای خنک آنکس که عقلش نر بود / نفس زشتش ماده و مضطر بود

He writes: "Know that the husband is intellect and the wife is greed and avarice" عقل را شو دان و زن را حرص و طمع. He equates women with infants, telling his readers that both have deficient intellects, which is why the Prophet said, "Consult her but do the opposite of what she says and go on your way:"

گفت با او مشورت کن و آنچ گفت / تو خلاف آن کن و در راه افت

The difference between men and women, he points out, is not physical strength, or the power and opportunity to earn a living (otherwise some animals like lions and elephants would have been superior to humans), but that men are more mindful of the end:

فضل مردان بر زنان ای بوشجاع / نیست بهر قوت و کسب و ضیاع

15 For other examples of Rumi's use of a symbolic configuration that can be conceptualized as the phallus, see Tourage, *Rumi and the Hermeneutics of Eroticism*.

ورنه هر شیر و پیل را بر آدمی / فضل بودی بهر قوت ای عمی
فضل مردان بر زن ای حالی پرست / زان بود که مرد پایان بین تراست

Rumi generally associates women with the material world "This world is a strong and clever sorcerer" ساحره دنیا قوی دانا زنیست, or the earth: Omran, Moses' father tells his mother, "I am like a cloud, you are the earth and Moses is the offspring" من چو ابرم تو زمین موسی نبات. He believes them to be inherently defective, thus inferior, beyond remedy. In a passage that reads as if he is benevolently excusing women, he writes: woman's "imperfection" is from nothing but being a woman, "like that of a donkey, [whose imperfection has no other cause except] from being a donkey" آفت او همچو آن خر از خریست. As if anticipating an objection to his sexist generalization, in the next line he goes on to explain that portraying woman as a beast of burden like a donkey is "because she is inclined towards color and scent."

وصف حیوانی بود بر زن فزون / زآنک سوی رنگ و بو دارد رکون

Rumi advises the male seeker: "If on the path of the Religion you do not want to be a highway thief / do not worship color and perfume like women."

گر نئی در راه دین از رهزنان / رنگ و بو مپرست مانند زنان

Deficiency of women's intellect and weakness of their souls, he believes, prove that even their dreams are less than that of a man:

خواب زن کمتر ز خواب مرد دان / از پی نقصان عقل و ضعف جان

Rumi not only equates women and infants because of their deficient intellects, but also equates them on account of their deficient bodies. He finds the evidence of inherent deficiencies of women in their defective bodies that uncontrollably menstruate, noting that when women menstruate, they are like infants who have no control over their bodily functions and discharges and who soil the ground where men pray:

مستحاضه و طفل و آلوده پلید / کرده مستعمل به هر جا که رسید

In another passage he likens the world to a female sorcerer, "a black devil" *siyah div* سیه دیو, "a ninety-year old hag with a rotten pussy" نود ساله عجوز گنده کس. It is to counter the "sorcery" *jādu* جادو of these "stinking old hag[s] with potent spells" هین فسون گرم دارد گنده پیر that God has sent (only male) prophets:

ور گشادی عقد او را عقلها / انبیا را کی فرستادی خدا

In the *Divan* too Rumi repeatedly uses the feeble nature of woman as a trope. In one ghazal he advises men not to be afraid because the thought of fear is a female defect

در بیشه شیران رو وز زخم میاندیش / کاندیشه ترسیدن اشکال زنان است

The inherent weaknesses of women in battle and on the spiritual path is repeated in many ghazals in the *Divan*. Here are some examples:

چون که از دور دلت همچو زنان می‌لرزد / تو چه دانی که در آن جنگ دل مردان چیست

Since like women your heart shivers with fear even at a distance [from the battlefield] / How would you know what men's hearts are like in that battle?

در راه رهزنانند وین همرهان زنانند / پای نگار کرده این راه را نشاید

There are highway robbers on this path and these companions are [like] women / ornamented feet are not suitable for this path

چون هیچ نیابی تو پهلوی زنان بنشین / از حلقه جانبازان بگذر به کنار آخر

Since you do not find anything, go sit beside women / just leave the circle of devotees aside

زین دمدمه‌ها زنان بترسند / بر ما تو مخوان که مرد مردیم

Only women would fear these clamors / Do not recite them to us because we are manly men

مردانه کنیم کار مردان / پنهان نکنیم آنچ کردیم

We perform men's work like men / we do not hide what we have done

صبر سوی نران رود نوحه سوی زنان رود

Patience gravitates towards males, lamentation towards women

One passage in the *Divan* reads like a typical rude spat between uncouth men (of any time and place) where they express their anger towards each other through verbal violent sexual aggression towards women. In this passage Rumi is telling another man that if he is not to give him the promised "wine" (likely a term referring to something they are fighting about), then, "go put it in the vagina of your own women"

سالار دهی و خواجه ده / آن باده که گفته ای به من ده
ور دفع دهی تو و برون جه / در کس زنان خویشتن نه

Again in the *Divan* he records his fight with a man by calling him "donkey's ass," کون خر and goes on to swear at him so: "May a hundred donkey's penises be in his ass, a hundred dog's farts in his beard."

صد کیر خر در کون او / صد تیز سگ در ریش او

In addition to these sporadic passages, the *Masnavi* contains allegories, cautionary and didactic tales that elaborate on the theme of women's inferiority and fear of chaos resulting from their uncontrollable sexuality. For example, Rumi narrates the tale of a woman who concocts a plan to be alone with her lover. She climbs a pear tree to gather some fruit. Atop the tree, she bursts into tears, yelling at her husband: "Who is that pederast who is on top of you, oh you wicked effeminate man!"

گفت شوهر را که ای مابون رد / کیست ان لوطی که بر تو میفتد

The husband becomes angry at her ridiculous charges and asks her to come down so he could climb the tree to pick the fruit himself. As soon as he goes up she embraces her lover who has been hiding around the corner. The husband angrily yells from the treetop, "Who is that [man] on top of you, you whore?"

گفت شوهر کیست آن ای روسپی / که به بالای تو آمد چون کپی

The wife responds,

> There is no one here except me, you have become crazy / this illusion is from this pear tree! On top of it I too saw things crookedly.

While highlighting how cunning women could be, this story becomes the background for a lesson that follows: our egoism is like the pear tree, only by coming down from it can we see things correctly.

Another similar story in the *Masnavi* is the tale of a man who uses his attractive wife's sexuality to trap notables of the city for extortion. He sends her to seduce the judge into their secluded house, then arrives when they are together and extorts money. Even though the text is clear that this was a plan hatched by the husband, Rumi blames women for their cunningness: "The deception of women has no end" مکر زن پایان ندارد. This particular line is a reference to the tale of the young Joseph in the Qur'an where Joseph, the paragon of male beauty, is seduced into having an affair by the wife of his master in whose house he was raised. As the story goes, Joseph refuses her sexual advances and the affair never takes place. Yet in a twist of the story Joseph's master catches them together, and realizing his own wife is at fault he utters these words: "This is from trickery of you women; indeed your guile is enormous!"[16] Like all the classical commentators of the Qur'an that saw this verse as a condemnation of women,[17] Rumi presumes these words of the husband, uttered in anger and addressed specifically to his wife (or the notable women of Egypt at the time), is a categorical denunciation of all women across time and place. In fact he blames women for their negative contributions to the entire narrative of humanity: from Eve who, unlike Satan, was successful in getting Adam to eat the forbidden fruit

چند با آدم بلیس افسانه کرد / چون حوا گفتش بخور آنگاه خورد

to Noah's wife who undermined his prophetic mission

نوح چون بر تابه بریان ساختی / واهله بر تابه سنگ انداختی

to Cain killing Abel for the sake of a woman

اولین خون در جهان ظلم و داد / از کف قابیل بهر زن فتاد

Joseph is quoted as saying that he does not know whether he should complain about being betrayed by his brothers or about women who caused his downfall just like Adam from paradise.

ناله از اخوان کنم یا از زنان / که فکندندم چو آدم از جنان

Rumi and Mary

As much as Rumi claims to be pointing to the inner meanings of things and events beyond the literal sense, he fails to rise above his own patriarchal cultural context and see beyond it even when he is writing positively about exceptional women. For example, he speaks highly of Mary (Maryam) whose elevated station as mother of Jesus is attested in the Qur'an. In his *Divan* he writes: "Who is not pregnant, through the breath of the Holy Spirit, like the pregnant Mary?"

کیست که از دمدمه روح قدس / حامله چون مریم آبست نیست

In another ghazal in the *Divan* he writes:

> Like Mary we have become pregnant with God's light / Even though we are bound by this body, like Jesus who was tied to his cradle

16 Qur'an 12:23-28.

17 Barbara Freyer Stowasser, *Women in the Qur'an, Traditions, and Interpretation* (Oxford and New York: Oxford University Press, 1994).

Do not search about these matters through your own rationality / Because in the plain of love we are outside of these matters.

همچو مریم حامله نور خدایی گشته‌ایم / گر چو عیسی بسته این جسم چون گهواره‌ایم

از درون باره این عقل خود ما را مجو / زانک در صحرای عشقش ما برون باره‌ایم

These lines are rich with allusions and meanings until we read them through a gender justice lens. Exceptional women like Mary with the potential to empower all women are to be found in Islamic and Sufi traditions. Yet, Mary's potential for empowering women—for example, some consider her to be a prophet, therefore upsetting the common belief that God has only sent male prophets—is lost when by emphasizing only the virgin birth of Jesus she is rendered so exceptional that no woman can ever be like her.

In fact, in the *Masnavi*, Rumi himself points out Mary's exceptionality in a self-contradictory, woman-hating passage where he argues that since a woman cannot do physical battle (considered to be "minor jihad," according to the prophetic tradition), she will never be able to do the "greater jihad" either (battle with the carnal self). Rumi himself never engaged in physical battle in his lifetime, but that does not prevent him from moralizing that women and effeminate men (a category of males that Rumi repeatedly mocks for their penile dysfunction) are as suitable for physical combat as aloe-wood and musk are for a donkey's ass. In the next line he becomes conscious of the inconsistency of his own position about women, that there are great notable women, and great male war heroes, like the ancient Iranian national hero Rustam, who are born of a woman. So he goes on to say these are exceptionally rare cases: "Except rarely, a Rustam may be concealed in a woman's body, like a Mary."

نیست لایق غزو نفس و مرد غر / نیست لایق عود و مشک و کون خر

چون غزا ندهد زنان را هیچ دست / کی دهد آنک جهاد اکبرست

جز بنادر در تن زن رستمی / گشته باشد خفیه همچون مریمی

He continues to assert that the reason some men are faint of heart is because the feminine *mādegi* مادگی is hidden in their bodies, something that becomes manifest in the next world to expose any man who did not prepare for manliness *mardi* مردی.

آنچنان که در تن مردان زنان / خفیه‌اند و ماده از ضعف جنان

آن جهان صورت شود آن مادگی / هر که در مردی ندید آمادگی

Seemingly female-positive passages like these misappropriate the female biological function of birthing as the analogy of the divinely inspired creative process of men's mystical writings in ways that disempower women who embody this reproductive process. For example, consider this line in the *Masnavi* where Rumi characterizes mystical creativity as feminine: "Like Mary through that touch [of the divine] upon the bosom / the soul became pregnant with a heart-captivating Messiah."

همچو مریم جان از آن آسیب جیب / حامله شد از مسیح دلفریب

Here pregnancy is presented as a mystical category to be distinguished from its cultural/biological correlation, the woman, and appropriated. If pregnancy is a good analogy for divine inspiration shouldn't women who embody this potentiality have a better understanding of it, and therefore have greater propensity for the mystical path? (It is worth noting that in the Islamic mystical context, terms like the "path" or "wayfaring" are gendered terms that privilege men because of the many limitations, such as restrictions on travel without a man's permission, that are placed on women.) In the male-centred world of Rumi the answer is no!

Stripping and Appropriating the Feminine

As these examples show, Rumi spares no effort of imagination to strip away any connection between women and the spiritual significance of the feminine. Rumi's male supremacy is therefore a result of his belief that with their inherent spiritual-intellectual flaws, as reflected in their defective bodies, women are irrelevant to the mystical path except to highlight men's superiority by contrast. The true Sufi on the mystical path is therefore by default male, either a biological man, or in rare cases an exceptional woman who is admitted in the path as an honorary man. It follows that for Rumi the ultimate object of love of a male mystic cannot be a woman, but a man, Shams, to whom he dedicates his entire book of more than 30,000 verses of lyrical ghazals, the *Divan*.

Thus, according to Rumi, a male mystic must find the creative feminine within his own body. Rumi tells us that the body of a male mystic "is like Mary," giving birth to his own Jesus تن همچون مریمست و هر یکی عیسی داریم.[18] It is in this spiritualized sense that a male mystic gives birth to the "spiritual child" *valad-e ma'navi* ولد معنوی.[19] The "spiritual child" is like Jesus of the soul, a formation that in Rumi's patriarchal context, and considering his disparaging views of women, denigrates and discards the biological necessity of having a womb and requisite sexual encounter with a female for the purpose of pregnancy. The male mystic becomes pregnant by the divine breath, just like Mary (a reference to the Qur'an 66:12, where God says: "We breathed our spirit into her"). The purpose of the abstraction of pregnancy is to avert the anxiety threat produced by women's unique biological capability and denying them any creative capacity. Put simply, Rumi's male-centred logic of invitation to patriarchal power is: if a woman gave you physical birth, we give you spiritual rebirth; if a woman gave you life, we give you eternal life; if a woman nursed and nourished you, we nourish you spiritually. Moreover, any female (human or animal) can produce biological offspring, but only a male mystic contemplating the divine can give birth to spiritual children. Here, spiritual children are volumes of divinely inspired poetry, which Rumi presents as proof of his claim to be the conduit of the divine presence.

The Divine Poetry

Just as the infant Jesus spoke in the cradle, testifying to Mary's purity (Qur'an 19:29), Rumi argues that his poetry is the speaking proof of the divine source of his work: "Although this written statement (i.e., the *Masnavi*) is itself only a claim / what is written is itself an evidence of the inner meaning (of this assertion)."

این نوشته گرچه خود دعوی بود / هم نوشته شاهد معنی بود

He starts his *Masnavi* with the lofty claim that this book is a divinely revealed text equal to the Qur'an. In the opening line of the *Masnavi*, he writes (in Arabic):

> This is the Book of the *Masnavi*, which is the roots of the roots of the roots of the religion in unveiling the mysteries of attainment (to the Truth) and of certainty; and the doctrine of God the Great, and the clearest path of God, and the most manifest evidence of God.
>
> هذا كتابُ المثنوى و هُو اصول اصول اصول الدين، فى كشف
> اسرار الوصول واليقين، وهو فقه الله الاكبر، و شرع الله الازهر، و
> بُرْهان الله الاظهر

Later on in the book he has a spat with a man who calls the *Masnavi* a trivial book of stories. His anger at the unfavourable comments of this man is clear in these lines:

> Suddenly a great idiot raised his head / out of a donkey's stable, like a backbiting woman
> (Saying) that these words, namely, the *Masnavi* / is simply the story of the Prophet and imitation (of others)
> There is no mention of investigations and grand mysteries / so that saints would run their steeds in that direction
> From the stations of asceticism to the passing away from self (*fanā*) / step by step up to meeting God
> It does not have the explanation and limitations of every station and state (on the mystical path) / so that by means of those wings a man of heart should soar.
>
> خربطی ناگاه از خرخانه‌ای / سر برون آورد چون طعانه‌ای
> کین سخن پستست یعنی مثنوی / قصه پیغامبرست و پی‌روی
> نیست ذکر بحث و اسرار بلند / که دوانند اولیا آن سو سمند
> از مقامات تبتل تا فنا / پایه پایه تا ملاقات خدا
> شرح و حد هر مقام و منزلی / که بپر زو بر پرد صاحب‌دلی

Then he goes on to explain that his *Masnavi* is divinely inspired, just like the Qur'an, and issues the same challenge that the Qur'an offers to its detractors: bring a chapter like it if it is such an easy book to compose:

> When the Book of God (the Qur'an) was revealed / the unbelievers attacked it just like this (the way they attack the *Masnavi*)
> Saying: These are just legends and worthless tales /

18 Rumi, *Kitab-i Fihi ma Fihi*, 21.

19 For the concept of the Messiah of the soul and "spiritual child," a term by Rumi's commentator Ismail of Ankara, see Henry Corbin, *Creative Imagination in the Sufism of Ibn 'Arabi* (London and New York: Routledge, 1969), 202, 405.

> not a deep inquiry and sublime investigations
> ....
> He (God) said, If this seems easy to you / then easily compose one chapter (like it)
> Let the *Jinn* and mankind and all the skilled people / produce a single verse like this "easy" (book)
> چون کتاب الله بیامد هم بر آن / این چنین طعنه زدند آن کافران
> که اساطیرست و افسانهٔ نژند / نیست تعمیقی و تحقیقی بلند
> ....
> گفت اگر آسان نماید این به تو / این چنین آسان یکی سوره بگو
> جنتان و انستان و اهل کار / گو یکی آیت ازین آسان بیار

Why then would one of the greatest mystics of all times so readily believe and promote patriarchal sexist notions, such as the ridiculous idea that women get uncontrollably sexually excited at the sight of a donkey's erect penis? How can Rumi's own claim of mystical insights be reconciled with his sexism evidenced in many of his tales and passages? Isn't Rumi's claim to be the master of esoteric sciences and his *Masnavi* a timeless, divinely revealed scripture equal to the Qur'an, therefore, dubious at best?

Putting Rumi in Perspective

Rumi wants us to be awakened to a spiritual world beyond ours. But was he himself able to transcend his own cultural context? The vulgar passages and bawdy tales are not hidden away or collected in a separate section. They are deployed in the midst of a highly acclaimed mystical work by a great mystic himself. When they are not overlooked, they do pose a problem for readers of Rumi. For example, Annmarie Schimmel, a great scholar of Sufism viewed them as literary devices used by a master storyteller to attract the audience's attention[20]—though one can argue that no subsequent didactic lesson justifies jubilantly relating the tale of a young slave's repeated violent rape for expressing his desire for his master's daughter. Reynold Nicholson, whose monumental English translations of Rumi remain unmatched to this day, dismisses them as the result of "the failing power" of an aging mystic, and goes on to translate these passages into Latin to make them less accessible to the English reader.[21]

As demonstrated above, many passages of the *Masnavi* show that, for Rumi, the woman is rendered secondary and derivative; exceptional women, who are not rare in Islamic and Sufi traditions, are absorbed into the masculine as honorary men; and the feminine (differentiated from its cultural/biological correlate, the woman) is contained within the masculine. What these passages demonstrate is that Rumi's access to a divine source, if such a source exists at all, is severely limited by his patriarchal cultural constraints and by his gendered and embodied self that he evidently cannot overcome. They also show that being inevitably a gendered and embodied subject firmly rooted in his own male-centered world hinders Rumi from an ethical-egalitarian reading of the Qur'an. It is of course possible that, instead of reading male supremacy into the Qur'an, "liberation" from cultural constraints be read from it.[22] Similarly, it is surely possible, and more in tune with the quranic imperative of justice, that we read gender justice from the Qur'an according to what Amina Wadud calls the Qur'an's "tawhidic paradigm."[23] However, Rumi's salient flaw lies in his reading male-supremacy into the Qur'an even though his entire mystical enterprise comprises of illuminating the mystical path of transcending such cultural constructs. Hence, these violent passages in Rumi's poetry are better placed along the continuum of androcentric interpretations of Islam institutionalized by the political, religious, and legal authorities during the classical age of Islam that continue to be maintained by the "enforcers of orthodox, androcentric Islam."[24]

It is the same with Rumi's take on the institution of slavery. Islam accepted slavery as a social fact of seventh-century Arabian society, but limited and modified it through its teachings and practices to the point that many contemporary scholars argue the trajectory of quranic teachings is towards the elimination of slavery, even though this is not articulated in definite terms. The Qur'an views slaves as moral equals to the free people and favors emancipation of slaves as an act of piety, a work of charity for which public funds can be used, and for the expiation of sins.[25] Verse 36 of the Qur'an's fourth

20 Annmarie Schimmel, *The Triumphal Sun: A Study of the Works of Jalaloddin Rumi* (Albany: State University of New York Press, 1993).

21 Jalal al-Din Rumi, *The Mathnawī of Jalālu'ddīn Rūmī*, 8 vols., ed. and trans. Reynold A. Nicholson (London: Luzac, 1925–1940).

22 Asma Barlas, "Believing Women" in *Islam: Unreading Patriarchal Interpretations of the Qur'an* (Austin: University of Texas Press, 2002).

23 Amina Wadud, *Inside Gender Jihad* (Oxford: One World, 2007).

24 Leila Ahmed, *Women and Gender in Islam: Historical Roots of a Modern Debate* (New Haven and London: Yale University Press, 1993), 66.

25 Robert Brunschvig, "ʿAbd," in *The Encyclopaedia of Islam*, 2nd ed., ed. P. Bearman, et al (Leiden: Brill Publishing Online, 2012).

chapter mentions slaves among those who specifically should be treated with *ehsān* احسان, a word rich with significance, often translated as "kindness," but also denoting performance of deeds in the most beautiful way possible—the others grouped along with slaves in the same verse to be treated with *ehsān* are one's parents and relatives, the orphans, the needy, the neighbor, and the stranded traveller. Cognizant of the perils of master-slave power differences, Prophet Muhammad, in many of his sayings, instructs believers to act with "real kindness towards this inferior social class."[26] Yet we do not get any hint of compassionate sympathy or exemplary prophetic kindness in Rumi's violent treatments of the young Hindu slave or of the slave girls in the stories I cited in previous sections. It seems clear that Rumi is at home among Muslim male jurists before him who saw "[s]laves and women as overlapping categories of legally inferior persons."[27] Exactly as the male jurists had a vested interest in the overlap of slavery and marriage in their rulings because of "their own status as slaveholders,"[28] in these tales Rumi too is more invested in upholding the self-serving sexist arrangements of power and dividends of racism than any transcendental love or universal compassion. Rumi, therefore, like any other man, is a product of his time and place. How then are we imposing our own modern sensibilities upon this thirteenth-century mystic?

The New Age Rumi

Rumi's popularity as a New Age spiritual guru gives rise to the caricature of a gentle mystic for the capitalist market economy; and the apologetic approaches that uncritically recycle his mystical ideas, mythologize him in the process. Therefore, the question remains: how are we to reconcile the evidence of Rumi's common sexism, racism, homophobia, and anti-Semitism, with his purported mystical significance for our times? The problem posed by the "non-mystical" passages exemplified above is not a problem of interpretation. Had they been odd literary tensions in a thirteenth-century mystical text they would have remained of interest to a handful of obscure scholarly publications. However, Rumi is one of the better-known mystics of all times. People continue to make pilgrimages to his gravesite in Turkey, attend performances of whirling dervishes, and find solace in his comforting words. Scholars continue to publish on his ideas and spiritual insights and on the significance of his mystical concepts. Dismissing these passages as incongruently "vulgar" and "obscene"—as some of Rumi's commentators have done—in favour of the otherwise more "mystical" trajectory of his works therefore assumes an untenable mystical versus non-mystical dichotomy. These passages are not "exceptions" to Rumi's otherwise egalitarian mystical system of ideas. They are symptoms of Rumi's normative perspective. In the mystical world of Rumi, women and slaves are not random targets of abjection. They are violently and publicly disciplined—with a large erect penis as an instrument of punishment—because they inhabit desiring bodies that threaten the cohesion of the sanctified patriarchal, class, and racial hierarchies. The "disgraceful" death of the mistress as a result of sexual intercourse with her donkey is a punishment for her unauthorized sexual excitement: "Out of joy that woman's vagina became a nightingale / restless and inflamed in sexual urges for the donkey."

از طرب گشته بز آن زن هزار / در شرار شهوت خر بی قرار

The textual display of her lifeless bloodied body for all to see with graphic details of her intestine torn apart by the donkey's penis is both a proof of women's disruptive sexual urges at the site of an available erect penis (albeit a donkey's), and a cautionary lesson in its consequences. It is in this context that Rumi asks the male reader: "A bad death with a hundred disgraces, O father / have you ever seen a martyr for the ass's penis?"

مرگ بد با صد فضیحت ای پدر / تو شهیدی دیده‌ای از کیر خر

The same could be said about the tale of the Hindu slave who is severely punished with sexual violence for miscegenation. His "ass, torn like a beggar's cloak" کون دریده همچو دلق تونیان is put on display in the text for all to see as a testament for the consequences of simply expressing a desire for (not actually committing any!) class and racial transgression.

My point is not to merely show how patriarchal and racist Rumi is, or how male-centered and short-sighted his worldly

26 Brunschvig, "ʿAbd."

27 Kecia Ali, *Marriage and Slavery in Early Islam* (Cambridge, MA: Harvard University Press, 2010), 8.

28 Ali, *Marriage and Slavery in Early Islam*, 22.

views are, though these are sufficient causes for seriously doubting the veracity of his mystical claims. Nor should we be scandalized by his use of vulgar words and imagery. Rather, I argue that by focusing only on the positive aspects of his work while neglecting tensions and contradictions in his poetry and flaws in his character we provide perfect excuses for spiritual patriarchy to function seamlessly with all its violent abuses and prejudices. Is it too much to expect recognition and respect for the inherent dignity of all humans, regardless of their gender, sex, social status, or religious loyalties from a great mystic who by all accounts has ascended to the heights of spiritual worlds and has delved into the depths of human soul?

Leaving Rumi

There is an argument that racism and sexism are modern constructs that cannot be categorically applied to pre-modern times. However, because the universality of Rumi's message and his mystical authority rest upon his claim to have transcended his own cultural context, it is not useful to excuse him by calling him "a man of his time," a product of his particular patriarchal context. To the extent that Rumi's mysticism is relevant to our time, we are justified in applying these descriptive terms to his context and ideas—not to confine him to our sensibilities but to hold him accountable to his own standards of the Qur'an and prophetic tradition, while examining the universality and timelessness of his spiritual relevance.[29] What then is the relevance of this great mystic to our contemporary concerns?

The answer is not found in polished academic studies of his work that cherry-pick sublime, if obscure, mystical concepts from his poetry; nor in affirming his bond with the sacred sources of Islam that inspire him; nor in clichéd aphorisms and pop-psychology memes attributed to him. We should ask: can we separate Rumi from his sexism and racism? This is similar to asking in our time: can we make a distinction between a male artist who commits sexual assault or promotes sexism and his art? My answer is, to the extent that the artist and his art support a violent, unjust, sexist structure, the distinction between art and the artist breaks down.[30] Moderated only by the degree of our passion for justice and compassion, the relevance of Rumi to our lives lies in our honest assessment of the man, his ideas and the structures of injustice they support. I do not think Rumi is relevant to our time and our concerns. I am certain that because of his inexcusably harmful beliefs and ideas he was harmful to his own time in so far as he upheld elite male supremacist, patriarchal, sexist, and racist aspect of his culture. We should then be asking ourselves, why do we need a guide in the spiritual path, especially where in the case of Islam and some branches of Sufism no intermediary with the higher powers is admitted and necessary?

Much as I prefer to meet the gentle Birkenstock-wearing gray bearded "Rumi" who reads his poetry to the tune of double bass—because his Rumi is closer to the sacred sources that should have inspired the original—I believe that commodifying and mythologizing Rumi and his mystical ideas do not hold the promise of a panacea for our contemporary condition. Our salvation, which is to say, possible answers to the spiritual urgencies and socio-political imperatives of our time, does not come from Rumi or any spiritual guru of the East or the West, no matter how universalized his teachings sound, how authentically they are accessed, and how eloquently they are presented. The character flaws of a globally celebrated mystic like Rumi illustrate that spiritual achievements and mystical claims are not guarantees against social and personal failings. This reminds us of the many contemporary instances of abuse and exploitation of vulnerable people by religious-spiritual leaders. For example, consider Frithjof Schuon (d. 1998), the Swiss German Shaykh (spiritual leader) of the first traditional European Sufi order, who relocated to the United States in the last years of his life. Schuon is ranked among the greatest Sufi masters of the past and present. The academy's most prestigious names consider him to be a man who "directly 'apprehended the Truth,'" the one who "seems like the cosmic intellect itself," and "unaffected by the limitations of historical circumstances."[31] In 1991 a grand jury in Bloomington, Indiana indicted Schuon for child molestation and sexual battery (charges later dropped for lack of sufficient evidence).[32] We

29 See Tourage, "Studying Sufism."

30 Janna Thompson, "Friday Essay" separating the art from the badly behaved artist – a philosopher's view." In *The Conversation*, May 9, 2019. https://theconversation.com/friday-essay-separating-the-art-from-the-badly-behaved-artist-a-philosophers-view-116279.

31 Gregory A. Lipton, "De-Semitizing Ibn ʿArabi: Aryanism and the Schuonian Discourse of Religious Authenticity." *Numen* 64 (2017): 263, 264.

32 Mark Sedgwick, *Against the Modern World: Traditionalism and the Secret Intellectual History of the Twentieth Century* (Oxford: Oxford University Press, 2004), 174-5.

can also note other examples, such as the cases of Bikram Choudhury of Bikram Yoga,[33] Maharishi Mahesh Yogi of Transcendental Meditation,[34] and Mahatma Gandhi.[35] Another prominent example is one of the most brutal dictators of our time, Iran's Ayatollah Ruhollah Khomeini (d. 1989). Khomeini is known for his exquisite poetry about selfless love, wine and mystic union, all of which informed his political views.[36]

"There is a crack," Leonard Cohen, the bard sage of our time reminds us, "a crack in everything." For years I was fascinated by and found solace in the spiritual insights of Rumi's poetry. I read, memorized, studied, and taught Rumi. But, when I was awakened to his shortcomings as a mystic, a Muslim, and a man, and when I considered Rumi's immense popularity in the West at the cost of erasing his religious identity and questionable ideas, I felt betrayed, and, for the sake of scholarly honesty, stopped teaching my course on Rumi. And yet, as Cohen points out, it is through the crack in the wall that "the light gets in." Now I do not believe Rumi betrayed my trust. Rather, I am thankful to him because by his failures he taught me that it is not internally inherent impediments that keep us from spiritual growth and self-transformation. Rather, the main barriers are the structural injustices that we construct and sustain, in our narratives, institutions, societies, and relations. Rumi's works stand as relics of the still-reverberating injustices of the past, and his own flaws as a warning against the perils of following any master on the spiritual path. Again it is Cohen's words that sets the frame for such a relationship:

Follow me the wise man said,
But he walked behind.

33 Eliza Griswold, "Yoga Reconsiders the Role of the Guru in the Age of #MeToo," *New Yorker*, July 23, 2019, https://www.newyorker.com/news/news-desk/yoga-reconsiders-the-role-of-the-guru-in-the-age-of-metoo.

34 Elisabeth Garber-Paul, "How a New Book Exposes the Dark Side of Transcendental Meditation," *Rolling Stones*, June 7, 2016, https://www.rollingstone.com/culture/culture-news/how-a-new-book-exposes-the-dark-side-of-transcendental-meditation-54282.

35 Arundhati Roy, *The Doctor and the Saint: Caste, Race, and Annihilation of Caste, the Debate Between B.R. Ambedkar and M.K. Gandhi* (Chicago: Haymarket Books, 2017).

36 Asghar Seyed-Gohrab, "Khomeini the Poet Mystic," *Die Welt des Islams* 51, 4 (2011): 438-58.

Mahdi Tourage is Associate Professor of Religious Studies and Social Justice and Peace Studies at King's University College, London, Ontario. He is the author of *Rumi and the Hermeneutics of Eroticism* (2007) and the edited volume *Esoteric Lacan* (with Philipp Valentini, 2019). His publications have appeared in *Iranian Studies*, *International Journal of Zizek Studies,* and *Body and Religion Journal*.

jayce salloum

indefinite allusions in a limitless sky

going to leaving in or between Kabul, Panjaw, Band-e-Amir and or Bamiyan,

space of being, spatial being, between understanding
and being, that of love –the greater of being, defining
the undefinable existence
lending light the dust will settle
nothing from the air but the air, nothing from the sea
but the water
I do not pretend to know this direction only the aim

During a year-long residency in the mountains of Banff I was initiated in Sufi stories via the translations of Idries Shaw, introduced to me by Hu Hohn, fables such as, *The Exploits of the Incomparable Mulla Nasrudin* and *The Subtleties of the Inimitable Mulla Nasrudin*. These books were chock-full of stories for contemplation and meditation. I would read them riding the bus at night to get me through trying times in the late 1970s while living in San Francisco. Much later in 2008, I'm in the central highlands of Afghanistan, where the colossal Buddha statutes once stood in Bamiyan. A stark, arid, severe, beautiful landscape; people scrapping by with subsistence farming, much like my grandparents did in Syria. I'm filming scruffy country boys in a new school built by Western troops. The boys are speaking Hazaragi (a Farsi dialect) –of which I don't understand a word. At the end of each session, we ask them to tell a joke or a song, something other than the conversation I've tried to record. Six months later when I'm back home in Vancouver and the translations have been sent to me from Quetta, I discover, then and there were the very same Sufi stories—thirty years after I was introduced to them—being told by those little boys at Laisa-e-Aali Zukoor school. These temporal and spatial rifts go hand in hand with other displacements of our overarching crisis time and space –proving how connected across this shared earthly landscape we all are.

Many thanks to the impeccable Khadim Ali, and to the translator and eternal wunderkind Muzafar Sanji; to Mohammad Zia, our stalwart driver and safe-keeper who deftly transported us over unspeakable rutted goat trails aka roads; and to all who shared with us a mat to rest or sleep on, stories, food, curious minds, and warm hearts.

These photographs are originally from the installation project, "the heart that has no love/pain/generosity is not a heart," a collaboration with Khadim Ali (2008-2010), curated by Haema Sivanesan. The texts found here were written, now, for this book, as in the spirit and essence I could draw from the subject and place.

Jayce Salloum, 2023

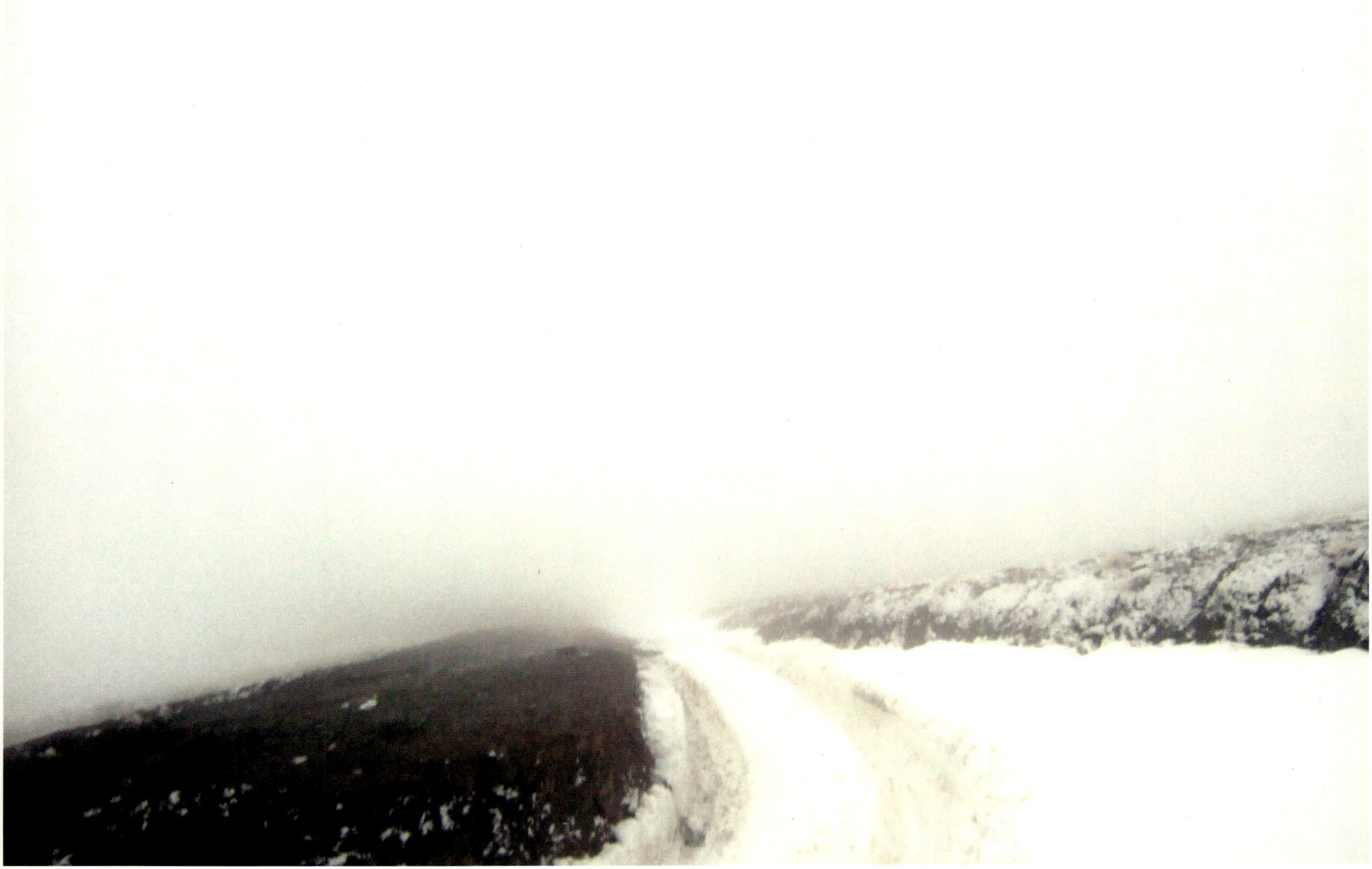

moving through w/here to there this place space as a substance object, materially expectations so detrimental,
trust fixed points on an ephemeral landscape screens seens scenes

through brilliant gilded light life shimmering shining fields of windswept dryness, sedimentary air silvery spring crystal lining sky blue sky pungent near starkness beauty a scarred sacred land thaw wet damp before the dust becomes us, *upon arrival*

sense the space of being, spacial being, between understanding and being, stretches that of love – the greater of being, the undefinable existence the place means, belonging passes passages elusive, *indefinite allusions of a limitless sky*

swaths layers local colour imbedded earth, from a ways up the hill - vestiges shrouded.. carved of stone *etched*
marking oneself writing to the future *sounding the past* remnants, part it be, *memoria*, was written by the victors
ultimately to be crowned, thus *inscribed* scraping the tabula rasa cycle of state what means this site now the statues gone frescos effaced
disappeared , and to what to them to us, a void *presence of the absence* precious survival but more than that

forms of more than *resisting* more than this bordering the impossible now the notion of compassion the possibility of *imaginations*
still life lives momentary pause wonders, scenes to aspire to, arid *the dust pervades the mud perspires.*
are we being torn apart for our own protection or protecting ourselves from tearing each other apart. we inhabit separate spaces
existing in the same world. Mulla Nasr al-Din on the road, stripped bare unwrapping themselves written or spoken divulging a *presence*

the most heavily mined country in the world. moving together respect each *terms of existence.* Khadim recalls a story by Sheikh Sa'adi: in a visit to a soup kitchen Sa'adi was attacked by a pack of stray dogs. as he picked up a stone to defend himself he found the stones all frozen together and wondered, *what kind of place it was where all the stones were fixed in place and all the beasts roamed free*

they who invaded us   many vanquished   sides taken   the profound vacuity   ripped asunder   apart   stacked   *circles to ponder*
occupied our   domains   their unbelief — *routes to determine* our future   embellish theirs   *Aryan, Bactrian, Achaemenian, Greek, Kushan, Indian, Mongol, Safavid, Mughul, British, Soviet, American, Europeans, Canadians, NATO*   *a cumulative effect*   a chronology *of what remains,*
what taken,   closed,   why destroy   why memories   an array of gestures   beyond the surface,   entrenched   the histories,
presence (out of) places,   occupations,   conflicts   cartographies   this absence   *for the future*

a school in Dasht-i Barchi, where girls once were taught, 6am assembly the singing is mesmerizing, chanting rumi *the heart that has no love / pain / generosity is not a heart* a promise back and forth to the group to the individual a resonance wave-like communing at heart. like lulling waves by the shoreline the future beckons, bright is the hope all is at stake, there is a singular importance solely of the individual and equally of the group and both *in relationship to each other* a commitment for the community to be Hazara here elsewhere

why attempt a *nation state* forcing irrelevant goals or impositions disjunctive *taking stock* who have you given power to
serving whom and to what end can one re present serve as *epitome* displacement making home while fleeing
that which becomes permanent dispossession beyond words *what has been lost*

wrapped ruins, *bodily* discarded, detritus sheltered, saved quotidian lives a daily history monuments of incompleted
and current wars a *history of the present* destruction reign of the day dissolution diffusion persecution why is anyone
what threat to whom *represented in the imaginary* belief our leaders' lies complicit we die early *drawing the days*

metaphors useless how is dreaming *still possible* if Afghanistan was a being *what would it dream* a mapping turning constellations of contiguity no society can survive without equality tolerance social justice resisting representation far afield but intimately connected *a close impenetrable distance*

cascading demarcating markers of *our continual history,* contested *for and against us,* (this) place today
living lending light the dust will settle, in non-errant time is it once or never has been
~~though bombs rain from the sky and within~~, if we live *hope springs eternal*

Editor's note:

In the text under the 8th plate in this series, the line "the heart that has no love / pain / generosity is not a heart" has been mis-attributed to Rumi. This line is a translation of

> هر آن دل را که سوزی نیست دل نیست
>
> har ān del rā ke suzi nist del nist

which is part of the second line in the opening passage of *Farhad-o Shirin*—a romantic narrative in verse—by Vahshi Bafeghi (1532-1583). A closer translation may be: "the heart that has no burning is not a heart." *Suz* سوز is not love but literally means burning, often used to mean longing for unattainable (or departed or separated) love. Rumi predates Vahshi Bafeghi, and *Farhad and Shirin* was inspired by *Khosrow and Shirin* by Nizami whose work inspired Rumi too. The attribution of this line to Rumi is not too far-fetched given the shared inspiration, and it is possible that somewhere within his vast ouvre Rumi may have a similar line. It could also be that Rumi overshadows other poets when it comes to expressions of love and longing, so this beautifully concise line has become associated with Rumi for some.

Jayce Salloum, as if an itinerant geographer of conflicted territories, observes the world and creates/collects images/texts to make meaning from. A grandson of Syrian immigrants, raised on Sylix land, now on the territories of the Xʷməθkʷəy̓əm, Sḵwx̱wú7mesh and Səl̓ílwətaʔɬ. Recognizing and acting on this is an everyday practice, but let's face it, he could do a lot more.

gita hashemi

پرسه با رومی roaming with rumi

1

جلال الدین محمد Jalāl al-Din Mohammad was born in وخش Vakhsh in lower Central Asia in 1207 CE.[1] That is 604 AH by his Islāmic lunar calendar. We do not know much about his mother except her name, مؤمنه خاتون Mo'mene Khātun. His father is known as بهاءالدین ولد Bahā' al-Din Valad. A self-titled Sultān al-Ulamā سلطان العلما King of the Clerics, he was an Islāmic teacher and preacher with a small following. We do not know for sure, but he might have been born and possibly educated in بلخ Balkh, a city inhabited continuously for over 2500 years. Balkh was a highly developed cosmopolitan and enlightened city and a major trade hub on the *Jādeye abrisham* جاده ابریشم Silk Road before the مغول Mogul warlord چنگیز خان Ghenghiz Khān deployed one hundred thousand horsemen to sack the city and kill its inhabitants in 1220 CE.

Balkh survives today as a small town near مزار شریف Mazār-e Sharif, one of the strongholds of the Talibān in their return campaign in 2021. More than two and a half millennia earlier, in the 6th century BCE, *Zartosht* زرتشت Zoroaster had taught in Balkh after it had been invaded by the *Hakhāmanesh* هخامنش Achaemenid king, *Dāriyush* داریوش Darius. Later, in 329 BCE the *Maghduni* مقدونی Macedonian *Eskandar* اسکندر Alexander invaded Balkh and its region. By the start of the Islāmic conquest in 705 CE, Buddhism had flourished in Balkh, as monks traveled westward from India to preach their religion. Although Islām became dominant after the conquest, the older religions managed to keep their centres and congregations. Then, unlike now, elimination of religious minorities was not a state priority. Balkh also had a Jewish quarter. The Arab geographers describe the city in the 9th and 10th centuries CE as having several gardens and bazaars, including one called *Bāzār-e Āsheghān* بازار عاشقان Lovers' Market. Love probably was not in short supply then as it is today.

Balkh, *Marv* مرو Merv (which was also razed to the ground by the Moguls), *Samarghand* سمرقند Samarkand and *Bokhārā* بخارا Bukhara were the four major cities in lower Central Asia, an area known as *Māwarā al-Nahr* ماوراء النهر in Arabic, *Farā-rud* فرارود in Persian, and *Varāz-rud* written as *Варазруд* in Tajik, all literally meaning beyond the river. The term Transoxania (Beyond Oxus) found currency in the West because of the exploits of Eskandar/Alexander whose army's eastward

1 The historical information and inferences related to Rumi's life in this writing is culled and adapted principally from Lewis, Franklin. *Rumi: Past and Present, East and West*. London: Oneworld, 2020. Questionable speculations and meanderings are mine. All transliterations are based on Persian pronunciations common in central Iran.

expansion came to a halt in this area in the face of strong local resistance. He was wounded himself. Ὦξος Oxus, from *Vaxš* وخش Vakhsh, is the Greek name for آمو دریا *Āmu Daryā*, the river which expands into (or through ?) the highest desert in the world. Vakhsh is the largest tributary of Āmu Daryā. There a Hellenistic kingdom was briefly established as the easternmost part of the Greco-Macedonian empire. It survived for about a hundred and fifty years, from c. 256 to 120-100 BCE. Āmu Daryā, also known as *Jeyhun* جیحون Jayhun, and its northern twin سیر دریا *Syr Daryā*, are the two major rivers that pour into now nearly vanished *Daryāche Ārāl* دریاچه آرال Aral Sea. *Daryā* دریا is a Persian word that means sea or a vast river resembling a sea. *Daryāche*, composed of *daryā* plus the Turkish suffix *che*, means small sea.

The rivers Amu Daryā and Syr Daryā defined the borders of the area that is referred to in *Shāhnāme* شاهنامه *Shahnameh Book of Kings* as *Turān* توران, the land inhabited and ruled by Turks, the enemies of ancient Irānians. فردوسی Ferdowsi, a native of توس Tus, a town one thousand kilometers west of Balkh, wrote the *Shāhnāme* between c. 977 and 1010 CE. Being the first major book written entirely in *Farsi* فارسی Persian after the Islāmic conquest, the *Shāhnāme* is considered the national Persian epic both for its highly dramatic stories and because of the significant role it played in re-establishing *Farsi* فارسی Persian as the main literary language in the region after nearly three centuries of Arabic domination. The *Shāhnāme* includes 50,000 lines of rhyming couplets, a poetic form known as *masnavi* مثنوی, a form that lends itself more readily to long stories as attested by the many narrative volumes composed in masnavi form in Persian by famous and not-so-famous poets before and after *the Masnavi* by Jalāl al-Din Mohammad Balkhi. In any case, to be fair, the first famous masnavi in the annals of Persian literature is arguably the *Shāhnāme*, an interweaving of myth and history retold through stories of variously antagonistic, amorous, or otherwise artful encounters involving a host of now legendary characters whose lives and deeds unfold in the context of the animosity between Irān and Turān. Then, as now, stories of forbidden love, betrayal, filicide, monsters in the mountain caves, brain-eating snakes emerging from the shoulders of cruel kings, and blacksmiths leading popular uprisings were even more sensational against the backdrop of political intrigue and ethnic war. Ultimately, nothing is new and original. We know that, don't we?

In Bahā' al-Din's time, and long after, the area between the two rivers (the *Shāhnāme's* Turān) was known as *Khārazm* خوارزم Khawrazm, also known as *Khorāsān* خراسان Khorasan. Dialects of *Farsi* فارسی Persian dominated the vernacular in most of it then as they do today. Although Islāmic teaching was in Arabic and all clerics and scholars had to learn that, *Farsi* فارسی Persian was the administrative and the literary language. Bahā' al-Din and his son, Jalāl al-Din Mohammad Balkhi aka Rumi, spoke دری Dari, a version of *Farsi* فارسی Persian that is current in much of Afghānistān today. Bahā' al-Din was not a keen writer and only a collection of sermons attributed to him remains. Jalāl al-Din Mohammad Balkhi aka Rumi, uttered (because we know he did not write them down himself) his oeuvre—including the *Masnavi*, *Divān-e Shams*, and *Fih mā Fih*—in *Farsi* فارسی Persian with some splattering of Arabic, perhaps to display his knowledge of that exalted religious language or because it was necessitated by the Islāmic subjects he engaged in. Arabic in Islām = Latin in Catholicism. The majority of the practitioners are not conversant in it, but its use gestures to authenticity, accuracy, and, most importantly, authority.

2

In *Farsi* فارسی Persian, the suffix *i* relates what precedes it to a place or a tribe or group of people or an ideology or a person. The toponyms Balkhi and Rumi mean from Balkh and from Rum respectively. The first is used in *Farsi* فارسی Persian (sometimes) and the second in Western contexts (almost exclusively) to refer to the same historical figure. Both are valid but neither is clear-cut. Bahā' al-Din's centre of activities and his family's residence was in Vakhsh وخش, a few hundred kilometers to the northeast of Balkh, near Vakhsh River, the main tributary of Amu Daryā. There he had a number of wives and children, his mother, and a modest appointment and income from *beyt al-māl* بیت المال public funds as a minor *faghih* فقیه jurisconsult. *Faghih* is a type of Islāmic scholar who has *ejāze* اجازه permission to interpret Islāmic laws and traditions. *Velāyat-e faghih* ولایت فقیه meaning, literally, guardianship of *faghih*, is a political theory in Twelver Shia Islām that asserts that the *faghih* has custodianship over people, not unlike the priest being the shepherd of his flock. However, advanced in the 1970s by Ruhollah Khomeini, the guardianship of faghih goes beyond spiritual and religious concerns and extends to all aspects of governance. It was enshrined in the constitution of the Islāmic Republic of Irān after the 1979 Revolution, and is the basis of the legitimacy and far-reaching and unaccountable powers of the institution of Supreme Leadership in IRI. But this is not (or is it?) directly related to Bahā' al-Din nor to his son Jalāl al-Din Mohammad Balkhi aka Rumi.

What we know about Bahā' al-Din comes from hagiographic accounts written after his son Jalāl al-Din became famous on the other side of the *Daryā-ye Khazar* دریای خزر Caspian Sea. One of those accounts is by سلطان ولد Sultān Valad, Jalāl al-Din's second son with his first wife, گوهر خاتون Gowhar Khātun. Yes, Sultān Valad, like his father, was the second son, not the first as commonly thought. Jalāl al-Din's first son, like his namesake uncle, did not make a name for himself. That might explain why both the uncle and his nephew are commonly excluded from the family tree in hagiographies. Jalāl al-Din's first son did not excel in anything. Even though he was well-educated, his father had to intercede with people of means and influence from time to time to secure a position for him which he apparently could not keep for long. But Sultān Valad exceeded his brother and became one of the founders of the *Tarighat-e Molavi* طریقت مولوی Mevlevi Order which is centred in *Ghuniye* قونیه Konya. According to Sultān Valad's account, his grandfather Bahā' al-Din was an ascetic and had a dislike of unjust and unreligious rulers as many Sufis did. That might explain why he was not able to attain a secure appointment in his native land and eventually had to migrate with his family in tow. It is also possible that he made the decision to migrate because of the looming Mogul invasion, as some have said, but the timeline does not support that, unless we accept that Bahā' al-Din had foreknowledge of the war through his mystical powers. There is also the story that he was the target of malicious machinations in the court by Fakhr al-Din Rāzi فخرالدین رازی, a contemporary influential philosopher and pioneer of inductive logic. Clearly mysticism and logic are not of the same cloth but this story is likely more apocryphal than historical.

In any case, in Islāmic *madrese-ha* مدرسه‌ها madrasas — literally meaning places of study, usually operated through charitable endowments—and *masjed-ha* مسجدها mosques appointments were made by those who endowed them, typically rulers and their families and cronies. Because his name does not appear in any of the biographical dictionaries—Who's Whos—from his own time we can deduce that he was not favoured and famous as a great scholar. The disfavour of Khorāsān's rulers, however, might be the very reason his own small circle considered him the *sultān* سلطان king of the clerics. It may also be that such a title came about by his own design. In his *Ma'āref* معارف *The Knowings*—a generic title for a collection of sermons by a scholar—Bahā' al-Din relates that the title *Sultān al-Ulamā* سلطان العلما King of the Clerics came to him in a dream where he saw himself standing at a distance from a sage who pointed to him and told someone else "There stands the King of the Clerics." The stories written in hagiographies about a century later, including in Sultān Valad's *Ebtedā' nāme* ابتداع نامه *The Book of Beginnings* surely exaggerate that Bahā' al-Din appeared around the same time in three hundred clerics' dreams and they all saw someone telling them, "There is the Sultān al-Ulamā."

The toponym Balkhi might have stuck through another self-perpetuated legend. Maybe Bahā' al-Din was tired of his modest lot in Vakhsh and dreamt of going to more important places: "My heart began to wander, why Vakhsh? Others are in Samarghand or Baghdād or Balkh, in majestic cities. I am stuck in this bare, boring, and forgotten corner." Immediately after this wondering "[Then] God inspired me with this thought: If you are with Me and I am your companion, you will not be in any place—not Vakhsh, not Baghdād, or Samarqand." Divine inspiration notwithstanding, he uprooted his family and went to Samarqand sometime around 1210 or1212. His old mother stayed in Vakhsh. He did not succeed in securing a position in Samarghand either, so the family and a small following left Farārud/Khāwrazm/Khorāsān/Central Asia around 1216 or 1217. It is said that three hundred camels carried Bahā' al-Din's rare and valuable books and the household belongings of the migrants. Clearly, this was a major undertaking not embarked upon lightly. The first-born son and a married daughter stayed behind. We do not know if they survived the Moguls' descent a few years later, but we know that a decade later Jalāl al-Din named his first son Alā' al-Din after his then deceased older brother. Carrying the burden of a distant loss from the moment of his birth may be why the boy never became anything. But that is a different thought trajectory. This one is to trace how Balkhi came to be a designation for Jalāl al-Din.

So, Bahā' al-Din and his progeny traveled from the north-east toward the southwest of the Irānian plateau, a journey that would have taken at least two months and whose route we cannot be sure of. It is fabled that along the way in *Neyshāpur* نیشاپور Neyshabur, a likely stop, they met the famous Sufi صوفی poet Farid al-Din Attār فریدالدین عطار. Attār's masnavi, *Mantegh al-Teyr* منطق الطیر *Conference of the Birds*, was already famous in his own time as it remains today. Such fame was no small feat because, although by this time the Chinese had already been printing texts using printing blocks and then moveable type, the printing technology had not travelled westward and copies of Persian manuscripts, as is obvious from the term, had to be produced by hand. The story goes that Attār was so impressed with the 10-years-old Jalāl al-Din that he gifted him a copy of his *Asrār nāme* اسرار نامه *The Book of Secrets*. Indeed that would have been a great gift before the printing press. But Rumi himself and the hagiographers close to him, his family and his time do not mention such meeting. This story was first mentioned two and a half centuries later in a *Tazkerāt al-sho'arā* تذکره الشعرا *Biography of Poets*—a fairly established book genre that often mixes historiography with myth-making. Many things we think we know about Balkhi aka Rumi are myths created over the centuries after his death.

It is true, however, that the Valad family eventually arrived in *Baghdād* بغداد. There a great and famous Sufi figure, Shahāb al-Din Omar al-Sohravardi شهاب‌الدین عمر سهروردی—not to be mistaken with Shahāb al-Din Yahyā al-Sohrevardi شهاب‌الدین یحیی سهروردی, aka *Sheykh-e maghtul* شیخ مقتول Murdered Sheykh, who was also a Sufi master but lived a hundred years earlier—was *Sheykh al-Shoyukh* شیخ الشیوخ Leader of the Clerics, and the advisor to Khalife al-Naser al-Din Allāh خلیفه ناصرالدین الله, the last effective *Abbāsi* عباسی Abbasid *khalife* خلیفه caliph who ruled for forty-seven years uninterrupted, undoubtedly a great accomplishment in those tumultuous times. Bahā' al-Din, not famous and not a native Arabic speaker, could not play Sultān al-Ulamā where there was a Sheykh al-Shoyukh at work already. He also did not have much to recommend him for a position there. Baghdād was an important Islāmic centre and a thriving city that attracted many ambitious scholars and students alike, an altogether different city from the den of corruption and field of ruined monuments that the West has made of it today. It was the legacy of that brilliant past that got loaded on planes leaving Baghdād for auction houses in London and New York. But let us not digress. Bahā' al-Din took his family via *Kufe* کوفه Kufa to *Makke* مکه Mecca to undertake the *Hajj* حج, the ritual of pilgrimage to *Ka'be* کعبه The House of God, performed in the month of *Zo al-Hajje* ذوالحجه, the last month of the Islāmic calendar. *Hajj* is mandatory for every adult Muslim who has the means. This is why performing *Hajj* is not only the testament of devoutness but also the proof of a modicum of material wealth. From Makke the Valads must have joined a pilgrims' *cāravān* کاروان caravan heading for *Suriye* سوریه Syria. The Valads stayed for a time in *Halab* حلب Aleppo and then *Dameshgh* دمشق Damascus.

These were great cities respectively with twenty-one and thirty-four madrases only in the Hanafi حنفی order, not to mention the multitude of madrases belonging to the other major sects, *Māleki* مالکی, *Shāfe'i* شافعی, and *Hanbali* حنبلی. To remain focused, we will not let the present war and destruction in *Suriye* سوریه Syria enter the chorography here, even though it would deepen our humility to remember that what is now a *from* in the demographic movement descriptions used to be *a to*. Humility is the gate we have to walk through to cast our eyes on other lived lives and the unlived ones too, the ones that could have been, the ones that should have been, and the ones that almost were. Bahā' al-Din's was an amalgam of the last three. He belonged to the Hanafi sect, but there were no positions for him in *Halab* حلب Aleppo. That could be in part due to his deficiency in vernacular Arabic. Giving sermons for ordinary masjid/mosque-goers in their vernacular is a major requirement of an appointee teacher and religious leader, and vernacular Arabic is vastly different from the formal and Qurānic Arabic that non-Arab Muslim theologians learn in the course of their education. Bahā' al-Din's best chance for securing a position for himself and his son Jalāl al-Din who was coming of age, therefore, would be to settle in a Persian-speaking region. Irān was already full of scholars like him and he was, in his late seventies, probably too old to compete or maybe too tired to retrace the journey back to Irān. So the family went from Suriye to adjacent *Rum* روم Rome that had lately come under the rule of Farsi-speaking *Saljugh* سلجوق Saljuq kings.

Derived from the Arabic name *al-Rum* الروم for ancient Roman Empire, Rum was the name Muslims used to refer to what is known in the West as Byzantium. When the Valads arrived in the area, it was a mere two decades after the end of the Fourth Crusade during which the Europeans sacked *Ghustantaniye* قسطنطنیه Constantinople; Christians killing Muslims *and* Christians presumably on their way to recapture Jerusalem. So Rum, aka Anatolia aka Asia Minor aka present-day Turkey, was the exposed frontier of the Islāmic world at this time, as it remains today. It was inhabited by a large number of non-Muslims, including Greeks, Armenians and Turkmens. The Saljugh rulers were eager to populate the frontier cities with Muslims, particularly Farsi-speaking ones because, although they were a Turkic tribe, they had already adopted Farsi as the language of the court. Farsi/Persian is a prime example displaying the linkage of language, power and colonialism. For the Valads, this was advantageous. Bahā' al-Din and his family settled briefly in *Āghshahr* آق‌شهر, invited by Esmati Khātun عصمتی خاتون, who was either the wife of prince Fakhr al-Din Bahrāmshāh فخرالدین بهرامشاه—known as the patron of *Makhzan al-Asrār* مخزن الاسرار by the famed poet Nezāmi نظامی—or the paternal aunt to Sultān Alā' al-Din Kayqobād علاءالدین کیقباد. Esmati Khātun had met Bahā' al-Din somewhere near Āghshahr, probably while she was on an outing, and encouraged Bahrāmshāh to invite him to settle in Āghshahr. This probably would have been the winter of 1217.

Jalāl al-Din was ten years old, or eleven or twelve. It is possible that Esmati Khātun built a *khāneghāh* خانقاه, a Sufi centre, named *Esmatiye* عصمتیه after its patroness, where the Valads and their entourage lived. Khāneghāh was and is different from madrase: The former is a place for Sufi gatherings and rituals and the latter is a place for teaching formalized Islāmic knowledge, but in those times the same building could be used as one or the other depending on who funded and controlled it. If Bahā' al-Din was indeed settled in the khāneghāh, that indicates that he was known as a Sufi Sheykh شیخ not necessarily a scholar of Islāmic law. In Āghshahr Bahā' al-Din taught *dars-e 'ām* درس عام general teachings in Islāmic theology for the public, not intended for students in religious studies. That broad non-specialized teaching could be another indication that he was not ranked as a great *'ālem* عالم cleric. The Valads stayed in Āghshahr until their patroness and patron died around 1221 and the patronage stopped as it was not supported by a *vaghf* وقف which is a long-term charitable trust. Bāhramshāh's daughter, Saljuqi Khātun سلجوقی خاتون, who was married to Ezz al-Din Kay Kāvus عزالدین کیکاووس, a member of the ruling Seljughs in Konya قونیه, must have met Bahā' al-Din or heard about him from her father. It is possible that on her recommendation he was invited to *Lārende* لارنده, present-day *Karāmān* کرامان or *Gharemān* قره‌مان, by its Saljugh governor. A digression here seems appropriate: Although we know that there were women who were agents and players of some note in the lives of notable men, we don't know much about them. Noted?

By this time because of Mogul attacks progressively expanding east and south, refugees were flocking out of Khorāsān and Irān and heading to Anatolia, not unlike the present day, minus the Mogul attack. Lārende that had been under Christian rule and reconquered by Saljughs only recently had a large Greek population, and its governor Amir Musā امیر موسی wanted to Islāmicize the town by settling Muslim refugees there. It is said that at Bahā' al-Din's request, Amir Musā built a madrase for him to teach at. The family stayed in Lārande for about seven years. There, at the age of seventeen, Jalāl al-Din married Gowhar Khātun, the daughter of one of Bahā' al-Din's friends/disciples who along with his family had accompanied the Valads in their journey from Samarghand. The young couple bore two sons between 1224 and 1226. Jalāl al-Din's mother, Mo'mene Khātun مومنه خاتون died in Lārande and was buried there. We do not know much more about Jalāl al-Din's life in Lārande but he probably had fond memories of this town as later he mentioned its great peaches that were brought to Ghuniye/Konya.

امروز به قونیه، می‌خندد صد مه رو / یعنی که ز لارنده می‌آید
شفتالو

Today in Ghuniye smile a hundred beauties /
meaning that peaches are arriving from Lārande

According to all hagiographers, around 1228 Sultān Alā' al-Din Keyghobād ibn-Keykhosrow سلطان علاءالدین کیقباد بن کیخسرو, the ruler of Rum and also a second son, invited Bahā' al-Din to relocate to Ghuniye. Under Keyghobād's rule, the Seljuq Sultānate and its capital Ghuniye were expanding. Bahā' al-Din and family moved to Ghuniye and settled in Altunpā آلتونپا, the only madrase in town, no longer visible on Google Earth, and there he took a position as an Islāmic scholar. He died in Ghuniye two years later, in 1230 or 1231. That is when and where Jalāl al-Din's rise begins and his story flourishes.

A second son to Bahā' al-Din Valad, an aged mystically minded migrant cleric whose ability to survive and support his family depended on the tides of time and the whims of the rulers and a great deal of roaming in search of better circumstances, Jalāl al-Din was not old enough nor sufficiently educated and accomplished at the time of his father's death to assume his position, unlike what the legends claim. He had to travel and train for almost a decade before coming back to Ghuniye and assuming the teaching position inherited from his father. He remained in Ghuniye for the rest of his life, but the designation Balkhi was how he, and probably his father, introduced themselves. After all, Vakhsh, their town of origin was a bare, boring and forgotten corner that probably few on the other side of the rivers and the sea had heard of. Balkh, in contrast, was a majestic city whose fame as a centre of learning and culture had spread throughout the Islāmic world. It was more advantageous, in those times as it is today, to connect oneself to a known place than to an unknown place. What place of origin would you want to be associated with if you were a displaced person in need of patronage? The one that nobody has heard of or the other that has historical and cultural prestige?

3

In the Arabic preface to the *Masnavi Ma'navi* مثنوی معنوی, Jalāl al-Din introduces himself thus:

الْعَبْدُ الضَّعیفُ الْمُحتاجُ اِلی رَحْمَةِ اللهِ تَعالی مُحَمَّدُ بنِ مُحَمّدِ بنِ
الْحُسَینِ البَلْخی

بنده‌ی ناتوان نیازمند به رحمت خداوند تعالی، محمّد بن محمّد
بن حسین بلخی

The weak servant in need of the mercy of the
Almighty God, Mohammad the son of Mohammad
the son of Hossein from Balkh

That requires an explanation. His given name was Mohammad as was his father's. It was customary in elite families in their time to give a byname to male progeny, something related to *al-din* الدین faith/religion. Jalāl al-Din means the Glory of Faith, and Bahā' al-Din means the Splendour of Faith. That affirms the greatest mystic poet's and his father's deep roots in Islām, regardless of the de-Islāmicization efforts of many of the contemporary so-called translators—who do not know Farsi but ride on Rumi's fame nontheless. Within his own circle, his disciples addressed him as *Mowlavi* مولوی My Master. Pronounced *Mevlevi* in Turkish, this is a fairly generic honorific address for one's religious guide and guru. Early non-Mevlevi sources refer to him as *Mowlana* Jalāl al-Din Mohammad Balkhi.

Mowlānā مولانا is composed of *mowlā*, master, and *nā*, our. When his fame spread, some Persian and Arab sources referred to him as *Mollā-ye Rumi* ملای رومی The Mullah from Rum or *Āref-e Rumi* عارف رومی The Sage from Rum. Mollā ملا, mowlā مولا, and āref عارف all refer to an educated person of status, but they diverge in connotation for present-day Farsi speakers. Mullāh is a preacher with traditional Islāmic learning, considered pedantic knowledge by the Sufis, while mowlā and āref both indicate persons with access to deeper and higher knowledge, the esoteric and mystic knowledge, the knowledge that is not arrived at through learning alone but requires self-denying experience and conscious rejection of the trappings of the material world. For example, nobody ever refers to Khomeini or Khamenei as mowlā or āref. They are devious mullāhs through and through. But, through usage, Mowlānā, our master, and Mowlavi, my master, have come to function as proper names for Jalāl al-Din Mohammad Balkhi aka Rumi. With many other mystics and Sufis already circulating and influential, the Mevlevi Order did not spread in Irān in the same manner as it took hold in Ghuniye/Konya. But that is a different story and I am fast running out of space. That should not be a concern, however, because stories about Balkhi aka Rumi abound, in truth or falsehood or in-between shades.

یکی میگفت که مولانا سخن نمی‌فرماید، گفتم آخر این شخص را نزد من، خیال من آورد، این خیال من، با وی سخن نگفت که چونی یا چگونه‌ای، بی سخن، خیال، او را اینجا جذب کرد، اگر حقیقت من او را بی سخن جذب کند و جای دیگر برد، چه عجب باشد. سخن سایهٔ حقیقت است و فرع حقیقت، چون سایه جذب کرد حقیقت بطریق اولی سخن بهانه است، آدمی رابا آدمی آن جزو مناسب جذب میکند، نه سخن، بلک اگر صدهزار معجزه و بیان و کرامات ببیند، چون درو از آن نبی و یا ولی جز وی نباشد، مناسب سود ندارد، آن جزوست، که او را در جوش و بی قرار میدارد، در کَهْ، از کهربا اگر جزوی نباشد، هرگز سوی کهربا نرود، آن جنسیت میان ایشان خفی‌ست، در نظر نمی‌آید، آدمی را خیال هر چیز با آن چیز می‌برد، خیال باغ بباغ می‌برد و خیال دکان به دکان، اما درین خیالات، تزویر پنهان‌ست، نمی‌بینی که فلان جایگاه می‌روی پشیمان می‌شوی، و می‌گویی پنداشتم که خیر باشد، آن خود نبود، پس این خیالات بر مثال چادرند و در چادر کسی پنهان‌ست، هرگاه که خیالات از میان برخیزند و حقایق روی نمایند، بی چادر خیال، قیامت باشد، آنجا که حال چنین شود، پشیمانی نماند، هر حقیقت که ترا جذب میکند، چیز دیگر غیر آن نباشد، همان حقیقت باشد، که ترا جذب کرد «یَوْمَ تُبْلَی الْسَّرَائِرُ» چه جای اینست که می‌گوییم: در حقیقت، کشنده یکی‌ست، اما متعدد می‌نماید، نمی‌بینی که آدمی را صد چیز آرزوست، گوناگون می‌گوید، تُتماج می‌خواهم، بورک خواهم، حلوا خواهم، قلیه خواهم، میوه خواهم، خرما خواهم، این اعداد می‌نماید و بگفت می‌آورد، اما اصلش یکی‌ست، اصلش گرسنگی‌ست و آن یکی‌ست[2]

Someone said: Mowlānā does not speak. I said: Well, it was the thought of me that brought this person to me. This thought of me did not speak to them, asking, "How are you?" or "How are things with you?" The thought, without speech, attracted them to this place. Why would it be strange if my truth attracts them and takes them to a different place? Speech is the shadow of truth, an offshoot of truth. Since the shadow could attract, the truth would do much more. Speech is an excuse. People are attracted to others by that suitable element not by speech. Even if they see a hundred thousand miracles and expositions and graces, there is no benefit in these if there is no element of that prophet or saint in them. It is that element that keeps a person aroused and unsettled. If there were no element of amber [kahrobā] in a straw [kāh], the straw would never go toward the amber. That sameness of element in them is hidden and not apparent to sight. Humans are attracted to a thing by the thought of that thing. The vision of a garden takes them to the garden and the vision of the shop takes them to the shop. But hidden in these thoughts are deceptions. Do you not see that you go to a place and then regret it, saying that, 'I imagined that it would be good but it wasn't?' So these thoughts are like veils, and somebody is hidden under the veil. When the thoughts disappear and the truths appear, without the veil of thought,

2 *Fih ma Fih*, chapter 1. https://ganjoor.net/moulavi/fhmfh/sh1. Last accessed January 20, 2022.

that is an upheaval. Where this becomes the state of being there will not be any regrets. When any truth attracts you, nothing remains but that truth that attracted you. "The day when the secrets become apparent."[3] Why would we speak then? In truth, the attractor is one but it appears manifold. Do you not see that the human desires a hundred different things? S/he says, 'I want pottage, I want bread, I want halwa, I want fish stew, I want fruits, I want dates.' S/he utters these words and varieties but in truth the origin is only one thing. The origin is hunger...[4]

3 From Qur'an, sureh 86, "Al-Tareq," verse 9.

4 In translating this passage I have consulted and benefited from the translation in Arberry, A. J. *Discourses of Rumi*. London: John Murray, 1961, pp 18-19.

the border | train to skopje, april 4, 2016 | from the series *nth movement*, part of the *declarations diptych* | gita hashemi | 2016

http://hdl.handle.net/10315/41085

dust in the sunlight

oneness of being, 3 | gita hashemi | 2022

recorded at bellamy ravine and scarborough bluffs, unceded territory of the mississauga of the credit first nation

Not from the east nor from the west   a sun shone from the soul
    stirring our walls and doors   as dust dancing in sunlight
Because we are motes searching   for the rays of that sun
    we live as dust   whirling day and night

Rumi, ghazal 136

Āftābi ney ze shargh-o ney ze gharb az jān betāft
    zarre vār āmad be raghs az vey dar-o divar-e mā
Chon mesal-e zarre-im andar pey-e ān āftāb
    raghs bāshad hamcho zarre ruz-o shab kerdār-e mā

آفتابی نی ز شرق و نی ز غرب از جان بتافت
ذره وار آمد به رقص از وی در و دیوار ما
چون مثال ذره‌ایم اندر پی آن آفتاب
رقص باشد همچو ذره روز و شب کردار ما

مولوی، غزل ۱۳۶

rumi

ghazal 2131

Abandon your guile   lover   Go mad   go mad
Step into the heart of fire   Become moth   become moth
Turn yourself into a stranger   Tear down your house
Then come here and   board with lovers   board with lovers
Go rinse your heart through   seven waters[1] like a plate   Rinse off the malice
Then for the wine of love   become chalice   become chalice
You must become all soul   to be worthy of a soulmate
If you go to drunkards   become drunk   become drunk
Wondrous pearl earrings   are companions to the beloved
If you want the beloved's ear   become pearl   become pearl
As your spirit rises in the air   from the sweetness of our tale[2]
perish and like lovers   become legend   become legend
You are the Night of the Grave   go become the Night of Power
Like the Night of Power   for spirits   become shelter   become shelter[3]
Your thoughts go in a direction   and drag you there
Abandon thinking   Like destiny   become forehead[4]   become leader

1 Referencing seven seas, standing for all the seas of the known world.

2 The wording of my translation here incidentally coincides with the translation by Franklin D. Lewis, *Rumi; Swallowing the Sun (*London: One World, 2013), p 121.

3 The Night of the Grave, *leylat al ghabr*, is the first night in the grave when angels Nakir and Munkar visit the deceased and ask questions about religious matters the correct answers to which save the soul from torment. The Night of Power, *leylat al-ghadr*, is mentioned in the Qur'an as the night when revelations came to Mohammad. Some believed *leylat al-ghadr* or *ghadr* for short to be the night when angels and spirits descend and wishes of the pious are granted.

4 It is believed that a person's destiny, *ghazā*, is written on their forehead, *pishāne* or *pishāni*. As in many of his lines, Rumi uses the capacity of the language to evoke multiple images with the same word. *Pishāne* could also mean leader and *ghazā* could mean happenstance.

read by elena basile

مولوی
غزل ۲۱۳۱

Hilat rahā kon ‘asheghā   divāne show divāne show
    Vandar del-e ātash darā   parvāne show parvāne show
Ham khish rā bigāne kon   ham khāne rā virāne kon
    vāngah biyā bā āsheghān   hamkhāne show hamkhāne show
Row sine rā az sinehā   haft āb shu az kinehā
    vāngah sharāb-e ‘eshgh rā   peymāne show peymāne show
Bāyad ke jomle jān shavi   tā lāyegh-e jānān shavi
    Gar suy-e mastān miravi   mastāne show mastāneh show
Ān gushvār-e shāhedan   hamsohbat-e ‘ārez shode
    Ān gush-o ‘arez bāyadat   dordāne show dordāne show
Chon jān-e tow shod dar havā   zafsāne-ye shirin-e mā
    fāni show-o chon ‘āsheghan   afsāne show afsāne show
Tow leylat-ol ghabri borow   tā leylat-ol ghadri shavi
    Chon ghadr mar arvāh rā   kāshāne show kāshāne show
Andishe-at jāyi ravad   vāngah tow rā ānjā keshad
    Zandishe bogzar chon ghazā   pishāne show pishāne show

حیلت رها کن عاشقا دیوانه شو دیوانه شو
و اندر دل آتش درآ پروانه شو پروانه شو
هم خویش را بیگانه کن هم خانه را ویرانه کن
وآنگه بیا با عاشقان همخانه شو همخانه شو
رو سینه را چون سینه‌ها هفت آب شو از کینه‌ها
وآنگه شراب عشق را پیمانه شو پیمانه شو
باید که جمله جان شوی تا لایق جانان شوی
گر سوی مستان می‌روی مستانه شو مستانه شو
آن گوشوار شاهدان هم صحبت عارض شده
آن گوش و عارض بایدت دردانه شو دردانه شو
چون جان تو شد در هوا ز افسانه شیرین ما
فانی شو و چون عاشقان افسانه شو افسانه شو
تو لیلة القبری برو تا لیلة القدری شوی
چون قدر مر ارواح را کاشانه شو کاشانه شو
اندیشه‌ات جایی رود وآنگه تو را آن جا کشد
ز اندیشه بگذر چون قضا پیشانه شو پیشانه شو

Lust and desire   are locks placed on our hearts
    Become the key   in the key   become the groove   become groove
The light of the Chosen One   embraced the Wailing Pillar[5]
    You are no less than a piece of wood   Become wail   become wail
Solomon advises you   Listen to the speech of birds
    You are the snare   birds scuttle from you   Go   become nest   become nest
If your idol reveals their face   like a mirror   become full of them
    If they let down their hair   become brush   become brush
How long two-headed like a rook   How long a peon like a pawn
    How long go crooked like a queen[6]   Become enlightened   become enlightened
You offer money and tributes   in gratitude for love
    Abandon the wealth   give yourself   Become offering   become offering
You were element for a time   you were animal for a time
    for a time you became animating spirit   Give it all   become beloved
O Speaking Self[7]   how long scurry to the door and the roof   Fly inside the house
    Abandon the speaking tongue   Stop jabbering   stop jabbering[8]

5 Mohammad, the Chosen One, used to lean against a pillar made of the trunk of a palm tree when preaching in Masjid al-Nabi in Medina. When a pulpit was built, the pillar felt abandoned and wailed. Mohammad embraced the pillar until it became quiet. It is said that the pillar—*Oston-e Hannane*, also translated as the Moaning Pillar or Yearning Pillar—was then cut and buried under Mohammad's pulpit.

6 See note 2. Here my understanding of the second hemistich differs from Lewis'. I keep closer to the actual words used in the original.

7 Originating in Aristotle's hylomorphic conception of individual, the Speaking Self, *nafs-e nāteghe* or *nāteghe* for short, is understood in *Erfān* or Islamic mysticism as the soul that materializes temporarily within the body to give it its expression in the world.

8 See note 2 to Ghazal 1759 on page 32 in this volume. Even when the term "silent" itself is not present, as in this line, he signs off by evoking the concept of silence.

Ghofli bovad meyl-o havā   benhāde bar delhā-ye mā
    Meftāh show meftāh rā   dandāne show dandāne show
Benvākht nur-e mostafā   ān oston-e hannāne rā
    Kamtar ze chubi nisti   hannāne show hannāne show
Guyad Soleymān mar tow rā   beshnow lesān-ol teyr rā
    Dāmi-o morgh az tow ramad   row lāne show row lāne show
Gar chehre benmāyad sanam   por show az u chon āyene
    Var zolf bogshāyad sanam   row shāne show row shāne show
Tā key doshākhe chon rokhi   tā key cho bizagh kam toki
    Tā key cho farzin kazh ravi   farzāne show farzāne show
Shokrāne dādi 'eshgh rā   az tohfe-hā-o māl-hā
    Hel māl rā khod rā bedeh   shokrāne show shokrāne show
Yek modati arkān bodi   yek modati heyvān bodi
    Yek modati chon jān shodi   jānāne show jānāne show
Ey nāteghe bar bām-o dar   tā key ravi dar khāne par
    Notgḥ-e zabān rā tark kon   bichāne show bichāne show

قفلی بود میل و هوا بنهاده بر دل‌های ما
    مفتاح شو مفتاح را دندانه شو دندانه شو
بنواخت نور مصطفی آن استن حنانه را
    کمتر ز چوبی نیستی حنانه شو حنانه شو
گوید سلیمان مر تو را بشنو لسان الطیر را
    دامی و مرغ از تو رمد رو لانه شو رو لانه شو
گر چهره بنماید صنم پر شو از او چون آینه
    ور زلف بگشاید صنم رو شانه شو رو شانه شو
تا کی دوشاخه چون رخی تا کی چو بیذق کم تکی
    تا کی چو فرزین کژ روی فرزانه شو فرزانه شو
شکرانه دادی عشق را از تحفه‌ها و مال‌ها
    هل مال را خود را بده شکرانه شو شکرانه شو
یک مدتی ارکان بدی یک مدتی حیوان بدی
    یک مدتی چون جان شدی جانانه شو جانانه شو
ای ناطقه بر بام و در تا کی روی در خانه پر
    نطق زبان را ترک کن بی‌چانه شو بی‌چانه شو

rumi, ghazal 2131 مولوی، غزل ۲۱۳۱

nika khanjani

broken hands and feet

a transmission of rumi's ghazal 2131 across generations, countries, time zones, and centuries

http://hdl.handle.net/10315/41082

broken hands and feet
nika khanjani | 2022

nika
roxana
May Panah

What follows are the traces of a process. The title is a rough translation of a Persian expression about speaking a language badly, *dast-o pāshekaste*.

In creating a new work under some difficult circumstances, I had several email exchanges with curator and editor Gita Hashemi. I include my emails, mostly intact and unedited, to give background and context to the video that I made in collaboration with my mother and daughter.

This is an honest peek into the process, in working with constraints of the pandemic, burnout, and imperfect technology as well as more subterranean themes of exile, the trauma of losing one's ancestral homeland and language, and the earnest attempts to transmit old mystical lyrical poetry into days that are clogged with bad news, bad internet connections, climate anxiety and unresolved family dynamics. We are simply doing the best we can.

I used this imperfect work around faulty transmissions as an opportunity to push back against perfectionism and pull myself closer towards acceptance. I may never speak Persian as well as I would like. I may not have taught my daughter as much Persian as I would have liked; but against many odds, I am still holding onto these beautiful threads that keep me tethered to a distant home, one that I carry within me as I live as a guest on other occupied lands.

DECEMBER 11, 2021

I'm considering co-creating an audio piece (maybe some visual) with my mother. She'll be visiting soon and I feel confident we can carve out space to record her teaching me how to recite one of the poems. Me, with my diasporic accent; her, with her own broken Persian after so many years of surviving in North America. I imagine asking her a few questions or offering word prompts for us to explore. I imagine the tone to be warm, measured, vulnerable, with one voice reading a phrase of the poem, the other voice trying to repeat it. I would include a written piece to accompany it.

I think so much about how the disorientation from displacement and trauma limits our capacity to be more curious about the lands on which we've arrived and settled. About the cultures and people who had relationships with this land. It feels like a double-grief of displacement and exile: loss of one's ancestral connections, and difficult access to the ancestors of our new home. Something I've been feeling out.

JANUARY 25, 2022

Checking in briefly to give you an update. My mother couldn't visit us in the end for all the pandemic reasons/travel restrictions/etc.

We recorded our project through Zoom and ... it's interesting. I'm not sure how it will read to viewers but I'm in the process of editing and working with the material—recitation of the first part of one of the poems by each of us, phrase by phrase—and I'll see what kind of shape I can get it into by February 1.

FEBRUARY 04, 2022

Thanks for the note. So, yes, we incorporated video and leaned into zoom — with its glitchy sound and frozen video. I'm working on a rough edit and I can send something along to you shortly for feedback. I think there's something real in there. I just have to sculpt and finesse a bit to find the rhythm of it. I'd like it to be no more than 5 minutes, or somewhere around there.

FEBRUARY 07, 2022

Here's the draft of this video collaboration I did with my mother and daughter through zoom. I left a lot out (the frustrating tech bloopers, which are somewhat hilarious but also mostly embarrassing) but I'm still thinking of putting some other shots in, and taking others out.

APRIL 20, 2022

My apologies for the radio silence. I appreciate you

reaching out, yet again, to check in with the project. The video is edited and much tighter, but that's all I could muster in the past couple of months. We've simply been managing a series of family challenges and financial/time scarcity and, what I thought would be a fairly simple, enjoyable writing exercise has been hard for my overwhelmed brain to articulate. I realized the deadline came and went amidst a death in the family that had us traveling back to the US last minute and I didn't have it in me even to let you know.

I'm in production this week for a film I'm shooting on Sunday. I know I can't do anything until then. I just wanted to write back before another day passed.

I've been trying to connect some simple dots around the resonance I feel with the discourse of language transmission and renewal that Indigenous peoples on Turtle Island have been fighting for. It inspires me and also touches on some shame that I didn't learn Persian well enough to read, to write, to speak and to understand Rumi.

There are entanglements that, when I start following the threads, touch up against vulnerability I'm not quite ready to throw into the world publically. My parents didn't actively teach me Persian (they were in survival mode) and yet were embarrassed by the way I spoke it poorly. I made efforts to learn and yet, at some point, I got tired of walking around with a posture of apology with Iranians because I didn't properly speak our mother tongue.

I've been trying to accept myself as Iranian enough even if my efforts aren't measuring up to some standards. But then as I learn from the Algonquin community of Barrier Lake, and Lakota language programs on Standing Rock, and the importance they give to reclaiming their own languages in order to heal and reconnect to the land and themselves, I find my shame bubbling up—that I speak to my child in English and send her to a French public school rather than prioritize teaching her one of her ancestral languages. This shame, though, is bound up with trauma—and writing about it takes a delicacy of mind and pen that I just haven't been able to access. There's grief when I see the extent to which colonization has disconnected me from my own language, how imperialism has wrecked my parents and countless others and how capitalism threw them into perpetual survival mode.

I DO want to disentangle the threads and I DO want to learn publicly, but it feels like the stress of the past two years has quite literally made me dumber. I don't want to send you something sloppy, and I don't have the brainpower or agility to think clearly about this—so I've been stuck.

Nika Khanjani is an Isfahan-born, Houston-raised, NYC-skooled filmmaker, writer and somatic-based trauma healer residing as a guest on the unceded lands of the Kanien'kéha Nation, known as Tiohtià:ke or Montreal. She is the librettist for the opera *Vanishing Point*, adapted as her most recent film.

elena basile

making room for rumi

You were element for a time   you were animal for a time
for a time you became animating spirit   Give it all   become beloved[1]

Anthropocentric exceptionalism may have its roots in theocentric exceptionalism and there is not much we can do about it except repeat after me God is dead, God is dead, God is dead.

And so is Man.

But spirit isn't, spirit isn't—

Spirit is not dead because spirit belongs. Everywhere and to each place. And because of this, spirit can be recognized but is not everywhere the same. Each place expresses spirit otherwise. Each place extends the tendrils of spirit differently through the thick tangle of animate matterings reaching up, rooting down, traveling through. Murmuring in sonorous tongues for ears attentive enough to welcome their gifts.

I can read Rumi only in English translations, and yet every time I do, I feel invariably summoned into a kind of deep attention that requires humility and decluttering. Humility, as in, becoming receptive to the humbling strike of an encounter with the sacred that disarms and decentres. Decluttering, as in becoming aware of centuries of orientalist western receptions of his poetry and finding myself called to peel open my (corporeal and linguistic) senses steeped in colonial logics of epistemic certainty and mastery. Despite this, I keep being assailed by anxieties about how to imagine the absent Persian text behind the translation. A language I do not know how to read, how to listen to. However much I delight in the concept and practice of translation as a mode of engaging with the unknown, and however much I nominally subscribe to Édouard Glissant's anticolonial championing of the right to opacity in translation, here I am, fretting over what I do not know, what I do not understand, what I may not be properly feeling of his poetry. So much Rumi has been rendered banal and postcard-like by American new age constructs, that I hesitate to even venture to speak. What I can do, maybe, is to attend closely to the difference Rumi makes for me here and now, in a way that unfolds and reveals the necessary situatedness of my approach.

Rumi—I can't get over the fact that the most beloved Persian poet is recognized in the West by way of a name that is first and foremost a toponym of dense political resonance. For me, born and raised in Italy, where the centre of the Mediterranean

1 Rumi, ghazal 2131, translated by Gita Hashemi, page 140 in this volume.

empire of old that goes by the name of Rome continues to extend its self-mythologizing tentacles across centuries and continents, the imperial reach of the cultural geography inscribed in the name "Rumi" is inescapable. Whatever the attempts to play it down, it is a fact that the geographic area in which Rumi eventually settled (contemporary Anatolia) had nothing to do with the by-then-long-gone Roman Empire, but instead was at the time under the domain of the (waning) Islamic Seljuq Empire. So why do countries in the West insist on calling this poet, known to people in the Persianate world as Molavi Balkhi and to Turkish readers as Mevlana,[2] with a name, Rumi, that is technically little more than a topographic anachronism, "a man who lived in Rum"? What energies keep emanating from inside names? What residual symbolic resonance do they keep producing despite the layering of centuries of conquest that traverses lands and the way human societies—cultures and economies—lay claim to them? I am compelled to dig deeper.

Culturally, I find myself sensing only an incremental kind of separation from this Sufi poet that Dante must have certainly known of. And yet, I am also deeply aware of the steep cultural chasms dividing the lands I grew up in from his. Rumi's lifespan roughly coincides with the time of the last crusades—that fundamentalist botched attempt on the part of the Catholic Church to 'conquer' Jerusalem and more deeply monopolize its cultural hold on Europe by asserting a clear-cut difference from the Islamic world. I know, the crusades were not a factor in Rumi's life wanderings—if anything, his geographic trajectory from Afghanistan in the East to Anatolia in the West seems to have been spearheaded by the Tatar invasions from the north-east. But my cultural provenance compels me to linger on the crusades' proximity to Rumi, and the ongoing effects of the sharp cultural edges and cuts they asserted after the thirteenth century.

Such sharp edges are made even sharper here on Turtle Island where I have been given an easy chance to settle thanks to a whitened italianness—this land assaulted by centuries of creeping colonial invasion enabled by the Roman Catholic "doctrine of discovery" and the arrogant assumption of the 'natural' superiority of the Christian man, racially whitened into the monstrous vampirizing abstraction of modern Man, keen on feeding its own machine of destructive greed. Over and over and over.

I don't remember ever reading Rumi in Italian translation in Italy, but I must have been exposed to the orientalist mystique that's been wrapped around him ever since the eighteenth century particularly through English and German translations (think Goethe, think Sir William Jones). I don't know how else to explain how I did not hesitate to buy a hard copy of *The Essential Rumi*, 'translated' by Coleman Barks with John Moyne at a graduate student book sale at the University of Toronto in the mid 1990s, shortly after I had arrived in Canada. This, I believe, must be the edition that has made Rumi the best-selling poet of the twentieth century and likely the one that feeds contemporary ubiquitous memes and hallmark postcards all over the English-speaking world. I don't remember the book leaving a particular impression on me, although I know that buying it responded to a deep spiritual yearning, and particularly a deep dissatisfaction with the temporal projections of sin and salvation typical of Christianity and the historical arrogance of its institutional morphing into a universalist philosophy for the colonial production of Man. What I had read, a couple of years earlier, was an Italian translation of Henri Corbin's 1964 *Histoire de la philosophie islamique*, which introduced me to Sufi ideas, and especially the sense of a deeply immanent rather than transcendent understanding of the deity, whose revelation is not entrusted to an apocalyptic end of times but to a chain of teachers/prophets each incrementally dedicated to manifesting and deepening humanity's sensate spiritual becoming. I was attracted and fascinated by this Sufi god, which reminded me of the pervasive immanence of Spinoza's god—the heretic Dutch Jewish philosopher of the seventeenth century sidestepped by the Cartesian champions of modernity, whose god energetically pervades and animates all worldly bodies.

It must have been the adjacency I perceived between the

2 See Hashemi's conversation with Fatemeh Keshavarz about this topic "Being the Astrolabe," on page 41 in this volume.

immanence of the Sufi god and the Spinozist god, which kept the Coleman Barks edition of Rumi on my bookshelves despite the typical itinerant life I led as a graduate student, changing rental rooms every other year or so and shedding a few books at every move. So, when, while conversing about *rumi roaming*, Gita Hashemi encouraged me to write something about my experience of Rumi, I found the book and started leafing through it with an attention I had never given it before. More than the poems themselves, my attention was caught by the "Note on These Translations and a Few Recipes" that is appended at the very end of the collection. Here Barks tells the story of how he came to 'translate' Rumi, giving a circumstantiated historical, geographical, and spiritual account of his encounter with the Persian poet, first spearheaded by the injunction of another American poet, Robert Bly, who put some mid-century translations of Rumi by J.A. Arberry in his hands, telling him "these poems need to be released from their cages,"[3] presumably meaning the cages of Arberry's literal translations. What follows is the narrative of a spiritual awakening first prompted by a dream and then the encounter with a "Sri Lankan saint," "sufi sheick," and "teacher," Bawa Muhaiyaddeen, who de facto authorizes his work on Rumi in an "apprenticeship" of love "beyond religion." Barks writes: "My apprenticeship continues, and whatever else they are, these versions or translations or renderings or imitations are homage to a teacher."

While reference to his "teacher" explicitly inserts Barks with the teleological chain of teacher-student relations of the Sufi tradition, the chain of synonyms that morphs the translation into a rendering and an imitation leaves me wondering why the word 'translation' still appears on the front cover, especially when Barks himself posits his English poems on the outer edges of a 'proper' idea of translation as traceable equivalence to an original foreign text. The insinuation of a New Age modality of orientalist appropriation is right under my nose—and indeed scholars and recent translators have pointed that out[4]—but what catches my attention is the imperial geography that structures Barks' following paragraph. Recalling his own childhood as a "geography freak," Barks recalls being tested one day by his Latin language teacher on the capital of Cappadocia. He recalls being nicknamed 'Capp' at school after being unable to name the region's capital. The narrative then returns to interpret that nickname as a sign of destiny, as the adult self realizes that "the central city of that Anatolian area was Iconium, now Konya, where Rumi lived and is buried." Here it is, again, the question of names and their symbolic resonance. A good colonial subject steeped in an education that draws a straight line of continuity between the Roman and the American Empire, Barks does not hesitate to name the Latin Iconium before Konya and place Rumi there. The weight of Latin and of Rome carries the day, excusing him from any acknowledgement—nowhere present in this autobiographical account—of his ignorance both of Persian and of the Islamic theology underlying much of Rumi's poetry. If his creative rewriting of Arberry's English translations seems genuinely instigated by a spiritual quest mediated by Sufi teacher Bawa Muhaiyaddeen, naming the book a translation squarely belongs to the mythologizing, space-time-boundary-stretching powers of Empire. And this book definitely benefitted from Empire—the way Barks placed Rumi within "the strong tradition of American free verse" having become ground zero for the contemporary proliferation of spiritual banalities attributed to the mystic.[5]

Despite this, the last segment of his afterword does something that might be worth reading against the grain of common modern assumption about cultural and spiritual value. Barks writes:

> Cooking and the grace of eating together have been important parts of the tradition that descends through Rumi . . . When transformation reaches a certain point, one goes into the kitchen to help fix food for the long table. Bawa Muhaiyaddeen improvised this meal on December 17, 1978.

There follow three recipes, each progressively more generous than the other in quantity, "with enough to carry some home for those who could not be there." It is easy to dismiss this as the most orientalist gesture of all—an introduction to exotic food that will enhance the western reader's experience of the poems as a 'flavor' of the exotic other—but may it be

3 All direct quotes are from *The Essential Rumi*, trans. Coleman Barks with John Moyne (Edison, New Jersey: Castle Books, 1997), 290, 295.

4 See Manijeh Mannani's introduction to her recent collaborative translation with E. D. Blodgett of selections from Rumi's Masnavi, titled *Speak Only of the Moon: A New Translation of Rumi* (Toronto: Guernica, 2017), 12.

5 Omid Azadibougar and Simon Patton persuasively show how Barks' version of Rumi's ghazals and of stories from the *Masnavi* "maximizes the popular cultural element [of Rumi's work] but reduces the spiritual ones to the level of a platitude" ("Coleman Barks' Rumi in the U.S.A.," in *Translation and Literature* 24, 2 [2015], 186).

possible to read this extended reference to the transformative force of food sharing against the grain of its own reductive exoticism? That is, as the account of a spiritually grounded commensal ritual that nurtures connection rather than separation between the spiritual and the material worlds? In other words, I am wondering if the force of Bawa Muhaiyaddeen's teaching can still be recognized and salvaged from Barks' account. Indeed, what kind of lesson might be at work in Muhaiyaddeen's humble act of preparing a meal for many and of sharing the recipe with students and, through Barks, with readers? Can the recipes listed at the end of the book be understood as an attempt to reintroduce the poetic text into the metabolic circle[6] that links food to culture to spirit—an attempt that foregrounds the humble, nurturing, and democratizing aspect of that experience?[7]

Truth is, I can't tell how democratic Rumi's writings actually are. The more I become familiar with Rumi's work—in translations offered by careful scholars such as Franklin D. Lewis—the more I have trouble separating his mysticism from what appears to be his deep embeddedness in the social, ethnic, and sexual hierarchies of his time. Even when his encounter with Shams forced him into a revelatory opening to the powers of mystical love, it was ultimately Shams, not Rumi, who paid the price of the deep social transgression enacted by the exclusivity of their relation (it matters little whether they were sexual with each other or not, as it is obvious that they were spiritually exclusive lovers). Part of me believes that Rumi's abiding by such hierarchies stems from the human- and male-centric dimension of the monotheistic tradition he belongs to—something Islam shares with both Christianity and Judaism. Although Rumi's god is neither the omnipotent patriarch of the Torah nor the self-sacrificing son of god of the Gospels, humans and particularly 'male' humans in his poetry seem to enjoy a privileged relation to spirituality, which is not afforded to women, animals, or non-Muslim peoples (who are frequently featured as slaves in his didactic stories).[8] In addition, the more I am exposed to the animacy and non-anthropocentric worldviews that pervade

6 I am making a slant reference here to Karl Marx's notion of "metabolic rift"—the estrangement of nature from culture—which environmental Marxist thinkers use to refer to the conditions that produce ongoing ecological crises. See John Bellamy Foster, *Marx's Ecology: Materialism and Nature* (New York: NYU Press, 2000).

7 During discussions about this piece, Gita Hashemi reminded me that at the time of Coleman Barks' publication in the 1990s a major (and very profitable) trend towards 'world cuisine' publications was taking hold, and it is very likely that considerations about the greater profitability of the book went into the addition of the recipes in its appendix. This is an avenue of research I did not have the time to get into when writing this piece, but which I want to signal here. I don't believe that this takes away from the value of the questions I ask about the wider metabolic processes of matter, culture, and spirit, but it does act as a reminder of the insidious capacity for appropriative cooptation present in the current political economy of the global north's culture industry.

8 See Mahdi Tourage's essay "Rumi Is Irrelevant" on page 102 in this volume for a more detailed discussion of this problematic aspect of Rumi's production.

the stories and teachings of many Indigenous peoples here on Turtle Island,[9] the more I feel the need to divest from those hierarchical tendencies present in the adjacent monotheistic traditions of the Mediterranean region I grew up in.

As I reorient myself towards a less superficial understanding of what it means to acknowledge the livingness of the land and to enter in deeply respectful relations of gratitude and reciprocity with the entangled life forces of other than human kin, I feel called to set aside the anthropocentric hierarchies I see playing out in some of Rumi's work in order to respond more fully to the spiritual entreaties I also read in his poetry. So, when I read Gita Hashemi's translation of the penultimate couplet of ghazal 2131, there is a refreshing sense that Rumi too can be made to speak differently to the entangled urgencies of the present moment:

> You were element for a time   you were animal for
> a time
>   for a time you became animating spirit   Give it
> all   become beloved

This is a line that resonates with me far more powerfully than Manijeh Mannani and E.D. Blodgett's translation of the same as

> Once the elements you were, and beast
> Then human soul, now be Soul, at least

or Franklin D. Lewis's rendition that reads in turn thus:

> For a while you were matter
> For a while you were animal
> For a while you were soul
>   Become the soulmate
>   Meet your soul

I am in no position to evaluate the accuracy of the translations, but I trust that each one of them is tapping into a seed present in the ghazal in Farsi. This said, against Mannani and Blodgett's explicit reinscription of Rumi's spiritual exhortation into a pyramidal scheme in which the human soul stands above the "elements" and "beasts"; and against Lewis's emphasis on the mystic union with one's own "soul," Hashemi's translation eliminates hierarchies and exhorts the reader to become beloved rather than the Soul (an absolute, capitalized entity in Mannani and Blodgett's translation and an article-less noun in Lewis).

9 I have learned and am learning from the words of John Croutch, first introduced to me by Gita Hashemi during her site-responsive collaborative performance *passages iii: like flesh and blood* in 2015. Together with members of the TiP Collective, I interviewed John Croutch in the summer of that same year for another participatory project, *Transitions in Progress. Making Space for Place*. I have learned and am learning from historian Victoria Freeman who introduced me to Ange Loft, artistic director of Jumblies Theatre and leader of *Talking Treaties*, a workshop she conducted with me and my students at Glendon College in 2018; I keep learning from the writings of Leanne Betasamosake Simpson; and most recently from Vanessa de Oliveira Andreotti's book *Hospicing Modernity* and the online course she conducts with the GTDF collective, *Facing Human Wrongs*, at UBC, which I am presently exploring with the with-nessing guidance of Lisa K. Taylor.

The difference is crucial and timely. What, indeed, might it mean for each of us readers to engage with such an entreaty to surrender into becoming beloved (be loved) rather than to ascend and fully disappear into an absolute "Soul"? Might this entreaty require that we engage in a lovingly circular rather than vertical continuum with the materiality of our being 'element' and 'animal' at some point of our metamorphic existence? Might the seed of a response-able play of reciprocity-in-difference with the full heterogenous beauty of earthly life uncluttered by Man-made hierarchies be something this Rumi-in-translation is suggesting?

A direct invitation, refreshing in its simplicity, radical in its demand. Reader, open yourself to the world, put your ear to the ground, feel the ongoingness of its becoming, of your own. Surrender the world's love, become beloved—become

Elena Basile, born and raised in Italy to an English mother and an Italian father, writes, researches, and teaches in Tkaronto, Treaty 13. She has spent most of her life writing about the entangled layers of language, culture and place that make belonging possible, collaborating with artists and writers along the way. She is currently working on decolonizing her own approach.

rumi

ghazal 294

Water has been cut off   from this world's river[1]
O spring   return   bring back the water
The water that even the springs of Khidr and Ilyas[2]
have never seen and   will never see
Glory upon that springhead   from whose gushing splendour
water flows every moment   from the eye of the soul
Where there are waters   bread grows
but never o my soul   did water grow from bread
Like beggars   for a morsel of bread
o guest   do not cry because of poverty
The entire world is   but half a mouthful
Greed for half a mouthful   disappeared the water
Earth and sky are   bucket and pitcher
but water is   beyond earth and sky
You too go fast   beyond earth and sky
till you can see water   flowing from no-place
Your life's fish will   slip out of this pool
and it will drink   from the boundless sea
In that sea   where Khidrs are the fish
therein immortal are the fish   immortal the water
From that visitation   comes light to the eyes
From that roof   flows water into the rainspout
From that garden   come these blooming faces
From that waterwheel   this garden drinks water
From that palm   come Mary's dates[3]
This water is not from any   portals and contraptions
Your body and soul   become contented when
water flows toward you   from this place
Don't keep beating your drum   like guardsmen
for these fish   are guarded by water

1 In translating this ghazal I have consulted, benefited, and in a few places borrowed some wordings from A. J. Arberry, *Mystical Poems of Rumi*, annotated and prepared by Hasan Javadi (Chicago: University of Chicago Press, 2009), pp 64-5. In some places, however, my understanding of Rumi's words is significantly different.

2 In the Islamic lore, Khidr (pronounced Khezr in Persian) and Ilyas (Eliās) are prophets who continue to live in the physical world, and are present on earth. Khidr, a pre-Islamic figure, is associated with springs and oceans, with water that gives life. Ilyas is associated with land and its bounties.

3 Referencing Qur'an, chapter 19, verses 23-27: "When her time came the pains of childbirth drove her to the trunk of a palm tree. Realizing her condition, she cried out: Would that I had died before this and had been quite forgotten. The voice of the angel reached her from below: Grieve not; for thy Lord has provided a rivulet below thee, wherein thou mayest wash thyself and the child. Then take hold of the branch of the palm tree and shake it; it will shed fresh ripe dates upon thee. Thus eat and drink and be at rest. Shouldst thou see anyone approaching, call out: I have this day vowed a fast to the Gracious One. I will, therefore, hold no converse with any person." *The Quran*, translated by Muhammad Zafrulla Khan, (New York: Olive Branch Press, 1997) pp 290-91.

read by jayce salloum

translated by gita hashemi

مولوی

غزل ۲۹۴

بریده شد از این جوی جهان آب
بهارا بازگرد و وارسان آب
از آن آبی که چشمه خضر و الیاس
ندیدست و نبیند آن چنان آب
زهی سرچشمه‌ای کز فر جوشش
بجوشد هر دمی از عین جان آب
چو باشد آب‌ها نان‌ها بروبند
ولی هرگز نرست ای جان ز نان آب
برای لقمه‌ای نان چون گدایان
مریز از روی فقر ای میهمان آب
سراسر جمله عالم نیم لقمه‌ست
ز حرص نیم لقمه شد نهان آب
زمین و آسمان دلو و سبویند
برون‌ست از زمین و آسمان آب
تو هم بیرون رو از چرخ و زمین زود
که تا بینی روان از لامکان آب
رهد ماهی جان تو از این حوض
بیاشامد ز بحر بی‌کران آب
در آن بحری که خضرانند ماهی
در او جاوید ماهی جاودان آب
از آن دیدار آمد نور دیده
از آن بام‌ست اندر ناودان آب
از آن باغ‌ست این گل‌های رخسار
از آن دولاب یابد گلستان آب
از آن نخل‌ست خرماهای مریم
نه ز اسباب‌ست و زین ابواب آن آب
روان و جانت آنگه شاد گردد
کز این جا سوی تو آید روان آب
مزن چوبک دگر چون پاسبانان
که هست این ماهیان را پاسبان آب

Boride shod az in juy-e jahān āb
Bahārā bāzgard-o vārasān āb
Az ān ābi ke cheshme Khezr-o Eliās
nadidast-o nabinad ān chenān āb
Zehi sarcheshme-i kaz farr-e jushesh
bejushad har dami az ein-e jān āb
Cho bāshad āb-hā nān-ha beruyand
vali hargez narost ey jān ze nān āb
Barāy-e loghme-i nān chon gadāyān
mariz az ruy-e faghr ey mihmān āb
Sarāsar jomle ālam nim loghmast
Ze hers-e nim loghme shod nahān āb
Zamin-o āsemān delv-o sabuyand
borunast az zamin-o āsemān āb
Tow ham birun row az charkh-o zamin zud
ke tā bini ravān az lā-makān āb
Rahad māhi-ye jān-e tow az in hoz
biyāshāmad ze bahr-e bikarān āb
Dar ān bahr-i ke Khezrānand māhi
dar u jāvid māhi jāvedān āb
Az ān didār āmad nur-e dide
Az ān bām ast andar nāvedān āb
Az ān baghast in gol-hā-ye rokhsār
Az ān dulāb yābad golsetān āb
Az ān nakhlast khormāhā-ye Maryam
Na z-asbābast-o zin abvāb ān āb
Ravān-o jānat āngah shād gardad
kazin jā suy-e tow āyad ravān āb
Mazan chubak degar chon pāsbānān
ke hast in māhiyān rā pāsbān āb

hjalmer wenstob, tim masso, annika benoit-jansson

hišukʔiš ćawaak

exploring rumi through nuučaańuł

nuučaańuł (Nuu-chah-nulth) is the traditional language of the nuučaańułʔatḥ, the peoples from the mountains to the sea. Our territories are located on the west coast of what is now known as Vancouver Island, British Columbia, and into Washington State where we share linguistic, cultural and familial ties with the qʷiniščiʔatḥ (Makah peoples).

nuučaańuł language comes from the land, it is grounded in our ḥaḥuułi (territories). Our ḥaḥuułi, right on the Pacific Ocean, can be beautiful, and it can be harsh. It's an environment that the nuučaańułʔatḥ have nurtured and cared for, and been nurtured and cared by, for centuries. We've heard from many of our Elders, that when they are teaching young children nuučaańuł, they compare it to our surroundings, our ḥaḥuułi. They compare language to the land we live on.

You can hear the sound of the harsh storms that pummel our shores, those southeast winds in the winter, in the rhythm of our language, with its roughness around the edges.

You can hear the different winds in the letters x, x̣, xʷ, x̣ʷ.

The elders talk about how the sound of letter š connects to the flowing water.

You can hear the sea lions and the quʔušin (raven) in our ʕ, a letter known as a pharyngeal that is made by tensing up the throat, a sound completely foreign to English but ever present in our land.

There are many dialects within the nuučaańuł language. We come from the ƛaʔuukʷiʔatḥ (Tla-o-qui-aht) First Nations, so we are speaking and learning the central dialect, with some specific translations and words unique to our own nation. Within the nuučaańuł language broadly, and even within the specific dialects, there is not one overarching dictionary as there is in the English language. While there are dictionaries being written, and some already in existence, within our communities our greatest resource is our remaining fluent speakers, of which there are very few.

We look to our Elders, and we also look to the land, and the slight differences between the ḥaḥuułi in each of the dialects. Where we are located, in ƛaʔuukʷiʔatḥ ḥaḥuułi, we are right on the edge of the open ocean, and the currents rip through the water at high speeds. Our language is a little harder, a little rougher on the edges, with multiple consonants and hard sounds right next to each other. The dialect south of us, though, is located in the calmer waters of Barkley sound, and you can hear how their dialect rolls a little smoother, a little rounder.

We explain all this, because it has been clear that when we are teaching the language, we are teaching it from the land's

hišukʔiš ćawaak | Hjalmer Wenstob | 2022 | Digital rendering of limited-edition serigraph print perspective. It is why we believe so strongly in revitalizing the language, because in learning the connections, we have a newfound respect for the land; it is not just something we live on, it is something we learn from. The land is connected to the language, and the language is connected to the land.

Over the last while, we have had the opportunity to read through a number of poems by Rumi, as translated from Persian by Gita Hashemi. We have thought about them through the lens of nuučaańuł language, art, culture and place, and worked through our own attempts and mis-attempts at translation.

When we get stuck, we come back to the land, as we do in our language. We feel connected to Rumi's words, yet lost in the translations to and from English. Take, for example, the following lines from ghazal 294:

Earth and sky are   bucket and pitcher
but water is   beyond earth and sky

We were drawn to this poem because of this line. Something so simple. Something so universal to everyone, the ideas of water, earth, and sky resonated throughout the poem, and throughout our own nuučaańuł worldview. Yet, when we went to break down, maybe build-up, from one language to another, something so simple transformed into something so multi-layered and complex.

Words of sky, earth and water, in English can be left as objects on their own, void of relationships to each other or ourselves. But in nuučaańuł, words are not isolated nouns as they are in English.

In our culture, we have a phrase—hišukʔiš ćawaak. In its simplest translation, hišukʔiš ćawaak means everything is one, and in that way interconnected. This concept—hišukʔiš ćawaak—is present throughout our stories, protocols, practices and histories.

In reading Rumi's words, Hjalmer's first thought—as an artist—was to attempt a visual translation. Art, like poetry (or rather, as poetry?), can be a way to bridge ideas without getting lost in the words. And yet, as soon as it came to speaking of art, we hit that same issue again, right from the very first word. Art.

Art, so simple a word in English, but in nuučaańuł, as in many Indigenous cultures, there is no word for art.

Of course, art was and is everywhere in our lives as nuučaańuł people. Our cultures, histories, and traditions were held in the art and cultural objects of our people: masks, totem poles, house fronts, weavings, tools, and regalia, to name a few. Our constitutions and histories, our political structures and lineages, our culture, was held in our art.

Without the use or need for the written language, our cultures recorded history, events, and law through oral and visual methods. Art could not be separated from everyday life, and for that reason, did not need defining or separation.

It was because of colonialism and attempted assimilation—which in many ways tie our stories to cultures across the world—that the realm of "Pacific Northwest Coast Art" or "First Nations Art" as we understand them in English, became separated from culture. To go back to language—in our English world, in our English tongues—we now have "Art." But when we translate to nuučaańuł, we talk about carving, and weaving, and painting—all action words, in relation to our world. There is no word for "Art."

There isn't, there wasn't, a word for art, because art wasn't something separate from life.

hišukʔiš ćawaak.
Earth, Sky, Water. Art, Culture, Truth.
hišukʔiš ćawaak.

We can see it in our art and we can see it in our language where the focus is on verbs, on movement and their relationships rather than centering nouns as in English. We see this in nuučaańuł, where a word such as water translates tenfold—what kind of water, in relationships with what around it? Flowing water? Stagnant water? Fresh, salt? In relation to a river, a lake, from our own mouth? Every word we looked to delve deeper into brought us both further and closer to Rumi's words.

Can we ever understand the original words as we read the words in English, and look to translate them into nuučaańuł? There's a certain beauty in this unknown. Two traditional languages, bridged, yet gapped, by a language that in many ways connects us, yet again disconnects us...

English is in many ways a collection of many languages, and the ambiguity in the spaces between the words is a space in which poetry can flourish. We see poetry, as we know it in English, as a way to push past the structures, to point out the possibilities in the spaces and the alternative understandings of words.

As learners, we dream of a time when we can write poetry in nuučaańuł, as we're sure our fluent speakers can and have done for generations—in songs, in stories, in words shared between family. We are at a point in our learning when we are still trying to grasp the structure, the many definitions, the many truths within the breakdown of the words. We hope that, if not us, our children will be able to know nuučaańuł so intimately that they can find the spaces in between, and play with the meanings and definitions within our words.

Until then, we wonder if maybe, using nuučaańuł as it is, within the English world we inhabit, is a way of poetry in itself, a way of pushing against the structures of English and finding the spaces in between. Take, for instance, the English phrase 'I love you.' When we asked our Elders how to say this in nuučaańuł, we were told the phrase:

yaaʔakuks suẃa

love/pain/aching/longing for — possessive — me   you

I love you, you are my pain.

In its own right, yaaʔakuks suẃa—you are my pain—is poetry in itself. At first, we may want to push against the notion of love being pain, but the beauty in that is its truth.
Water, Sky, Earth. Creation, Life, Death.

All in perfect balance, a cycle never-ending. Do we attempt to put question to it?

For now, that is all.

čuu.

Tim Masso and Hjalmer Wenstob are brothers from the Tla-o-qui-aht First Nations. Tim has been a language advocate and language learner since he was nine years old. At only 19 he is in the final year of a bachelor's of Education degree with a special focus in Nuu-chah-nulth language revitalization. Hjalmer is a renowned visual artist, specializing in both two- and three-dimensional Nuu-chah-nulth art, as well as many collaborative projects surrounding the language. Annika Benoit-Jansson is Hjalmer's partner and mother to their two beautiful children, Huumis and Cinkwa. Inspired by the work Hjalmer and Tim do together, Annika has been learning the language for over two years, and is in her final year of the language revitalization program, with the goal to teach her children their traditional language.

carly butler
mamaałni

You too go fast   beyond earth and sky
till you can see water   flowing from no-place[1]

The Nuu-chah-nulth word for white people, mamaałni, translates as people of floating houses and refers to Europeans who arrived by boat and were, 'people of no land'. In her video essay *Winter of Displacement*, Gita Hashemi writes of what it means to be landless, living on unceded territory, when your "ancestors are buried elsewhere."[2] I am a first generation Canadian and my ancestors are also buried elsewhere. Some are in Iran, like Gita's, where I may never go; and the rest are in England. I have no ancestors buried in Canada, or in North America. Unlike Gita, I am not landless. I own and occupy PID 000865028—Lot 25, Plan VIP27909, District Lot 282, aka 1595 Bay Street in Ucluelet, British Columbia. Ownership is an uncomfortable privilege for land that is the traditional territory of the Yuułuʔiłʔatḥ (yoo-thlew-ilth-uhht). Except as a settler on their land, I have no connections with the Yuułuʔiłʔatḥ territory and nation. I am still learning to properly pronounce Yuułuʔiłʔatḥ (yoo-thlew-ilth-uhht). The idea of borrowing Yuułuʔiłʔatḥ land is a more comfortable proposition as it implies the land will be returned. This is probably disingenuous—would I really ever give it back? Where would I go? The idea of home implies that there is a place I could return to. My discomfort comes from not knowing where home is.

With a personal family history of seafaring and living on boats, being a mamaałni makes sense to me: landless Europeans floating, wandering the globe in a never-ending search for more (home?). My parents did not have a sense of a homeland that they longed for or aspired to return to. Instead of stirring nostalgia, my family focused on fulfilling a somewhat unconventional dream of sailing around the world. Unconventional, but also perhaps just a version of the Western preoccupation of arrogantly wandering the world as entitled (white) backpackers—a veneration and romanticization of travel and exploration that continues unabated, often perpetuating colonialism. Is the culture of Instagram with its emphasis on discovery and empty landscapes, with only the solitary explorer ever featured, really that different than the colonial conception of terra nullius—land of no one, belonging to no one? In some ways sailing and the culture surrounding seafaring represent the pinnacle of this practice, for where better but in

1 Jalal al-Din Rumi, Ghazal 294, translated by Gita Hashemi, page 154 in this volume

2 Gita Hashemi, *fools in paradise, I: winter of displacement* (Toronto: SubversivePress, 2021), 12:43.

the open empty sea to stake your claim of privileged access, space, and adventure?

I admit, I also used to imagine the ocean as neutral territory. I was raised to believe the seas belonged to everyone, or at least to us as a Canadian family sailing the world. Six years ago I embarked on *The S Project*[3] with UK artist Gudrun Filipska, a collaborative project in which we used postal communication to send each other physical objects connected to where we live. Gudrun sent me packets of soil. I sent her bottles of seawater as my practice is almost always focused on the ocean. Given my family history, I felt ownership of this water. I thought that I was allowed to claim the sea where I lived. Feeling slightly self-righteous, I also imagined that sending water was more appropriate than sending a piece of earth that was not mine, as a settler on Yuułuʔiłʔatḥ territory. I did feel that the ocean was mine. I was going to add quotes around mine but the truth is that sense of ownership was quite unequivocal. Then Tla-o-qui-aht artist Hjalmer Wenstob pointed out to me that the traditional territory of the Yuułuʔiłʔatḥ actually extends well past the coastline. My smug good settler moment was over. The water had to be returned.

If my ideas about the ownership of water were problematic, so too were my ideas about the ownership of poetry. Originally it was the translation of Rumi's Ghazal 294 that I was drawn to, not surprisingly because the poem is all about water:

> The entire world is   but half a mouthful / Greed for
> half a mouthful   disappeared the water
> Earth and sky are   bucket and pitcher / but water is
> beyond earth and sky
> You too go fast   beyond earth and sky / till you can
> see water   flowing from no-place

Here I conveniently ignore the lines about the Islamic prophets Khidr and Ilyas—associated with oceans and land respectively. In the search for personal location and culture I can claim Persian ancestry through my grandmother and this leads to a parallel claiming of Rumi. But my grandmother was Baha'i not Muslim, and Baha'is are treated as outsiders and persecuted by the government in Iran.[4] My grandmother

3 Carly Butler and Gudrun Filipska, *The S Project*, multi media, 2017-ongoing, www.sprojectarchive.com.

4 See the Human Rights Watch 2021 Iran Report: www.hrw.org/world-report/2021/country-chapters/iran#814a01 (retrived 15 August 2022).

carly butler

attempted to teach me Farsi, but my teenage self was ambivalent at best—a lifelong regret, though have I taken real steps to learn the language myself? I have not. She also taught me to be wary of Islam. She angrily paged through the Qur'an with me and pointed out passages that offended her. So I am also guilty of what has been described as the "spiritual colonizing" of Rumi, that is, the removal by Western translators of Islamic references in Rumi's poetry. I ignore the references to the Qur'an—because they make me uncomfortable—in favour of the more New Age inspirational poster versions of the text.

It occurs to me that this is what settlers do, in this land I occupy, to Indigenous cultures. We appropriate. I live in an "alternative" surf community that has a dangerous tendency to appropriate Indigenous traditions as its own in the name of "good vibes only" (smudging, spirit animals, etc.). It is not a coincidence that my understanding corresponded with these presumed Rumi lines by Coleman Barks (the non-Persian-speaking "translator" whose "translations" started the Rumi craze in North America), another secular mamaałni: "I dip a jar in the ocean. / Filled containers become seawater. / Suddenly there is a world within this world, / ocean inside the water jar."[5]

The third couplet from Ghazal 294 as translated by Hashemi: "You too go beyond earth and sky / so you can see water flowing from no-place" reminds me of a line by Canadian artist Emily Carr that she wrote about Ucluelet, where I live: "One day I walked upon a strip of land that belonged to nothing."[6] I realize that I am drawn to these lines because my reading reinforces what led me to take bottles of water from the ocean, what I want to believe is true. I want to equate no-place (or in Arberry's translation the awkward "placelessness") to belonging to no one and therefore free to take.

My mamaałni self-of-no-land-floating-on-the-sea, wants to claim the space of water, to own what presumably belongs to no one. But focus on the Islamic references in the text, and the couplet becomes about a spiritual no-place, as in a higher state, beyond ego and ideas of ownership. The Indigenous conception of place is perhaps framed in the same way—the interconnectedness of all things and therefore the responsibility to protect the territory that is both land and extends into the sea. Would Rumi, the real Rumi, and not the "pop Sufi" version embraced with New Age earnestness in the West, reveal similar teachings if his work is allowed to speak its tongue?

5 Coleman Barks, *Rumi: Bridge to the Soul: Journeys into the Music and Silence of the Heart* (New York: Harper Collins, 2007), 107, 36.

6 Emily Carr, *Klee Wyck* (Toronto/London: Oxford University Press, 1941), 13.

Carly Butler (she/her) is a settler artist in Canada of British and Iranian descent. She currently lives and works on Vancouver Island in Ucluelet on the traditional territory of the Yuułuʔiłʔatḥ. Her interdisciplinary practice reinterprets nautical knowledge around navigation and survival to reflect on longing, regret, and nostalgia.

zainab amadahy

anti-oppression is not a healing modality

The product of my pain became the cure.[1] حاصل دردم سبب درمان گشت

While we see anger and violence in the streets of our country, the real battlefield is inside our bodies. If we are to survive as a country, it is inside our bodies where this conflict needs to be resolved.[2]

Traumatized people traumatize people.

I don't make that statement from a location of innocence. I am a traumatized person who has traumatized and otherwise acted unfairly toward others. What's more I am someone who has used the knowledge and skills I gained through anti-oppression training to perpetrate and justify acts of selfishness, irresponsibility and general bad behaviour. To balance that, as the universe has a way of doing, I've been on the other side of that coin, unfairly accused of oppressive behaviour. What's more, in my role as a community worker and consultant to the not-for-profit sector, I have also witnessed this dynamic play out among others, sometimes in the form of individuals from marginalized communities shaming and blaming each other. Systemic oppressions and complicity exist. And they almost always play some role in interpersonal conflicts and group dynamics. But that role can sometimes be blown out of proportion or considered foundational to a conflict when it isn't.

Resorting to false or exaggerated accusations of oppressive behavior is often symptomatic of trauma. Not excusable but trauma nonetheless. We all have our traumas: childhood, vicarious, collective, and intergenerational. When traumatized people come together in life partnerships, friendships, workplaces or collaborations, they are going to trigger each other. Despite good intentions, our unhealed wounds will paint us all in blood. There is a spiritual principle that says we tend to unconsciously attract into our lives those people and events best suited to mirror our wounds back to us so we see the need to heal. To a greater or lesser degree, that's the story of every type of relationship, and what makes us feel so vulnerable in intimate ones. Unfortunately, if you're lacking the self-awareness to understand what is happening, you may find yourself

1 Rumi, *Divan-e Shams*, Quatrains 261.

2 Resmaa Menakem, *My Grandmother's Hands: Racialized Trauma and the Pathway to Mending Our Hearts and Bodies.* (Las Vegas, NV: Central Recovery Press, 2017.)

looking to transform an undesirable reflection by changing the mirror, rather than the one looking into it.

آنچ در فرعون بود اندر تو هست
لیک اژدرهات محبوس چهست
ای دریغ این جمله احوال توست
تو بر آن فرعون بر خواهیش بست
گر ز تو گویند وحشت زایدت
ور ز دیگر آفسان بنمایدت
آتشت را هیزم فرعون نیست
ورنه چون فرعون او شعله‌زنیست

Alas, this is all about you
But you attribute it to the Pharaoh
That which was inside Pharaoh is inside you
But you hide your monster in the dark well
You are appalled if they talk about you
But you swell when the talk is of others
Your fire does not have the Pharaoh's woodpile
Otherwise it would raise flames like the Pharaoh[3]

The violence endemic (but not inherent) to human relationships and life experience has trained us to compete, protect, and defend in situations where it is not required. We project our traumas onto each other and then judge, blame and shame each other for reflecting back to us what we don't want to see and lack the capacity to deal with. This pattern has accelerated of late.

In the wake of extreme political polarization, increased economic precarity, climate change, and methods of coping with the pandemic, many lives, businesses and organizations have imploded. Because the old patterns of thinking and doing don't work anymore, we are in a position where adopting new patterns of behavior is mandatory to our survival as individuals, communities and a species. Consequently, interest in healing from trauma has soared. There are more publications, webinars, courses, and trainings than ever on the topic. Many of these resources recognize how forms of oppression contribute to, if not create, trauma and complicate the healing process. For example, it's impossible to heal from trauma when you are still in an actively harmful relationship, whether with an abusive life partner, an exploitative employer, or an unjust social system. This is obvious and recognized in our movements. But it's equally true that you can't heal from harm while you perpetrate harm on others.

Communities, organizations and relationships are reflections of the mindset of their members. We can't establish peaceful societies through practicing violence. Justice is not achieved through unfairness. We can't create institutional integrity by being under responsible or less than honest. Communities are not solidified by promoting division. We can't transform into better people by lashing out. When folks do any of these things it is a clear indication of their mindset and their spiritual injuries.

اشکال نو به نو چو مناقض نمایدت
اندر مناقضات خلافی مستریست
در تو چو جنگ باشد گویی دو لشکر است
در تو چو جنگ نبود دانی که لشکریست

When new things appear contrary to you
You see in their contrariness wrongdoing
You line up your armies if there is war inside you
You recognize combativeness when there is no war
inside you[4]

Many folks in our social movements attest to how anti-oppression frameworks have helped them recognize and acknowledge their traumas, while allowing them to shift the shame and self-blame they feel for the harm they have experienced. Furthermore, anti-O analyses have helped folks identify coping mechanisms they and others have developed in order to

3 Rumi, *Masnavi*, Book 3, Chapter 36. All quotes from Rumi in this piece were selected and translated by Gita Hashemi.

4 Rumi, *Divan-e Shams*, Ghazal 458.

normalize living traumatized in a traumatizing society. These are important and necessary first steps in the healing process, but they are not the end of the process.

Our justice and decolonial movements have been very good at teaching us how to think critically, particularly when it comes to anti-oppression theory, which trains us to look for, analyze, and critique power dynamics in all relationships. It trains us to understand how power dynamics of the past inform today's injustices. We learn how historical and current cultural narratives justify, rationalize, and reinforce injustice. Anti-O trains us to be vigilant about how we have internalized forms of inequality like white supremacy, colonialism, hetero-patriarchy, ableism, ageism, human superiority, etc. As a result, we expect each other to be transparent and accountable for our behaviors, to challenge unhealthy power dynamics whenever and wherever we find them, whether these show up within ourselves, in others, or in institutions and systems. We often acknowledge with each other how exhausting all this is. And we're allowed to be exhausted but we're not allowed to give up because, once we are aware, we become responsible for calling out and fighting injustice. Unfortunately, none of this guarantees an environment conducive to healing from our traumas. In fact, it can do the opposite.

Critical thinking, including anti-O, is crucial to our survival. Without it we wouldn't be able to make decisions, evaluate, or reason about how to improve the condition of our lives. Critical ideas can also inform our creativity. These are important functions of anti-oppression education. But anti-O is not a tool of healing. Nor is it a justification or rationalization for irresponsible behaviour, as too many of us have used it. Accusing someone of racism, homophobia, sexism, and other oppressive behaviours in order to derail uncomfortable dynamics is not only unfair to those being attacked, it trivializes movements that have cost people their lives, diminishes the credibility of legitimate grievances and creates a climate of cynicism, fear and resentment toward progressive change.

An emphasis on critical thinking to the detriment of other ideas can negatively impact our relationships. It is possible that Anti-O skills, tools and resources can be more weapons than medicine in the hands of people who have not done enough healing work. Our ability to identify unfair power dynamics doesn't guarantee we will interrogate our complicity in that unfairness or how we have possibly collaborated in our own victimhood. Nor will it magically provide us with the integrity needed to challenge such dynamics. A preoccupation with critical thinking will also limit our capacity to dream and create the world we purport to want. Allow me to illustrate with a Mayan teaching I received in my own healing journey.

The Maya were experts in thinking critically about our relationship with time. Their calendars demonstrate sophisticated knowledge around the intersections of cyclical rhythms found among the stars, on the Earth and within our bodies. Their astronomical and mathematical skills enabled them to predict the impact of cosmological alignments far into the future. One concept the Maya offer us is the idea of being stuck in time. That is, being so fixated on negative past events that they determine how we experience the present moment and impact our optimism about the future. You might say this is how the Maya conceptualized trauma.

Ask yourself: How often do you dwell on events that took place decades if not hundreds of years ago (or yesterday?), rerunning the story, fine-tuning it, expanding it, and feeling the intense emotions it evokes? You do this over and over, even when you are now in a completely new moment that demands a different response than you are offering, yet you continue to react based on past events.

The triggering of trauma invokes involuntary physical and mental responses. The partner who snaps at you today invokes the same reaction as your abusive parent. The boss displeased with your lateness invokes the same reaction as the teacher who humiliated you in front of the class. Every uniform you see invokes the terror you felt when the cops beat the crap out of your father (my personal example). Daily microaggressions can keep us locked in the stress response, unable to physically differentiate between the event(s) that traumatized us decades ago and today's minor annoyances that don't merit either the anxiety we feel or the rage we unleash.

هر اندیشه که می‌پوشی درون خلوت سینه
نشان و رنگ اندیشه ز دل پیداست بر سیما

Any thought that you hide in the privacy of your heart
Its colour and designs appear in what you display to the world[5]

Today's positive psychology is built on ideas that many wisdom and Indigenous healing traditions already knew: you create more of what you focus on and when you dwell on the negative it's measurably harmful to your wellness, including your relationship wellness. It also biases you in favor of a negative orientation to other aspects of your life. That's not an argument for repressing feelings or turning a blind eye to injustice. It's an invitation to consider how what you pay attention to can shape your perception and, consequently, your experience of life events and relationships.

Some researchers note that critical thinking and creativity light up different neural circuits in the brain and that these cannot be active at the same time. In other words, if you're working on a creative idea, you can't simultaneously think critically about it (or anything), although you can switch back and forth in an instant. You can be equally as skilled at critical thinking as you are at creativity. However, what if you devote eighty percent of your time mulling over past, present and potential future injustices and only twenty percent on what a just, decolonized society, workplace, or relationship might look like? We know from neuroplasticity that your brain will physically develop in a way that facilitates how you use it. A brain focused on anti-O is going to get really good at theorizing, analyzing, recalling, educating, and debating anti-O concepts.

But what you don't use, you lose. So, if you spend less time on creating the world you want and the relationships you desire, even if only to fantasize, your brain restructures itself to accommodate that. You will become less effective at imagining and practicing ways of living based on justice and equity simply because you've devoted more time, energy and gray matter to something else.

What's more, being on alert to find ideas, events, or people to critique, leaves you less likely to notice pro-justice and pro-equity activities, much less value and nurture them. However, if you turned that around and trained yourself to look for ideas, events, and people to appreciate, you will see them everywhere. That doesn't mean you'll cease to notice injustice but it might mean that you will invest more of your time and energy into creating the kinds of relationships, activities and events that promote just and equitable lifeways.

This is the idea behind Thanksgiving Addresses, gratitude rituals, and many other spiritual practices that measurably change brain structure and encourage us to focus our minds and hearts on life-affirming activities. It's simple, really: If you want to master a skill you need to practice it. Want society to be just and equitable? Being a role model for justice and equity helps you and the rest of us get there.

Many wisdom teachings tell us that one significant component of healing is taking responsibility. That is generally something traumatized people are reluctant to consider because they think the idea advocates self-blame. On the contrary, responsibility is not about self-blame and no one is responsible for someone else's behavior. Nevertheless, it is important to contemplate how assuming the persona of a victim and telling your victim story over and over again impacts your capacity to heal. Be honest. How much of your inability to show up, on time, live up to your agreements, and treat people respectfully is on someone else? How much is on systemic oppression? How much is on you?

Admittedly, in a reality where every life form and every event are interrelated there are no definitive lines of separation between me and you, us and them, this and that, etc. Like it or not, we all share some degree of culpability for our world's injustices. And of course, responsibility doesn't eliminate all obstacles and challenges from life. But consider the metaphor of the oyster living in an underwater environment where granules of sand will constantly penetrate its shell, creating an irritation that eventually transforms into a pearl. In confronting the challenges of life, we exercise our spiritual muscles and

5 Rumi, *Divan-e Shams*, ghazal 54.

become capable of creating finer and finer "pearls" with each endeavour.

Life events inevitably provide us with both joyful and challenging experiences. With this contrast, we make and refine our life choices, learning and growing along the way. As discussed above, we tend to unconsciously attract into our lives those people and events best suited to mirror our flaws and wounds back to us. We need to learn and teach each other constructive and compassionate ways of dealing with life's stressors. With response-ability comes the ability to consider responses in the present moment that can take us farther from or closer to the life, relationships and world we desire. The ways in which we treat our wounds and the wounds of others will determine whether we expand or contract our collective consciousness and at what pace.

This principle applies to all forms of relationships, including those forged in workplaces and across communities. When discomfort of any kind arises in a relationship, the formula that promotes expanded self-awareness and healing is to acknowledge its presence, explore it, learn what it has to teach, and allow that information to transform you. The triggering of wounds provides an opportunity to go inward and investigate what needs healing. As individuals heal so do communities. Communities that make space, provide encouragement and offer resources for healing their members accelerate the expansion of consciousness.

When we have healed from our traumas enough that we can enter a space with other traumatized individuals and hold an interest in learning more, being more, and helping others on their path to do the same, it's inevitably going to have impact across our species. We will no longer be traumatized people traumatizing people. We will be relatives enjoying healthy relationships.

Post-Script

After so many references to healing, it might be helpful to define how that term is used here. Healing is not a static state of being one can arrive at and rest in for all of time. It's an ongoing process of adjusting to life events in a way that provides you with a general sense of safety, confidence and connection in the world. There are many ideas about how one heals from trauma and many modalities and therapies available, from spiritual ceremony to psychedelics to somatic therapy, etc. Whatever modality, the process tends to fall into progressive steps that deserve a lot more space than can be taken here. Nevertheless, below is a brief overview of three steps:

1. Recognition that a traumatizing event has occurred and/or a trauma reaction has been triggered. You become aware of being triggered by noting your specific physical and mental reactions, such as tightness in some part of the body, fast beating heart, dizziness, nausea, loss of breath, a tendency to freeze, feelings of terror and/or rage, etc. The first concern after this recognition is to determine your level of safety and take action to remove yourself from danger (or danger from you), if that is necessary. Once safe, it is important to name and feel your feelings deeply without judging, storying, or rationalizing them.

2. Learning and practicing skills that reverse the trauma response and build resiliency. Some of these can be practiced when in the triggered state. There are many practices to choose from but examples include breathing techniques, tapping acupuncture points, and soothing self-talk. Other strategies that build resilience and awareness can be done consistently over time. These can include meditation, exercise, regular interaction with nature, journaling, certain yogic practices, etc. This is the phase where taking responsibility and making intentional choices that balance the best interests of yourself and others become important.

3. Reintegration. Trauma causes a fragmentation of the psyche. Or as my teachers have said, a fragmentation of the soul.

A part of who you are "flees" or is suppressed to keep you safe. After a traumatic experience you can lose your sense of innocence, trust, curiosity, personal sovereignty, self-control, freedom, safety and/or passion, for example. At your core you have trouble believing you are valuable, loved and worthy of enjoying life. When you can retrieve some or all those aspects of your soul, when they become a part of you again, you are reintegrated. At this point you may find a sense of meaning in the traumatizing experience because it taught you something or motivated you into a purposeful course of action. Consider the sexual assault survivor who becomes an activist or the refugee who advocates for political change.

Many modalities provide a framework for taking you through these steps, at different speeds. It's unfortunate that some proven processes are not covered by medical insurance, recognized as effective by health care professionals, or even legal (as in the case of psychedelics). The good news, however, is that there is a plethora of resources aimed at enhancing our collective understanding of trauma and exploring various approaches to healing. These should help you make the right choices for you as you embark on your own journey.

Editor's note: This essay was commissioned and written in the fall of 2021. Conversations within decolonial and justice movements about trauma-awareness and ways of healing and caring for ourselves and others have expanded since, yet Amadahy's perspective remains fresh and critical and is therefore included here without later revisions.

Zainab Amadahy lives in Nogojiwanong, Ontario, Canada and has authored works of fiction and nonfiction including *Wielding the Force* (2012), *Resistance* (2013) and *Life on Purpose* (2017), and published in magazines including *Muskrat*. Now semi-retired, she has worked in community arts, not-for-profit housing, Indigenous knowledge reclamation, women's services, and migrant settlement.

ghazal 1789

O lovers, o lovers   it is time to decamp from this world
   The drum of departure   reaches my soul's ear from the sky
Now the cameleer has arisen   and the caravan is arranged
   The driver has begged for discharge   Travelers   why are you still asleep
Ahead and behind these sounds   are sounds of drums and camel bells
   Every moment a soul and a breath   enter the no-place
From these upside-down candles   from these indigo planes[1]
   a wondrous disposition arises   to make the invisible visible
From the turns of this wheel   heavy slumber fell upon you
   Damned   this short life   Beware   this long slumber
My heart   go to your beloved   Friend   go to your friend
   Watchman   wake up   The watchman shouldn't sleep
Candles and torches everywhere   noise and excitement everywhere
   For tonight this pregnant world   will give birth to the world eternal
You were clay and you became heart   You were ignorant and you became smart
   Whoever has thus drawn you   will drag you there and yonder
In *ou*'s[2] draggings and trawlings   are pains that are pleasure
   Ou's flames are like waters   Do not frown upon them
Dwelling in soul is *ou*'s way   Breaking promises is *ou*'s way
   Before *ou*'s abundant guile   these flecks have trembling hearts
Grinning   you leap out of your hole to declare   I am the village chief
   How long will you leap   Bend your neck   or they will bend you like a bow
You sowed the seeds of deceit   You showed contempt
   You imagined truth nonexistent   Now see what you get you bastard
Donkey   you are better with straw   Cauldron   you are better with soot
   You who dishonour your clan and house   you are better in a well's depth
In me there is another   from whom this rage erupts
   If water burns and scalds   know that it is because of fire
I hold no stone in my hand   I hold no enmity with anyone
   I limit no one   for I am happy as a garden flower
Hence my rage is from another source   from another world
   This side a world   That side a world   I sit on the threshold
Only the person who is a mute speaker[3,4]   can sit on the threshold
   Enough that you revealed this secret   Say no more   Hold your tongue

1 An allusion to stars, "upside down candles," and the night sky, according to Shafiei-Kadkani. Molana Jalal al-Din Mohammad Balkhi, *Gozide-ye Ghazaliyat-e Shams* be kushesh-e doctor Mohammad Reza Shafiei-Kadkani (Tehran: Amir Kabir, 1365/1987) footnote 1, p 348.

2 *Ou* is the transliteration of او, the third-person pronoun in Persian. Persian is a genderless language, thus using gendered pronouns *she* or *he* as equivalent to *ou* would be inaccurate, prescriptive, and restrictive. Because the referent of the pronoun in these verses is special—the exalted object of desire and praise—rather than generic, I chose to keep *ou* rather than use a generic genderless *they*.

3 Mute speaker translates *nategh-e akhras*. See notes 7 and 8 in ghazal 2131 on page 140, and note 3 to ghazal 1759 on page 32 in this volume.

4 In the *sufi* and *bhakti* traditions muteness and silence occupy a prominent place. Words in many Asian languages carry three levels of meaning: the biophysical/empirical, the socio-cultural and the ontological/cosmological. Philosopher-poets use these levels of meanings to move between the three planes of existence. *Mute* at the biophysical/empirical level is the inability to speak. As a socio-cultural concept, *mute* is about witnessing. One must be mute to witness and know the Truth. Silence could follow from mute witnessing as when a person refuses to accept Untruth as an act of resistance. At the ontological/cosmological level being *mute* is the state of transcendence of the dualisms—*You* and *I*, *This* and *That*—so that it becomes possible to listen to the heart. As the body responds to instinct and the mind responds to worldly knowledge, the heart, the site of intuitive knowledge, responds to ontological/cosmological Truth. Only the heart can process instinctual and intellectual knowledge and guide a person to transcendence through intuitive knowledge. It is necessary, indeed a precondition, to remain mute to be able to listen to the heart; for the heart to be able to process instinctual and intellectual knowledge. This state of muteness—transcendent state—is not 'mysticism' as understood in European cultures. It is a deeper knowledge that puts both instinctual and intellectual knowledge into wider ontological and cosmological perspectives. Hence it is possible to become in Rumi's words 'a mute speaker'. —Note by Radha D'Souza. For more on philosopher-poets, read "What Can Activist Scholars Learn from Rumi?" by D'Souza, page 174 in this volume.

read by radha d'souza

translated by gita hashemi

مولوی

غزل ۱۷۸۹

Ey āsheghān ey āsheghān hengām-e kuch ast az jahān
  Dar gush-e jānam miresad tabl-e rahil az āsemān
Nak sārebān barkhāste ghattār-hā āraste
  az mā halāli khāste che khofte-id ey kāravān
In bāng-hā az pish-o pas bāng-e rahil ast-o jaras
  Har lahze-i nafs-o nafas sar mikeshad dar lāmakān
Zin sham'-hāy-e sarnegun zin pardehāy-e nilgun
  kholghi ajab āyad borun tā gheyb-hā gardad ayān
Zin charkh-e dulābi tow rā āmad gerān khābi tow rā
  Faryād az in omre sabok Zenhār az in khābe gerān
Ey del suye deldār show Ey yār suye yār show
  Ey pāsebān bidār show Khofte nashāyad pāsebān
Har suy sham'-o mash'ale Har suy bāng-o mashghale
  Kemshab jahān-e hāmele zāyad jahān-e jāvedan
Tow gel bodi-o del shodi Jāhel bodi āghel shodi
  Ān ku keshidat in chonin ān su keshānad kesh-keshān
Andar keshākesh-hāye ou nush ast nākhosh-hā-ye ou
  Āb ast ātash-hā-ye ou Bar vey makon ru rā gerān
Dar jān neshastan kār-e ou Towbe shekastan kār-e ou
  Az hileye besyār-e ou in zarre-hā larzān delān
Ey rish khand-e rakhne-jeh ya'ni manam sālār-e deh
  Tā key jahi gardan beneh var ney keshandat chon kamān
Tokhme daghal mikāshti afsushā midāshti
  Hagh rā adam pendāshti aknun bebin ey gholtabān
Ey khar be kāh owlātari Digi siyāh owlātari
  Dar gha'r-e chāh owlātari ey nang-e khān-o khāndan
Dar man kasi digar bovad kin khashm-hā az vey jahad
  Gar āb suzāni konad zātash bovad in rā bedān
Dar kaf nadāram sang man Bā kas nadāram jang man
  Bā kas nagiram tang man zirā khosham chon golsetān
Pas khashm-e man zān sar bovad vaz ālam-e digar bovad
  In su jahān ān su jahān benshaste man bar āstān
Bar āstān ān kas bovad ku nātegh-e akhras bovad
  In ramz gofti bas bovad digar magu darkesh zabān

ای عاشقان ای عاشقان هنگام کوچ است از جهان
در گوش جانم می رسد طبل رحیل از آسمان
نک ساربان برخاسته قطارها آراسته
از ما حلالی خواسته چه خفته‌اید ای کاروان
این بانگ‌ها از پیش و پس بانگ رحیل است و جرس
هر لحظه‌ای نفس و نفس سر می کشد در لامکان
زین شمع‌های سرنگون زین پرده‌های نیلگون
خلقی عجب آید برون تا غیب‌ها گردد عیان
زین چرخ دولابی تو را آمد گران خوابی تو را
فریاد از این عمر سبک زنهار از این خواب گران
ای دل سوی دلدار شو ای یار سوی یار شو
ای پاسبان بیدار شو خفته نشاید پاسبان
هر سوی شمع و مشعله هر سوی بانگ و مشغله
کامشب جهان حامله زاید جهان جاودان
تو گل بدی و دل شدی جاهل بدی عاقل شدی
آن کو کشیدت این چنین آن سو کشاند کش‌کشان
اندر کشاکش‌های او نوش است ناخوش‌های او
آب است آتش‌های او بر وی مکن رو را گران
در جان نشستن کار او توبه شکستن کار او
از حیله بسیار او این ذره‌ها لرزان دلان
ای ریش‌خند رخنه جه یعنی منم سالار ده
تا کی جهی گردن بنه ور نی کشندت چون کمان
تخم دغل می‌کاشتی افسوس ها می‌داشتی
حق را عدم پنداشتی اکنون ببین ای قلتبان
ای خر به کاه اولیتری دیگی سیاه اولیتری
در قعر چاه اولیتری ای ننگ خانه و خاندان
در من کسی دیگر بود کاین خشم‌ها از وی جهد
گر آب سوزانی کند ز آتش بود این را بدان
در کف ندارم سنگ من با کس ندارم جنگ من
با کس نگیرم تنگ من زیرا خوشم چون گلستان
پس خشم من زان سر بود وز عالم دیگر بود
این سو جهان آن سو جهان بنشسته من بر آستان
بر آستان آن کس بود کو ناطق اخرس بود
این رمز گفتی بس بود دیگر مگو درکش زبان

radha d'souza

what can activist scholars learn from rumi?[1]

If in the world thou art the most learned scholar of the time, behold
The passing-away of this world and this time! (I:2845)[2]

Historically, in Asia and the Middle East the poet-saint (also known as philosopher-poet) traditions produced scholars who were also social activists as we understand them today. Poet-saints were social thinkers and philosophers who were critical of the dominant scholarship, power structures, social inequalities, and injustice. They were the critics and conscience of society who promoted emancipatory social change. They argued that the purpose of scholarship should be to extend knowledge to ordinary people.

Colonization rewrote the social and intellectual histories of colonized societies in ways that introduced a disjuncture in the intellectual histories of these societies and their forms of knowledge.[3] In colonial historiography, poet-saints were recognized as poets and not as philosophers proper, and their writings were categorized as literature in the domain of aesthetics and not social philosophy. This representation of poet-saints mirrored the rupture between Aesthetics and Reason that the European Enlightenment introduced in Europe.[4] Consequently

1 This is an adaptation of a longer article originally published in *Philosophy East and West* 64, 1 (January 2014): 1-24.

2 Throughout this essay I use Nicholson's translations of Rumi, available in three volumes. See Reynold A. Nicholson, *The Mathnawi of Jalálu'ddin Rúmi: Edited from the Oldest Manuscripts Available: With Critical Notes, Translation, and Commentary* (London: Cambridge University Press, 1926), and Reynold A. Nicholson, *The Mathnawi of Jalálu'ddin Rúmi* (London: Cambridge University Press, 1977 [1930]). Nicholson's translations, published from 1925 to 1940 in six volumes with commentaries and extensive footnotes, is considered a monumental contribution in its own right. Nicholson provides extensive footnotes to his translations to make the meaning explicit without losing the poetic flavor of Rumi's writings. I have quoted the verses verbatim with the footnotes and provided the book and line numbers in the text for reference. Jalálu'ddin Rúmi's Mathnawi (also spelled Masnavi) comprises six books and 25,700 verses. The purpose of the Mathnawi is primarily pedagogic.

3 For example, see Bernard S. Cohn, *Colonialism and Its Forms of Knowledge: The British in India* (Delhi: Oxford University Press, 1997).

4 Jürgen Habermas, *Moral Consciousness and Communicative Action* (Cambridge: Polity Press, 1990), 225.

poet-saints came to be represented as mystics and spiritualists with little to offer toward ideas of equality, justice, or freedom. This way of representing dissident intellectual traditions in colonized societies made it possible to view Eastern people as intrinsically spiritual, a quality divorced from its materiality. At the same time it enabled the imperialist West to represent itself as the sole repository of ideas of freedom and emancipation.

In recent decades a distinctive branch of knowledge known as 'activist scholarship' has emerged simultaneously with market-driven reforms in the education sector. Drawing from a number of disciplines, including education, sociology, social anthropology, social theory, law, and human rights, activist scholarship proclaims as its core mission that philosophy should transform the world. Activist scholars affirm human emancipation as the goal of scholarship and have set themselves the task of building bridges between theory and practice. There is a spectrum of views on the theory-practice nexus that affirm (1) a relationship between knowledge and action, (2) knowledge as a condition for emancipation and freedom, (3) love for and solidarity in social change, (4) the importance of everyday life, and (5) the role of the activist scholar in social change. These themes form the subject matter of this essay.

Society has always been concerned with social change, but the emergence of activist scholarship as a field of academic specialization in social change has come with the emergence of globalized knowledge markets. In the context of the rise of commodified education markets in the service of monopoly finance capitalism, how do we understand the emergence of activist scholarship as if it were its Manichean other? Why is it that notwithstanding the critique of Eurocentrism, even critical postcolonial thinkers continue to see poet-saints through disciplinary lenses of art and literature and not philosophy and social theory? These questions mark the point of departure for this essay, which uses Rumi's philosophy as a trope to invite activist scholars to rethink their roles in social transformation and emancipation.

Contemporary debates in critical theory center on 'duopoly': universalism and relativism, multiculturalism and market-culturalism, fact and value, truth and reality, theory and praxis.[5] Others similarly list public-private, society-individual, science-religion, institutional religion–personal religion, secular-sacred, rational-irrational, and male-female as dualisms of modernity.[6] What is striking about the poet-saint traditions is the ways in which they have striven to overcome 'duopolies.' They did this by affirming ontology, i.e. the place of human beings in the larger universe, and by the extraordinary ontological awareness displayed in their works. These works have thus inculcated ontological awareness in people, i.e. sensitivity to human purpose, human destiny and ethics and aesthetics. Poet-saints share comparable conceptions of universalism, humanity, freedom, emancipation, ontology, epistemology, and action, and yet they demonstrate wide variations in the ways in which they have adapted universalist ideas to diverse local histories, cultures, and problems over extended periods of time. Poet-saints are far too numerous, spanning a long period from about the sixth century CE to the colonial era and spreading throughout Asia and the Middle East. Given this wide diversity and extended histories, the reason for choosing Rumi's works for this essay is strategic. Rumi, more than any other Eastern scholar, is best known and respected in the West. That the year 2007 was declared the United Nations Year of Rumi is testimony to his stature in the West. Celebrated as a mystic and a poet, the official celebrations did little to add to our understanding of his lasting influence among ordinary people in Asia and the Middle East, where pop groups, Bollywood vocalists, beggars on trains, and professional musicians continue to sing his songs and nurture the resilience he has instilled in them.

In each section below a theme of relevance to activist scholarship is interrogated through the insights offered by Rumi in his monumental work the Masnavi. What, if anything, can activist scholars learn from Rumi?

The Nexus between Theory and Practice

Activist scholars share theoretical orientations with wider trends in critical scholarship on disciplinary approaches to knowledge production. At one end of the spectrum is the postcolonial critique of disciplinary knowledge,[7] and at the

5 Uberoi, JPS. *The European Modernity: Science, Truth and Method* (New Delhi: Oxford University Press, 2002), 143.

6 Richard King, *Orientalism and Religion: Postcolonial Theory, India and 'The Mystic East'* (New York: Routledge, 1999).

7 Norman K. Denzin, Yvonna S. Lincoln, and Linda Tuhiwai Smith, eds., *Handbook of Critical and Indigenous Methodologies* (Los Angeles: Sage, 2008), 604; Ananta Kumar Giri, ed., *Creative Social Research: Rethinking Theories and Methods* (Lanham, MD: Lexington Books, 2004); Linda Tuhiwai Smith, *Decolonizing Methodologies: Research and Indigenous Peoples* (London and New York: Zed Books, 2006 [1999]), 208.

other end there are those who claim that scientific disciplines are a necessary starting point to understanding natural and social phenomena.[8] Social movements often represent specific sectional interests that reify disciplinary knowledge in the natural and social sciences—such as Greenpeace or the World Social Forum, or emerging environmental movements such as #RighttoBreathe in India or the UK-based Extinction Rebellion. Nevertheless, all share the view that scholarship must be creative and innovative if it is to promote just and equitable societies. These debates obscure a more fundamental question. Why should activist scholars be concerned about the primacy of practice over theory or vice versa? Activist scholars argue that the theory-practice relationship is important to unravel because it helps in understanding the ways in which knowledge can be empowering or disempowering. This argument is, in essence, an argument for improving the quality of knowledge by ironing out philosophical inconsistencies between various branches of knowledge or between the natural and social sciences in order to better affirm the theory-practice nexus. Does creativity mean doing scholarship differently? The debates conflate the scholar with scholarship. Activist scholarship focuses on the role of the scholar in society and overlooks the role of scholarship in providing access to ontological Reality. Can activist scholars glean insights from Rumi? Rumi decries disciplinary knowledge, but for different reasons. He writes:

> Because every pipe is connected with the reservoir.
> Dive, dive into (ponder deeply) the meaning of these words.
> (Consider) how the imperial grace of the homeless Spirit[9] has produced effects on the whole body;
> How the grace of Reason, which is of goodly nature, of goodly lineage, brings the entire body to discipline;
> How Love, saucy, uncontrolled, and restless, throws the whole body to madness.
> The purity of the water of the Sea that is like Kawthar (is such that) all its pebbles are pearls and gems.
> (I:2824–2827)
> For whatever science the master is renowned, the souls of his pupils become endued with the same.
> (I:2829)

Interdisciplinary approaches suggest that every underground water pipe is connected to every other pipe, as it were. No matter how much we uncover the network of pipes, this does not lead us to the reservoir that sustains all pipes. For activist scholars, that reservoir is Freedom. Disciplinary boundaries fetter our access to larger ontological truths. We fail to appreciate that Reason disciplines the body—and, we may add, the body politic. When the Spirit affects the whole body, it changes everything and transforms everything into unreason. We cannot privilege one type of knowledge over another, or one type of practice or theory, or prioritize any order, because, as Rumi says, "all the pebbles are pearls and gems." Activist scholarship limits knowledge to knowledge that can be accessed through reason. Rumi says that knowledge includes reason and unreason, the rational and the psychological dimensions of life, space-less/timeless and space-time contingent aspects. The mystique of Reason and Love animate the human spirit in every context and situation. We the scholars, Rumi says, circumscribe the souls of our students, the recipients of our knowledge, when we limit our knowledge to that which is accessible through reason alone. In activism and social movements, more than in any other social domain, the most transformative moments in human history have been moments when Reason was transcended and actions believed to be impossible became possible. Many large and small struggles that were predicted to fail based on reasoned analysis have succeeded. Mao's Long March was predicted to fail, as was the Bolshevik revolutions, or the defeat of Hitler in Stalingrad, or Vietnam's defeat of the biggest imperialist power. There are moments when the human spirit appears to confound Reason. Can activist scholars sharpen their sensitivity to the tempestuous attributes of freedom and emancipation? And if so, how? Rumi tells the story of a grammarian and a boatman:

> A grammarian once sat in a boat and asked to be ferried across a river. Appalled by the boatman's crude language he derided the boatman saying:

8 Roy Bhaskar, *The Possibility of Naturalism: A Philosophical Critique of Con- temporary Human Sciences* (London and New York: Routledge, 1998 [1979]), 194.

9 I.e., "the spirit, which has no spatial relations" (Nicholson's footnote).

"have you not studied any grammar at all?" "No" replied the boatman. "Half your life is wasted" the grammarian scolded. The boatman was quiet. Soon they were engulfed by a storm. "Have you never learned to swim?" the boatman asked the grammarian. "No," replied the grammarian. "Your entire life will be wasted," the boatman replied.

Stitching this story into his commentary, Rumi writes:

In self-loss,[10] O venerated friend, thou wilt find jurisprudence of jurisprudence, the grammar of grammar, and the accidence of accidence. (I:2847)

...

We are carrying jugs full (of water) to the Tigris: if we do not know ourselves to be asses, asses we are. (I:2849)

Here, language itself becomes an obstacle for the activist scholar, who is forced to work within the constraints of modernist languages of discourse. Modernist language segregates the language of philosophy and science from poetry and art. Rumi's boatman is the quintessential *fakir*. A *fakir* is literally a poor man, but also a mystic, a simpleton, an unassuming, unostentatious person, a humble person, someone who is not egotistical or self-centered. Thus, a *fakir* is not 'poor' or 'dispossessed,' standing in binary opposition to the rich or to the king or capitalism. The *fakir*, the boatman with appalling grammar, possesses attributes that help him weather the storms, attributes that the scholar lacks. At the activist end of the spectrum scholars recognize the attributes of the 'poor,' the 'working class,' or whatever, but require extensive footnotes and commentaries to articulate their thoughts.[11] While ideas are developed through epistemologies (scholarship), language has developed out of ontological/cosmological conceptions of the world that are more enduring.[12] By undermining ontology, modernist knowledge has introduced a hiatus between philosophy and literature, between science and the arts.

Activist scholars often work in creative and innovative ways and, like activists, are frequently criticized for their romanticism and utopianism. They must perforce choose the language of philosophy or the language of poetry, but not both. Consequently ontological knowledge, immanence and transcendence, become intellectualized as analytical categories distanced from the storms that engulf everyday life. Ontology is reduced to a problem for epistemological reflection and as such ceases to be the self-awareness that informs our ways of being in the world. It is as if we have lost our capacity to put our lives and our work into the larger perspectives of Life, Being, and human destiny.[13]

For the peoples of Asia and the Middle East, modernist language introduces another level of hiatus, a double disjuncture, as it were, between the psychological Self and the social Self. Fanon recognized this double disjuncture.[14] Their languages are grounded in a premodern ontology while their epistemology is modern. Modernist knowledge wrenches colonized subjects from the ontological premises of their languages and violates the depths of their Being.[15] To the extent that the poet-saint tradition nurtures that dismembered psychological Self it manifests as something 'spiritual.' To the extent that Western modernity forces its subjects to engage with their social Self in the language of philosophy and science, often foreign, it creates an uneasy relationship between their psychological Self and their social Self. Their unease manifests as discontent. Unease with the social world forces them to 'carry jugs of water to the Tigris' when their psychological Self knows that this makes 'asses' out of them.

Put the grammarian, the egotistical scholar, into the wider perspective of the infinity of Life, Rumi tells us. But he tells us this using syntax and grammar, using ghazals and ruba'is, carefully choosing his meter and rhyme. It is the ghazals that touch our hearts, transforming reason and logic into unreason and passion with transformative powers. The poet-saints of the East deliberately broke with the language of scholars to make philosophy accessible to ordinary people through combinations of poetry and stories. Rumi was one of the most celebrated scholars of his time. He gave up scholarship and academic positions altogether because he wanted to write for ordinary people. Rumi was accused by his peers of hanging out too much with "the tailors, the cloth-sellers and the petty

10 Literally, "in becoming less" (Nicholson's footnote).

11 Note the extensive footnotes that Nicholson needs to use to get across the message of the *Mathnavi*.

12 Clifford Geertz, *The Interpretations of Cultures: Selected Essays* (London: Fontana Press, 1993 [1973]).

13 I have capitalized words to signify an ontological as opposed to an ordinary level of meaning. Thus 'life' is used to convey ordinary meaning and 'Life' to convey ontological or transcendental meaning. So also other uses such as 'reality' and 'Reality,' 'self' and 'Self,' 'teacher' and 'Teacher,' and so on.

14 Frantz Fanon, *The Wretched of the Earth* (Harmondsworth: Penguin, 1990 [1961]), p. 255; Frantz Fanon, *Black Skin, White Masks* (London: Pluto, 2008 [1967]).

15 To the contrary, in premodern social movements the shared ontological premise of knowledge unified the arts and sciences. For the role of language in social movements in premodern times in India see A. K. Ramanujan, "Talking to God in the Mother Tongue," *Manushi* (1989): 9–14.

shopkeepers."[16] In India, Tulsidas wrote the *Ramayana* in vernacular verse (as opposed to classical Sanskrit) because he said he wanted to awaken the Ram that was in every *dhobi* (washerman) and *chamar* (cobbler).[17] Kabir sang to fellow weavers, and Bahinabai to housewives.

The poet-saints composed philosophy in verse. They did not abandon philosophy for poetry. Nor did they use poetry as a vehicle for philosophical contemplation. The poet-saints used words in activist ways to unravel Reality at all levels in order to unify the head and the heart. The activist scholar of today wishes to do the same: unify the minds and the hearts of people. The songs of Rumi and the Bhakti poet-saints of India have been sung everywhere in the East for centuries.[18] Sung over centuries by ordinary people, they infuse life into philosophy and make philosophy a living force. Their songs imbue ordinary people with a worldview and an outlook on life. Essentialist representations of nationalism, or reductionist representations like the 'Persian soul,' 'Islamic fundamentalism,' or the 'Hindu mind,' and catch-all terms like 'culture' fail to grasp what underlies the traits and attitudes that are captured by such essentialist characterizations, their material premise, as it were. The colonial representation of poet-saints as poets and not philosophers had two consequences. It recognized the dominant scholars in colonial societies—in contemporary terms 'the establishment' scholars—as the sole representatives of colonial subjects. Second, once dissident philosophers were 'downgraded' as poets it was an easy next step to brand popular resistances against the social order, including colonialism, as madness without intellectual foundation. Nevertheless, the songs of poet-saints define the psychological Self and the higher cosmic Self, unify the human with the Human (a higher humanity) in ways that aid people, de facto, to transcend the banality of everyday life, to sustain their humanity, and to resist the forces of oppression.

Of all the disciplinary divides of colonial modernity, the one between science and aesthetics has been the most devastating everywhere. The divide creates barriers in our capacities to unify our internal and external worlds in 'life' and Life. Social science speaks in the language of reason and intellect and produces its antithesis, the novel. Novels, the genre of modernity, speak the language of passion and the psyche. The poet-saint traditions recognized that language must unify thought and feelings, intellect and emotion, reason and passion in order for transformations in the individual and the world to occur. Nondualism requires finding ways of bringing together the immanent and transcendent in the human person and methods to unify the past and the future in the moment. To do this, philosophy had to switch to a different type of language from that of scholarship.

If the head and the heart speak in different tongues and genres how can the two be bridged? What language can the activist scholar invoke to be creative? The activist scholar's pathway to creative research and attempts to unify theory and practice face a roadblock from the outset.

Method and 'Madness'

At the heart of the theory-practice problematic is the transition from knowledge to action. Knowledge is an intellectual activity while action is driven by emotional and psychological motivators. At some point the heart must take over from the head for change to occur. Activist scholars assume that knowledge will lead to action and conversely attribute inaction to ignorance. Is there a necessary or logical connection between knowing and doing? Critical human rights scholars may not join a campaign to abolish the death sentence or to release political prisoners, and instead often remain indifferent to activism. A second type of person, who has little knowledge about human rights, may become an ardent campaigner. A third person, who is a distinguished human rights scholar, may also become an active campaigner. Activists are often disappointed or surprised by perceived gaps between the belief claims of people and their predisposition to act. Whatever the sociological and ethical explanations for such behavior, the fact remains that if there is no logical or necessary connection between knowing and doing, are activist scholars then right in assuming that good knowledge will lead to good action? Rumi's story of the drunken man and the police inspector provides

16 Afzal Iqbal, *The Life and Works of Jalauddin Rumi* (London: Octagon Press, 1983 [1956]).

17 See Amritlal Nagar's historical novel in Hindi, *Manas Ka Hans* (New Delhi: Rajpal and Sons, 1972), based on the life of the poet-saint Tulsidas.

18 On Bhakti poets in India see essays by A. K. Ramanujan in Vinay Dharwadker, ed., *The Collected Essays of A. K. Ramanujan* (New Delhi and New York: Ox- ford University Press, 1999).

some insights into the problem.

> A police inspector finds a drunken man lying along the wall. An argument ensues between them.
> "What did you drink?" the policeman asks. The man knows nothing about the properties of the drink except that it made him happy. "You are drunk," the inspector tells him; "get up—you are going to jail."
> Said the drunken man, "O Inspector, let me alone and go away. How is it possible to carry off pledges from one that is naked?
> If indeed I had the power to walk, I should have gone to my house—and (then) how would this (affair between us) have occurred?
> Were I (still) possessed of understanding and of contingent (unreal) existence, I should be on the bench, (giving instruction) like the Shaykhs." (II:2387–2391)

Knowing the rules, definitions, causes, and conditions of drunkenness is something entirely different from actually being drunk, which is not contingent on the knowledge of wine and its effects. A doctor knows a great deal about medicine but still falls ill just like anyone else with no knowledge of medicine.[19]

Indeed the powers that be, the police inspectors of this world, portray those who act, 'do the thing'—'get drunk' in Rumi's story—as 'mad.' Newspapers routinely refer to activists as irrational, unreasonable, 'loopy lefties,' 'weirdos,' and so on. Pictures of bra-burning women; tree-hugging, anti-logging activists; guitar-stringing 'peaceniks'; or suicide bombers are seldom represented as 'normal,' rational people. Rumi reverses dominant perceptions and ridicules the policeman instead. The policeman could see that the man is drunk and yet commands him to walk to jail as if his command could override the effect of drunkenness. Finding happiness in drunkenness, joy in renunciation, and fulfillment in activism requires the grasp of another more fundamental reality, namely that the human Spirit is not contained by or even contingent on scholarship. Scholarship is only one form of knowledge and by no means the exclusive repository of all knowledge.

Scholarship is about method; it is about interrogating the objects of knowledge, subjecting them to rigorous investigation, testing and evaluating according to the rules of inquiry that scholars set for themselves. Activism is about transcending method, about 'madness,' to be drunk in preference to knowing about the properties of wine. Rumi argues that the non-method, the 'madness,' does not stem from ignorance. To the contrary, it is a superior knowledge because it is a knowledge that transcends the intellect and grasps intuitively the human Spirit. As Rumi points out, intellect and reason are necessary but not sufficient conditions for transformative action. Intellectual knowledge takes us so far and no farther. There comes a point when there must be a reversal of roles between reason and unreason, intellect and intuition. Rumi says:

> When a man's understanding has been his teacher, after this his understanding becomes pupil.
> The understanding says, like Gabriel, "O Ahmad (Mohammad), if I take one (more) step, it will burn me;
> Do thou leave me, henceforth advance (alone): this is my limit, O sultan of the soul!" (I : 1065–1067)

Activist scholarship seeks to establish equivalence between scholarship and activism, knowledge and action, and put them on par in a reciprocal relationship. In contrast, Rumi invites us to consider them in an evolutionary order where the human mind transcends instinct, then intellect, then intuition. 'Madness' is a mature intellect that gives up method *because of its very maturity*. This is a profound difference and one that prompts us to reexamine the ways in which reason and unreason, method and 'madness' play out in emancipation. Irrationality, far from being a deviation from the normal, may have a positive role to play in keeping the flag of human freedom fluttering.[20]

Emancipation and Knowledge

Emancipation requires two types of knowledge: a knowledge of constraint, the cage that imprisons us, and a knowledge of how to be free, how to get out of the cage. Knowledge of constraint does not automatically or logically or necessarily show the way to freedom. Rumi highlights what is entailed in

19 Iqbal, *The Life and Works of Jalauddin Rumi*.

20 R. D'Souza, "How Shall We Remember Madan Lal Dhingra?" *Sanhati* (Kolkatta, India, 2010).

going from one type of knowledge to the other in his story of the parrot and the merchant (I:1547–1574; 1587– 1602; 1649–1658; 1691–1825–1848).

A merchant had a parrot that he loved and kept in a golden cage. He had bought the parrot in India on one of his business trips. When he set off on another business trip to India he asked his slaves, his handmaidens, and his parrot what they wanted from India. The slaves and handmaidens asked for different presents. His parrot said: "tell my fellow parrots in India I long to be free, tell them it is very unfair that they should fly in freedom while I live in this golden cage." When the merchant conveyed this message to the parrots in India, one of them collapsed and became motionless. The merchant thought the Indian parrot had died. He regretted conveying the message and unwittingly causing the parrot's death. When he returned home he told his caged parrot about what transpired. His parrot, too, collapsed and became motionless. Believing his parrot to be dead the merchant threw it out of the cage. No sooner was it out of the cage than it swiftly flew up, perched at a height, and looked down at the merchant. The distraught merchant asked the meaning of the Indian parrot's message. The parrot replied:

> She by her act counseled me–"Abandon the charm of voice and thy affection (for thy master),
> Because thy voice has brought thee into bondage": she feigned herself dead for the sake of (giving me) this counsel,
> Meaning (to say), "O thou who hast become a singer to high and low, become dead like me, that thou mayst gain release." (I:1830–1832)

Activist scholars focus on constraints, the cages that imprison ordinary people in various economic, political, and social institutions. They highlight the structures and sources of oppression and injustice and provide reasons for opposing various political and social practices. About their own 'cages,' the academic institutions, there is a positional ambivalence. Most activist scholars argue that it is possible to make use of the institutional spaces to develop 'movement relevant theory' or people-oriented public policy.[21] This qualified affirmation of institutional spaces keeps them 'caged' in, and activist scholarship itself emerges as the Manichean other to neoliberal transformations sweeping through academic institutions. It keeps activist scholarship trapped in a dualist and adversarial position, limiting the possibilities of transcendence. The dualist, oppositional, institutional context colors the forms of knowledge, the way problems are framed, the structure of knowledge, the disciplinary boundaries and concept formations, and produces what postcolonial scholars call the 'reverse gaze.' The very desire of activist scholars for emancipation embeds them deeper in knowledge institutions and prevents them from thinking through freedom and emancipation as ontological attributes of Reality at all levels. Activist scholars end up advocating for better rules of scholarship instead of freedom and ways of transcending the gaps between knowledge and action.[22]

What Rumi is telling us is to give up the very things we have come to love. The very generosity of the merchants of knowledge that we depend on stops us from making the transition from intellect to intuition. The revolutionary transformations of the early twentieth century were grounded in the most advanced theories of the times. The theoretical developments then current (which continue to influence theory and practice today) rarely developed within the existing dominant institutional contexts. Often they developed under conditions of extreme repression.

Miscommunications occur at every stage in the transition from knowledge of emancipation to the actual act of emancipating oneself, as Rumi's story illustrates. The merchant says one thing; the Indian parrot understands it as something else. The merchant thinks he caused the Indian parrot's death; the Indian parrot has something else in mind. The merchant does not discern the meaning of the message when he repeats it to his parrot, but his parrot grasps it straightaway. Activist scholars emphasize communication but do not give as much attention to misunderstanding (serendipity). Yet, history is testimony to the fact that wars were won or lost on miscommunication, and every activist will have stories of serendipity to tell in the success or defeat of their struggles.

21 Bevington and Dixon, "Movement Relevant Theory."

22 Radha D'Souza, "The Prison Houses of Knowledge: Activist Scholarship and Revolution in the Era of 'Globalisation,'" *McGill Journal of Education* 44, 1 (2009): 1–20.

Activists know that the outcomes of struggles are invariably unpredictable, but activists continue to struggle even when they know this. It is possible to argue that their actions are based on their faith in the justness of their cause. However, to say that activists persevere because of their faith says little about faith or their stamina to persevere. Is it possible that the source of their faith and perseverance stems from a taste of ontological freedom, Rumi's intuitive knowledge, which informs how activists are in the world, and points to their implicit awareness of Being?

Ontological awareness must lead to methodological practice in ways that help us reconceptualize Freedom. Grounded this way in ontology it is possible to argue that the struggle for life (survival) is an ontological attribute of all Life (ontological Reality). Following from this Reality, emancipation is a necessary attribute of society (social Reality), and the desire for freedom is an attribute of being human (psychological Reality). The growing emphasis on ontology in social theory ought to point to the inevitability of struggles for freedom, not because of determinism, but because it is an attribute of the ontological Reality, social Reality, and psychological reality of cosmological, social, and human life. This means that regardless of our theories and the consistencies or inconsistencies of our arguments, human beings as social beings will rebel against injustice, and their struggles will be informed by the specific forms that oppression takes in any geo-historical context. To be the handmaiden of emancipation, knowledge in specific geo-historical contexts must be consistent with the empirical/everyday world and ontological/cosmic Life. Activists grasp this Reality intuitively. Activist scholars are trapped in a paradox, however. Being activists, they too grasp that freedom and emancipation stem from deeper ontological truths about the nature of Being. The requirements of scholarship, however, introduce a tension in activist scholarship.

Scholarly knowledge, activist or otherwise, cannot accommodate that which is indeterminate, unknowable, infinite, or absent, except as an abstract theoretical idea, because scholarship is about certainty, about knowing, about the finite, and that which is present. Any talk of the unknown, the absent, the infinite, or the indeterminate becomes unscholarly, something mystical. Mysticism is usually cast in antithetical terms to reason and seen as the source of faith.[23] This representation of faith cuts it adrift from humanity and reason and gives it the appearance of something blind and inhuman (supernatural). Conversely, it limits freedom to something that remains within the bounds of Reason. If ontology is about Being then it follows that ontological awareness transforms the way we are in the world, how we see, act, and be in the world. Equally, it could be said that ontological understanding is implicit in the way we are in the world. Can we make it explicit though? The poet-saints did just that.

For Rumi, the mystical is an invitation to action and struggle, a gauntlet that must be picked up:

> Do thou arise and blow on the terrible trumpet,
> that thousands of the dead may spring up from the earth.
> Since thou art the upright-rising Israfil (Seraphiel) of the time, make a resurrection ere the Resurrection.
> O beloved if one say, "Where is the Resurrection?"
> show thyself, saying, "Behold, I am the Resurrection.
> Look, O questioner who are stricken with tribulation,
> (and see) that from this resurrection a hundred worlds have grown!"
> (IV : 1478–1481)

What is it that impels us to pick up the gauntlet, to step forward and say to the doubter, the 'questioner': "I am That, I am the proof and the participant, the subject and the object, the route and the destination"? A very different type of knowledge is needed to pick up the gauntlet, to be free and to fly from the cages that imprison us. Knowledge that addresses the intellect, that focuses on difference, explanations, causality, and such, does not provide knowledge of actions, why and how we act, what propels action and where. Action is beyond the realm of the intellect and belongs to the realm of emotion and the psyche. How do we transcend the realm of the intellect and enter the realm of intuition and passion?

For Rumi, Love is the key to action. Love is what helps us to transcend the knowledge of constraints, the cage that

23 King, *Orientalism and Religion*. Hence the impression of activists as idealists or out of the ordinary or 'weirdos.'

imprisons us, and to know how to be free, how to fly out of the cage.

Love and Knowledge

Why is it that some of us feel impelled to act when we see injustice, while others are content to stay on safer ground as witnesses from a distance, and yet others pro- actively defend the status quo. This point is pertinent for activist scholars. When workers go on strike, or when displaced peasants protest eviction from their lands, some support the workers and peasants and others the employers and landowners even though they are neither workers or peasants nor employers or landowners themselves. Both parties appeal to a higher ethic. The workers appeal to people's sense of fairness when they ask for fair wages, and the employer appeals to their sense of community by arguing that the strikers deprive people of cheap goods and services; the peasants speak of the unfairness of their eviction, the landowners of the need for economic development. Yet the question remains, why do the arguments of the workers and peasants appeal to some of us and the arguments of the employers and landowners to others?

Activist scholars invoke ethical and moral arguments to bridge the gap between knowledge and action and invite us to choose a superior ethic. All dualism requires conceptual bridging of some type. If the aim of activist scholars is to unify knowledge and action, then the appeal to a higher morality, a superior ethic, does the opposite: it reifies the knowledge-action dualism. Furthermore, the appeal to intellect does not guarantee that ideas will have a transformative effect. Marx said that when ideas grip the masses they become a material force. Can the appeals of activist scholars to superior reason infuse ideas with materiality and give these ideas transformative power—make people 'just do it'?[24] What can activist scholars learn from Rumi?

For Rumi, Love is the life force that animates, energizes, and activates everything. Love is not an idea capable of philosophical comprehension as an object of knowledge. It is not a philosophical category comparable to Beauty, Truth, Goodness, or Perfection, nor is it a unifying principle or a cosmological principle or a mediator between two contending forces, nor is it the arbiter between good and evil.[25] We cannot articulate Love in words or comprehend it, but we know it exists because of its transformative powers. However, Love does not exist in opposition to knowledge and reason or as something antithetical to it. Grasping its existence and its ways calls for higher, more advanced knowledge:

> By love bitter things become sweet; by love pieces of copper become golden;
> By love dregs become clear; by love pain become healing;
> By love the dead is made living; by love the king is made slave.
> This love, moreover, is the result of knowledge: who (ever) sat in foolishness[26] on such a throne?
> On what occasion did deficient knowledge give birth to this love?
> Deficient (knowledge) gives birth to love, but (only love) for that which is (really) lifeless.
> When it sees in a lifeless being the colour (appearance) of a desired one, ('tis as though) it heard the voice of a beloved in a whistle.
> Deficient knowledge cannot discriminate: of necessity it deems the lightning to be the sun.
> (II:1529–1535)

Love transforms nature; it transforms the way we see phenomena, the way we experience the world, yet it remains invisible. It provides us with the capacity to discriminate between the light of a candle and the light of the sun. What exactly is Love, though? Rumi replies:

> Then what is Love? The Sea of Non-Being: there the foot of the intellect is shattered.[27]
> Servitude and sovereignty are known: loverhood is concealed by these two veils.
> Would that Being had a tongue, that it might remove the veils from existent beings!
> O breath of (phenomenal) existence, whatsoever words thou mayest utter, know that thereby thou

24 D'Souza, "The Prison Houses of Knowledge."

25 Khalifa Abdul Hakim, *The Metaphysics of Rumi: A Critical and Historical Sketch* (Lahore: Institute of Islamic Culture, 1965).

26 I.e., "When did he (the fool!) in his vanity sit on such a throne?" (Nicholson's footnote).

27 I.e., "the intellect is unable to swim in that Sea" (Nicholson's footnote).

> hast bound another veil upon it (the mystery)
> That utterance and (that) state (of existence) are the bane of (spiritual) perception: to wash away blood with blood is absurd, absurd. (III:4723–4727)

Love is "Non-Being," that which is not (absent), that which is yet to be (come into being). As the absent Non-Being, Love transcends and subsumes paradoxes. It can only be lived and experienced. When we experience something and speak about it, we speak about the effect produced by our action, not the impulse that is the action. The phenomenal world can only swap one veil for another. Love is life's mystery, its greatest secret, that which makes life immanent and transcendent and unites the psychological Self with the ontological Self. Our capacities to wonder, to be amazed, to be confounded and surprised, to hope and fear, to laugh and cry, to be heroic and cowardly, to be inspired and depressed, to reach out to the sun with an immediacy, cannot be explained with words; it can only be experienced. Living means being open to the experience, to be receptive and sensitive to the unknown.

Love as Non-Being transforms the way we are in the world. When transformed by it we see the world differently. For those who speak about Love, Non-Being, ontology, and so forth without actually being in the world differently, their knowledge of these things is at best deficient.

> O balmer (of lovers), safety be thine! O seeker of safety, thou art infirm.[28]
> My soul is a furnace: it is happy with the fire; 'tis enough for the furnace that it is the fire's house.
> For Love, as (for) the furnace, there is something to be burned:[29] any one that is blind to this is not a furnace. (II:1375–1377)

To do is to Be; and to act is to be alive.

Where do these insights from Rumi leave the contemporary activist scholar? The kings under whom Rumi lived were despots. In his time despots demanded the bodies and minds of their subjects. The despots under whom the poet-saints lived could torment them psychologically and create social hardships for them, but they had no way of claiming their ontological Self, that substratum of Life we call Being. Activist scholars live under a 'market despotism' that demands Being itself, the very premise of our souls, our ontological Self. Activist scholars may speak what they wish, criticize, radicalize, internationalize, revolutionize things, be capitalist or communist or obscurantist—anything will do as long as what they do sells, as long as they obey the Market's diktats.[30] If the knowledge markets like activist scholarship, if it translates into metric values and monetary returns for the knowledge institutions, into funding grants and projects on social movements, it survives, not otherwise. Activist scholars are thrown into a catch-22 situation of means and ends: serve the Market to critique it, or critique the Market to serve it.[31]

What are activist scholars to do? Are they to abandon scholarship and become activists? Are they to become poets and wandering minstrels like the poet-saints? The poet-saints may have been their forerunners as activist scholars, but do the activist scholars not live in a vastly different historical and institutional context? It is possible to make a tentative beginning in developing an approach to the way these questions are answered by trying to grasp what the poet-saints *actually did*. What were their aims, their 'research objectives' and 'research methods,' if we wish to call them that?

Everyday Life, Love, and Knowledge

The poet-saints used words in activist ways to unify different levels of Reality: the psychological, social, and ontological. They sought to make knowledge accessible to ordinary people in ways that appealed to their heads and their hearts. In other words they transformed philosophy into common sense and an attitude to life.

In contrast, the activist scholar's heart is with the activists, and their head is with the scholars. The personality of the activist scholar becomes torn between head and heart, between method and 'madness,' reason and unreason. Often the activist scholar acts as a scholar to the activist and as an activist to the scholar—or remains equidistant from both. As a result the activist scholar fails to develop an autonomous identity. Who is the activist scholar writing for? The conventional scholar is

28 Literally, "having weak stays or handles" (Nicholson's footnote).

29 I.e., "the dross of sensual qualities" (Nicholson's footnote).

30 Incite! *Women of Colour against Violence: The Revolution Will Not Be Funded: Beyond the Non-profit Industrial Complex* ([Cambridge, MA:] South End Press, 2007), 256. Listen also to soul musician Gil Scott-Heron's songs "The Revolution will Not Be Televised" (". . . the revolution will be very loud") and "Who'll Pay Reparations on My Soul," in the album *A New Black Poet Gil Scott-Heron: Small Talk at 125th and Lenox* (Flying Dutchman/RCA, 1970; reissued as CD, 2001).

31 The problem of means and ends in activism, scholarship, and activist scholarship is problematic in its own right and merits proper consideration at another time. See Radha D'Souza, "Rights, Action, Change: Organize for What?" in Aziz Choudry, Jill Hanley, and Eric Shragge, eds., *Organize! Building from the Local for Global Justice* (Montreal: PM Press, 2012), 71–81.

clear on this count: they write for fellow scholars. The activists act. And the activist scholar?

Activist scholars at the activism end of the spectrum begin with everyday life as their point of departure and make the connections to social and institutional structures at the next level of social Reality.[32] They are, however, unable to make connections with the next level of ontological Reality. Scholarship more generally looks down on everyday life, treating it as something banal. The treatment of knowledge from everyday life as inferior or unprocessed knowledge justifies and rationalizes the specialist knowledge of scholars as something superior and valuable, and authorizes the use of the specialist's 'superior' language of scholarship. When scholars turn to everyday life, it is to transform everyday life into an object of philosophical contemplation. By objectifying it in this way they strip everyday life of the flesh and blood that sustain it. In emphasizing differences, opposites, contrasts, disputations, and contradictions they are unable to experience and promote Love, the life force that unifies everything and keeps the world going.

One of the salient features of modernist knowledge is its dismissal of stories. Modernist knowledge takes the demeaning of everyday life to extremes by reducing it to numbers, statistics, and generalizations; in other words it averages out human experience. The human spirit is thereby expunged from the accounts of the world. In fact, everyday life is the site where all levels of Reality, the psychological, the social, and the ontological, and all types of knowledge, converge. Thus, everyday life is a site of unification and the site where transcendence occurs.

Poet-saints reveled in stories from everyday life. Not only did they draw their inspiration from it, they broke with the methods of prevalent scholarship that relied on logical reasoning and conceptual abstractions removed from everyday life. Poet- saints developed a dialogic method that was very different from scholarly disputations. They advanced their dialogic method by interrogating the relationship between the three levels of the Self—psychological, social, and ontological. They sought out the universal within themselves and marveled at the particularities of the world around them. In order to unify the inner and outer worlds they took everyday life as their source of inspiration and the point of departure for their philosophy. From stories of everyday life they drew out the universal, everlasting nature of Reality, Life, and Existence. To this day their teachings remain intelligible to ordinary people for that very reason.

Poet-saints insisted that Being must dictate knowledge—ontology must lead epistemology—not the other way around. It is not enough to talk about Being and ontology; it is more important to walk the talk, as it were, to produce knowledge that is premised on reflexivity and awareness of Being and Reality. In this the poet-saints broke with the methods of scholarship and innovated new and creative ways of realizing their twin goals: making philosophy accessible to ordinary people and unifying different levels of Reality in nondualist ways. In doing so their works appealed to the heads and hearts of ordinary people. Above all, by turning to everyday life as an inexhaustible source of living stories, as Life's treasury, they unified theory and practice, the universal and the particular, the global and the local, in ways that ensured that philosophy would be supplied with inexhaustible resources upon which to draw.

Stories from everyday life help to describe, explain, and justify human experiences as well as to illuminate, reveal, and inspire. They provide knowledge of the world without snuffing out its mysteries. Stories provide analogies and metaphors that help us uncover layers of meaning, overcome dualities, and understand Reality in ways that inspire us to act. The poet-saints saw the purpose of their writings as being to help people transcend the difficult barrier between intellect and intuition that lies in the transition from knowledge to action.

Activist scholars seek to break with the modernist rules of scholarship—the re- search methods—but only to redefine them and reinstate them. A fleeting moment of dissidence becomes fossilized and lifeless after the moment has passed. For Rumi, it is the seeking itself that is evidence of the seeker's quest for Love, the life force we see around us every day. The 'research objective' is not to prove or disprove propositions but to unravel the mystery of life, what keeps it going, and our

32 George W. Smith, "Political Activist as Ethnographer," in Frampton et al., *Sociology for Changing the World*.

place in the larger schema of Life's majesty. Seeking is in itself evidence of the Love that unites our social Self with the cosmic Self. As Rumi says:

> In whatsoever state thou be, keep searching; O thou with dry lip, always be seeking the water,
> For that dry lip of thine gives evidence that at last it will reach the spring-head. Dryness of lip is a message from the water (to say) that this agitation (anxious search) will certainly bring thee to the water, ...[33]
> (III : 1439–1440)
> This search is the key to the things sought by thee; this (search) is thy army and the victory of thy banners.
> This search is like chanticleer crowing and proclaiming that the dawn is at hand. (III : 1443–1444)

The Activist Scholar as 'Activist Teacher'

Contemporary social theory remains preoccupied with power and knowledge.[34] This is even more so in activist scholarship that is oriented toward the redistribution of power through knowledge. The poet-saint traditions did not concern themselves with the transfer of power between social groups or culture and knowledge. Instead, poet-saints emphasized the *regeneration* of the 'self.' Regeneration of the 'self' is the condition precedent for transformative action. Scholarship may unravel structural conditions and mechanisms that generate oppression. At the human and psychological level oppression belittles and crushes the 'self'; it destroys the intrinsic self-worth of the oppressed person.[35] Belittling the 'self' is what sustains oppression, something Fanon discovered working as a psychologist in the colonial context of the Algerian struggle for national liberation. When the 'self' is restored and regenerated the person becomes *capable* of taking on power and cultural oppression. Self-worth is a non-dualistic state that comes with the unity of the psychological Self with the ontological Self, or, more simply, the unity of the individual human being with universal Humanity. A charismatic leader may intuitively grasp the structural class oppression and act to restore the self-worth of the oppressed in society through personal conduct, excellent oratory, and so forth, but this occurs fortuitously without a knowledge base that can provide guidance.

Activist scholars face a predicament. If they become participants in social movements they become embroiled in the organizational nitty-gritty, including the everyday politics, factions, and internal wrangling that are part of any social activity. They lose their capacity to develop 'movement relevant theory.' If on the other hand they stay away from social movements they become disengaged scholars.[36] Poet-saints did not face such predicaments.

Poet-saints were scholars who understood and played the role of 'activist teachers' in society. Their role was to 'show the way', to guide people from theory to action. They taught people 'how to be in the world' and believed that the transition from intellectual to intuitive knowledge was not possible without guidance. This is because going from theory to action, from intellect to intuition, is invariably a leap from the known to the unknown, from 'what is' to 'what is not yet.' Such leaps into that which has not yet come into being are at the heart of transformative action.

Rumi, like other poet-saints, gave teachers a preeminent place in life. 'Activist teachers' are more important than scholarship because 'activist teachers' illuminate the way and infuse life into prosaic scholarship. Real knowledge is contingent on finding an enlightened teacher:

> Choose a Pir, for without a Pir this journey is exceeding full of woe and affright and danger.
> Without an escort you are bewildered (even) on a road you have travelled many times (before):
> Do not, then, travel alone on a Way that you have not seen at all, do not turn your head away from the Guide. (I:2943–2945)

No doubt one must choose one's teachers carefully. As Rumi says:

> Look long on the face of every one, keep watch attentively: it may be that by doing service (to Sufis) you will come to know the face (of the true saint).
> Since there are many a devil who hath the face of

33 Or, "bring thee to us (to me)" (Nicholson's footnote).

34 Uberoi, *The European Modernity*, 143.

35 For a humane psychological depiction of how oppression belittles the self see the story by Lu Xun, "The True Story of Ah Q," in Lu Xun, *Call to Arms* (Beijing: Foreign Languages Press, 1981 [1922]).

36 Bevington and Dixon, "Movement Relevant Theory"; The Autonomous Geographies Collective: Paul Chatterton, Stuart Hodkinson, and Jenny Pickerill, "Beyond Scholar Activism: Making Strategic Interventions Inside and Outside the Neoliberal University," *ACME: An International E-Journal for Critical Geographies* 9, 2 (2010): 245–275.

Adam, it is not well to give your hand to every hand,
Because the fowler produces a whistling sound in order to decoy the bird,[37]
(So that) the bird may hear the note of its congener and come down from the air and find trap and knife-point. (I:315–318)

'Activist teachers' become one through the role they play in society; it is recognition by society that comes from society because of their value to society. Poet-saints emphasized renunciation as a way of life. By renunciation they did not mean withdrawal from society.[38] To the contrary, they remained actively engaged in society. Renunciation meant withdrawing from social institutions of power and knowledge, for example from public office, and limiting economic activity to minimal personal subsistence where necessary. Self-sacrifice was therefore an important value for the 'activist teacher.' This role contrasts with the role of the public intellectual in modern societies, which is premised on the public/private binary. The public intellectual is embedded in the power–knowledge equation. The public intellectual stands in opposition to institutions of state power and seeks to curtail public power through scholarship produced in knowledge institutions.[39]

Rumi gave up his influential academic position and scholarly writing. Typical of the poet-saint traditions, Rumi insisted on being a teacher with a message. He wrote the *Masnavi* for that purpose alone. And he chose his words, their structure, and their syntax in a way that was effective in conveying his message. In Rumi's words:

Does any painter paint a beautiful picture[40] for the sake of the picture itself, without hopes of conferring benefits?
Nay, (he paints it) for the sake of guests and young people who by diverting themselves (with it) may be relieved from cares.
From his picture (arises) the joy of children and the remembering of departed friends by their friends.
Does any potter make a pot in haste for the sake of the pot and not in hope of the water?
Does any calligrapher write artistically for the sake of the writing itself and not for the sake of the reading?
The external form is for the sake of the unseen form; and that took shape for the sake of another unseen (form).
Count up these corollaries to the third, fourth, or tenth in proportion to (your) insight.
As (for example) the moves in chess, O son: behold the results of each move in the next one.
They made this (move) for the sake of that concealed move, and that for the next, and that (again) for such and such. (IV : 2881–2890)

'Activist teachers' do not see knowledge and skills in instrumentalist ways. 'Activist teachers' *foresee* the outcomes concealed in what they write and speak. The 'external form is for the sake of the unseen form,' as with a chess player who sees the next move in each move that is made. They unify the message and the medium, and sow the seeds of freedom and the desire for emancipation such that what they sow becomes immanent in the actions of people in the future.

Uberoi writes:

[D]uopoly or the dualism of the European modernity, i.e. of fact and value, truth and reality, theory and praxis, howsoever efficient in calculation or enlightened in intention, is altogether bad for humanity because a person whose head, heart or hand (so to say) habitually acts without first consulting with the other two organs is very likely sooner or later to produce something misshapen or horrible, either an Auschwitz or a Hiroshima or both, whether this process of faith, knowledge and action appears as expediency (the end justifies the means) or alternatively as technicism (the means justifies the end).[41]

Activist scholars want, more than anything else, to avert Holocausts and Hiroshimas. To do this effectively they need to confront the fundamental premises of contemporary European modernity. It is not possible to return to the same 'duopoly' for knowledge, conceptual resources, and insights to find solutions to overcome it. Einstein famously said that no

37 Literally, "in order that the bird-catcher may decoy" (Nicholson's footnote).

38 J. P. S. Uberoi, *Religion, Civil Society, and the State: A Study of Sikhism* (Delhi and New York: Oxford University Press, 1996).

39 Ulrich Oslender, "The Resurfacing of the Public Intellectual: Towards the Proliferation of Public Spaces of Critical Intervention," *ACME: An International E-Journal for Critical Geographies* 6 (2007): 98–123.

40 Literally, "the beauty of the pictures" (Nicholson's footnote).

41 Uberoi, *The European Modernity*, 143.

problem can be solved from the same level of consciousness that created it. For this reason, if nothing else, activist scholars need to look further afield to intellectual traditions that have advocated nondualistic, 'counter-Enlightenment' approaches to social problems. Shorn of the verbiage of activist scholarship, of academic jargon, may it not be that deep down the activist scholar longs to be an 'activist teacher' treating the 'world as our classroom'?[42] That activist scholars are 'activist teachers' in search of a message and a medium? That the activist scholar is a teacher imprisoned by the iron walls of scholarship? How else can we break out of the prison except by 'just doing it'?[43]

42 David Austin, "Education and Liberation," *McGill Journal of Education* 44, 1 (2009): 107–118.

43 D'Souza, "The Prison Houses of Knowledge."

Radha D'Souza is critical scholar, writer, lawyer, and social justice activist from India. She teaches law at the University of Westminster in London, UK. She is co-producer of art projects *Court for Intergenerational Climate Crimes* (Amsterdam, 2021) and *Comrades Against Extinction* (Helsinki, 2022), and *Extinction Wars* (2023) based on her book *What's Wrong with Rights?* (Pluto Press, 2018).

ehab lotayef

i created you

I created you   a secret
and ordered you: Go
when your path is blocked
                                        Halt
but just for a moment
then go again

I created you   a mystery
and ordered you: Speak
when ears are shut
                                        Hush
but just for a moment
then speak again

I created you   a dream
and your dream was to conquer the universe

To see what has been and what never was
from the dawn of existence
to the edge of time

I created you
a lousy excuse
for a mistake that wasn't yours

إيهاب لُطيّف

خلقتُك

خلقتُك سِراً
أمرتك: سِـرْ
وحينَ يُسَدُ الطريقُ
توقف
ولكن للحظة
وعد للمسير

خلقتُك لغزاً
أمرتك: قُـلْ
وحين تُسدُ المسامعُ
اصمت
ولكن للحظة
وعد للكلام

خلقتُك حُلماً
وحُلمُكَ أن تستحل المكان

ترى ما يكون وما لم يكن
من بدء الوجودِ
لطرفِ الزمان

خلقتُك عذراً
قبيحاً
لذنبٍ لم تقترفه

read by the poet

I created you
a cruel revenge
for a crime you didn't commit

Yet you rise
and from you emerges
the meaning of life
and the essence of existence

Eons pass by
you wither
  and die

and I create
  a new secret
      a new mystery
          a new dream

And I order:
        Go

September 2018

خلقتُك ثأراً
غشيماً
لجرمٍ لم ترتكبه

لكنك تسمو
ومنك يفيض
فَهمُ الحياةِ
ووعيُ الوجود

وتمضي الدهورُ
وتذبُل
وتفنى

وأخلُقُ بعدَك
سراً جديداً
ولغزاً جديداً
وحُلماً جديداً

وآمره :
سِرْ

٢٧ سبتمبر ٢٠١٨

Ehab Lotayef is a poet, writer, activist, and IT Manager at McGill University in Montreal. He moved to Canada from Egypt in 1989 with a degree in electrical and computer engineerig. He has volunteered with and served on the boards of many local and international NGOs. His publications include the bilingual poetry collection *To Love a Palestinian Woman* (2010), the play *Crossing Gibraltar* (CBC, 2006), and numerous op-eds and articles in Canadian papers.

rumi

ghazal 648

Ahoy pilgrims who are on the road to *Hajj*[1]   where are you   where
  Come back   come   the beloved is right here
Your beloved is your neighbour   wall to wall
  Lost in the desert   what illusion are you under
If you could see the beloved's   formless countenance
  you would see   that you are the *Ka'be*[2]   the house and the master
So many times   you walked that road   to that house
  Come into this house for once   climb onto this roof
That house is pleasant   you have recited its signs
  Now show me   the signs of its master
Where is the bouquet   if you have seen that garden
  Where is the soul's pearl   if you have come from the creator's sea
In spite of all this   may your toil be your trove
  Alas   you are the veil   hiding your treasure

1 The annual pilgrimage to Mecca mandatory for all adult Muslims who have the financial means and physical ability for the journey.

2 Also transliterated as *Kaaba*, a cubic stone 'house' considered to be the *gheble* (*qibla*) for Muslims throughout the world, and the *Bayt Allah*, the House of God. It is at the centre of the Masjid al-Haram in Mecca, Saudi Arabia, and the site of the annual *Hajj* pilgrimage.

read by charles c. smith

translated by gita hashemi

مولوی

غزل ۶۴۸

Ey ghowm-e be haj rafte kojāyid kojāyid
    Ma'shugh haminjāst biyāyid biyāyid
Ma'shugh-e tow hamsāye-o divār be divār
    Dar bādiye sargashte shomā dar che havā-yid
Gar surat-e bisurat-e ma'shugh bebinid
    Ham khāje-o ham khane-o ham ka'be shomā-yid
Dah bār az ān rāh bedān khāne beraftid
    Yek bār az in khāne bar in bām barāyid
Ān khāne latifast neshānhāsh begoftid
    az khāje-ye ān khāne neshāni benamāyid
Yek daste-ye gol ku agar ān bāgh bedidid
    Yek gowhar-e jān ku agar az bahr-e khodā-yid
Bā in hame ān ranj-e shomā ganj-e shomā bād
    Afsus ke bar ganj-e shomā parde shomā-yid

ای قوم به حج رفته کجایید کجایید
    معشوق همین جاست بیایید بیایید
معشوق تو همسایه و دیوار به دیوار
    در بادیه سرگشته شما در چه هوایید
گر صورت بی‌صورت معشوق ببینید
    هم خواجه و هم خانه و هم کعبه شمایید
ده بار از آن راه بدان خانه برفتید
    یک بار از این خانه بر این بام برآیید
آن خانه لطیفست نشان‌هاش بگفتید
    از خواجهٔ آن خانه نشانی بنمایید
یک دستهٔ گل کو اگر آن باغ بدیدید
    یک گوهر جان کو اگر از بحر خدایید
با این همه آن رنج شما گنج شما باد
    افسوس که بر گنج شما پرده شمایید

travel boutique | izmir, near basmane station, april 18, 2016 | from the series *nth movement*, part of the *declarations diptych* | gita hashemi | 2016

http://hdl.handle.net/10315/41086

open fields

oneness of being, 4 | gita hashemi | 2022

recorded at bellamy ravine and scarborough bluffs, unceded territory of the mississauga of the credit first nation

From these confined prisons   my heart   you have a path to the open fields
    Are your feet so numb   that you imagine you don't have feet
You close your eyes and ask   where is the bright day
    The sun knocks on your eyelids and says   here I am   open now

Rumi, ghazal 54

دلا زین تنگ زندان‌ها رهی داری به میدان‌ها
    مگر خفته‌ست پای تو تو پنداری نداری پا
تو دو دیده فروبندی و گویی روز روشن کو
    زند خورشید بر چشمت که اینک من تو در بگشا

مولوی، غزل ۵۴

Delā zin tang zendān-hā rahi dāri be meydān-hā
    magar khoftast pay-e tow tow pendāri nadāri pā
Tow dow dide foru bandi-yo guyi ruz-e rowshan ku
    zanad khorshid bar cheshmat ke inak man tow dar bogshā

credits and acknowledgements

rumi roaming voices reading their own or Rumi's poetry: Radha D'Souza | Jayce Salloum | Trish Salah | Ehab Lotayef | Hajar Hussaini | Öykü Tekten | Elena Basile | Mahdi Tourage | charles c. smith | Zainab Amadahy | Gita Hashemi

between shadow and light performers: charles c. smith | Meryem Alaoui
Cameras: Kourtney Jackson | Zahra Saleki | Gita Hashemi | Maju Tavera (documentation) — Production support: Amira Alamary | Jon Vanneste

broken hands and feet performers: Nika Khanjani (director) | May Panah | Roxana Khanjani Rosadiuk

Book design consultation: Haleh Niazmand | Lauren Wickware | Allen Jomoc Jr.

CFP translators: Lida Nosrati (Persian) | Olivia Tapiero (French)

Early-stage book development with: Elena Basile | Bilal Hashmi

Publishing consultants: Elena Basile | Anjula Gogia

YorkSpace digital archive data management: Genny Jon | Jack Leong

rumi roaming ucluelet: Carly Butler (curator) | UMD Gallery and Projects

For their contributions at various states, stages, and spaces of this project, acknowledging: Krys Verrall | Bill Burns | Sarah AbuSharar | Hanan Hazime Bänoo Zan | Nour Bishouty | Kaya Juan | Lockchi Lam | Tannis Neilsen Manije Khanmohamadi | Katie Couchie | Greg Woodbury | Shlomit Nenookaasi | Lena Golubtsov | Tania Chahal | Shaghayegh Yassemi Marjan Moosavi | Sameer Farooq | Carrie Perreault | Ladan Eskandari Artemis Eskandari | Nuzhat Abbas | Erika Hennebury | Firooz Manji Charmaine Lurch | Negar Pooya | Lisa K. Taylor | Anguelina Ranguelova

Gratitude to all the families, friends, relations, advisors, and uplifters—of all species—of all the contributors whose support made the work sustainable.

Gita Hashemi: outside and inside covers, design, and typography | book design | performance research, direction and production | audio and video edit | web design | fundraising

Front cover: Crossing the Croatia-Hungary Border, 24 March 2016
Back cover: Leaving Port of Izmir, 15 April 2016
From the series Nth Movement, part of *Declarations Diptych*, Gita Hashemi (2016)

Inside cover and page 75: *I Love Chance and Popcorn Poets: Zoom transcription bloopers* | collected and designed by Gita Hashemi

Typefaces: Noto Sans and Serif, and Open Sans by Steve Matteson | Vazir Persian/Arabic by Saber Rastikerdar

oneness of being videos developed and recorded during a residency at Fool's Paradise through Ontario Heritage Foundation's Doris McCarthy AiR

Remembering the indefatigable radical activism and transformative friendship of Naomi Binder Wall

To the spirit of resistance and resilience in Turtle Island, Palestine, Afghanistan, Iran, Turkey, Syria, Iraq, Sudan, Cuba, India, Mexico, Congo, and everywhere in the decolonizing world. Liberation-in-progress

follow the project

colophon

rumi roaming: contemporary engagements and interventions

Guernica Editions Founder: Antonio D'Alfonso
Michael Mirolla, general editor

Gita Hashemi, curator and editor
Elena Basile, poetry and translation editor, and editorial consultant

Guernica Editions Inc. | www.guernicaeditions.com
1241 Marble Rock Rd. (ON), Canada K7G 2V4
2250 Military Road, Tonawanda, N.Y. 14150-6000 U.S.A.

SubversivePress | subversivepress.net | info@subversivepress.net
Founded by Haleh Niazmand, Gita Hashemi | Gita Hashemi, editor and publisher

Distributors:
Independent Publishers Group (IPG)
600 North Pulaski Road, Chicago IL 60624
University of Toronto Press Distribution (UTP)
5201 Dufferin Street, Toronto (ON), Canada M3H 5T8

First edition. | Printed in Canada.

Legal Deposit—First Quarter
Library of Congress Catalog Card Number: 2024942741
Library and Archives Canada Cataloguing in Publication
Title: rumi roaming : contemporary engagements and interventions / curated and edited by: Gita Hashemi
Names: Hashemi, Gita, editor
Series: Guernica world editions (Series) ; 93.
Description: Series statement: Guernica world editions ; 93

Identifiers: Canadiana 20240437489 | ISBN 9781771839709 (softcover)

Subjects:
LCSH: Jalāl al-Dīn Rūmī, Maulana, 1207-1273—Criticism and interpretation. |
LCSH: Jalāl al-Dīn Rūmī, Maulana, 1207-1273—Translations into English. |
LCGFT: Literary criticism. | LCGFT: Essays. | LCGFT: Poetry.

Classification: LCC PK6482 .R86 2025 | DDC 891/.5511—dc23

Guernica Editions Inc. and SubversivePress acknowledge funding support by:

Toronto Arts Council | Funded by the City of Toronto
Ontario Arts Council / Conseil des arts de l'Ontario — an Ontario government agency / un organisme du gouvernement de l'Ontario
Ontario
Canada Council for the Arts / Conseil des Arts du Canada
Canada

دلا زین تنگ زندان‌ها رهی داری به میدان‌ها

From these confined prisons   my heart   you have a path to the open fields